Approaches to Teaching
the Dramas of Euripides

Approaches to Teaching World Literature

Joseph Gibaldi, series editor

For a complete listing of titles,
see the last pages of this book.

Approaches to Teaching the Dramas of Euripides

Edited by

Robin Mitchell-Boyask

The Modern Language Association of America
New York   2002

© 2002 by The Modern Language Association of America
All rights reserved. Printed in the United States of America

For information about obtaining permission to reprint material from
MLA book publications, send your request by mail (see address below),
e-mail (permissions@mla.org), or fax (646 458-0030).

Library of Congress Cataloging-in-Publication Data

Approaches to teaching the dramas of Euripides / edited by Robin Mitchell-Boyask.
    p. cm. — (Approaches to teaching world literature ; 73)
    Includes bibliographical references and index.
    ISBN 0-87352-769-0 — ISBN 0-87352-770-4 (pbk.)
1. Euripides—Study and teaching. 2. Mythology, Greek, in literature—Study and
teaching. 3. Euripides—Criticism and interpretation. 4. Mythology,
    Greek, in literature. 5. Tragedy—Study and teaching. 6. Tragedy.
            I. Mitchell-Boyask, Robin, 1961– II. Series.
                    PA3978.A66 2002
            882'.01—dc21   2001059048
                    ISSN 1059-1133

Cover illustration for the paperback edition:
Greek black-figure amphora, c. 520 BC. Medea boiling a ram before
a daughter of Pelias. Courtesy of the Arthur M. Sackler Museum,
Harvard University Art Museums. Bequest of David M. Robinson.
Photograph by Junius Beebe

Set in Caledonia and Bodoni. Printed on recycled paper

Published by The Modern Language Association of America
26 Broadway, New York, New York 10004-1789
www.mla.org

CONTENTS

ACKNOWLEDGMENTS

Since this book is about teaching, I must begin by thanking my teachers. Since it focuses on Euripides, I must begin with my first teacher of Euripides. While the approach of my fortieth birthday increasingly blurs the memory of my early classical education, I am fairly sure that my first experience with Euripides was very unlike that of most undergraduates, for it was in a first-year Greek class with Anne Burnett at the University of Chicago. That experience instilled my love for Euripides and Greek tragedy more than any other. Teachers who fostered my intellectual development and provided my models for teaching in its most general and truest sense include (but are not limited to) A. K. Ramanujan, James Redfield, George Walsh, Karl Weintraub, and John Wyatt. I owe these teachers more than I can describe.

During the preliminary work on this volume I received the assistance of a research and study leave from Temple University in spring 1998. Since then I have been very grateful for the patience and editorial guidance of the MLA's Joseph Gibaldi.

My greatest debts remain as always to my wife, Amanda, and our two pupils, Nina and Oliver.

PREFACE TO THE SERIES

In *The Art of Teaching* Gilbert Highet wrote, "Bad teaching wastes a great deal of effort, and spoils many lives which might have been full of energy and happiness." All too many teachers have failed in their work, Highet argued, simply "because they have not thought about it." We hope that the Approaches to Teaching World Literature series, sponsored by the Modern Language Association's Publications Committee, will not only improve the craft—as well as the art—of teaching but also encourage serious and continuing discussion of the aims and methods of teaching literature.

The principal objective of the series is to collect within each volume different points of view on teaching a specific literary work, a literary tradition, or a writer widely taught at the undergraduate level. The preparation of each volume begins with a wide-ranging survey of instructors, thus enabling us to include in the volume the philosophies and approaches, thoughts and methods of scores of experienced teachers. The result is a sourcebook of material, information, and ideas on teaching the subject of the volume to undergraduates.

The series is intended to serve nonspecialists as well as specialists, inexperienced as well as experienced teachers, graduate students who wish to learn effective ways of teaching as well as senior professors who wish to compare their own approaches with the approaches of colleagues in other schools. Of course, no volume in the series can ever substitute for erudition, intelligence, creativity, and sensitivity in teaching. We hope merely that each book will point readers in useful directions; at most each will offer only a first step in the long journey to successful teaching.

Joseph Gibaldi
Series Editor

PREFACE TO THE VOLUME

This book has arisen out of the intersection of three related trends affecting the teaching of Greek drama in North American higher education: the comparatively recent intensive engagement by specialized classicists with teaching broad courses in translation; the interest among members of this same group with contemporary critical methods and thus with the work of their colleagues in other disciplines; and the often inadequate understanding of the subject among instructors in humanities departments who find themselves teaching Greek drama in a variety of different settings, such as courses in theater, English, women's studies, and history. The dramas of Euripides continue to strike a deeply resounding chord with modern readers and audiences , and yet they are the subject of an often perplexing, seemingly contradictory (and, for most teachers, overspecialized) range of scholarly studies. It is, therefore, very easy for student and instructor to remain at the level of the topical "relevance" of the plays or to continue to perpetuate the mistakes of previous generations (e.g., the "tragic flaw"), while overlooking the dramas' artistic complexity and Euripides's multifaceted engagement with his society and its problems. Contemporary audiences find Euripides strikingly modern and thus embrace him, but the closeness of this embrace often leads us to assume a facility that misleads. *Approaches to Teaching the Dramas of Euripides* attempts to negotiate between the Scylla of an oversimplistic modernity and the Charybdis of arid, particularized historicism.

This volume promotes, for the larger community of teachers and students, an understanding of the range of current scholarly work on Euripidean drama that can be successfully applied to the classroom experience. While this publication addresses mainly beginning instructors and nonspecialists, more-established teachers and scholars will find much that is interesting and useful here. The volume should guide teachers who use the dramas of Euripides in courses throughout the humanities and social sciences. While most of the essays in this book concentrate on a text or small group of texts, the ideas the authors present should be applicable to other parts of the Euripidean corpus, as well as to the tragedies of Aeschylus and Sophocles; this is especially true of the studies that present particular pedagogical techniques.

Indeed, it is the potential of these essays as models for other investigations that allows me to organize this volume with a broader palette than is typical for other editions in the Approaches series, which tend to concentrate on a single work. One could make a strong case for devoting a single volume to each of the most popular tragedies—*Bacchae*, *Hippolytus*, and *Medea*. But a more encompassing collection of studies will have a greater effect, I believe, on the teaching of Euripides and Greek tragedy in general, especially since the Euripidean corpus, with nineteen (or eighteen, depending on one's opinion about the disputed *Rhesus*) works extant (as opposed to the roughly seven each of Aeschylus and Sophocles), offers a widely diverse range of tones and styles that might present additional complications for beginning or unspecialized instructors (if they are even fully aware of this range). Readers interested in a more detailed examination of the three most popular tragedies should consult the works discussed in the bibliographical sections of this book. In editing this volume, I have sought to incorporate investigations of some of the more interesting but less frequently read tragedies, such as *Heracles* and *Hecuba*, to balance the fuller studies of *Bacchae*, *Hippolytus*, and *Medea* and to dispel some of the more commonly held stereotypes of Euripides through a fuller portrayal of the range of his artistry. My only real regret is that space does not allow additional examinations of other provocative dramas that are deserving of a wider audience, such as *Helen*, *Orestes*, and *Iphigenia at Tauris*, particularly as these three do so much to dislocate a modern reader's perception of the immediate legacy of the monolithic *Oresteia* of Aeschylus; many female students of *Iphigenia at Tauris* are elated to find that the Furies do not give up so easily after the trial of Orestes for the murder of his mother, Clytemnestra.

Euripidean diversity has found complements in the often divergent scholarly takes on the meaning of the dramatist's works, as well as in the different critical approaches. These divergences can be quite extreme. Is, for example, Euripides a radically innovative artist who subjects to scathing critique matters such as Athenian politics, the treatment of women, and the Olympian gods (see, e.g., the works of Michelini; Segal; Zeitlin)? Or does Euripides operate within the normative parameters of traditional Greek beliefs and Athenian tragic practices (see, e.g., Gregory; Kovacs)? Readers will find both views present in this collection, as well as essays that reflect the range of seminal approaches in current Euripidean studies, from Euripides's manipulation of mythical and folktale patterns to performance studies and feminist concerns. Despite this diversity and the conflicts that inevitably arise, the contributors to *Approaches to Teaching the Dramas of Euripides* all share a passionate commitment to undergraduate teaching and to broadening the understanding and appreciation of Greek tragedy.

The scholar-teachers assembled here participate in the movements I noted above toward a new emphasis on teaching classics in translation and to engaging in research beyond the parameters of traditional philology. For much of the history of classics in the United States and Canada, professional classicists focused their pedagogical energy on courses involving texts read in the original languages, leaving Greek drama in translation to be taught in departments of English and comparative literature, often by instructors who, for all their good intentions, had never studied Greek and might not know very much about the relevant historical contexts. As the numbers of students of ancient languages declined, however, and classics came to be seen as an elitist or even useless pursuit (despite, paradoxically, the continued popularity of the literature), many classicists came to see studying the Greek and Latin literature in translation as a key to the survival of the field in universities. Because many translations are now in print and because the vast numbers of resources available over the Internet vary widely in quality, one of the goals of this volume is to organize and interpret these tools.

To develop our understanding of how instructors are engaging such resources, both new and old, I began the preparation of this volume, as is the practice with the Approaches series, with a questionnaire. In 1997 the Modern Language Association surveyed a wide representation of Greek drama instructors and scholars from a cross-section of different academic institutions in the United States and Canada. This group included many classicists who normally have little contact with the MLA, as well as instructors from a variety of departments for whom Euripidean drama plays an important part in course work. Through a message broadcast over the most popular classics e-mail list, I was able to secure the further help of a number of additional colleagues, even some from South Africa and England. Their responses provided data on preferred editions and translations of the dramas of Euripides, bibliographical advice and background reading commonly given to students and other readings recommended for beginning instructors, useful audiovisual aids and computer resources, practical approaches to Greek drama, syllabi, and examples of successful classroom exercises. Throughout the process of compiling these materials, I was often moved by the enthusiasm of the respondents for improving the teaching of Greek drama and by the sheer generosity of many in sharing their pedagogical experiences; I would like to single out here Stephen Esposito, Adele Haft, and Ian Storey, whose contributions have particularly helped me shape the first part of this volume.

Robin Mitchell-Boyask

MATERIALS

The Classroom

Survey Result: The Most Popular Plays

This volume in the Approaches series differs in several respects from its associates, not least in the sheer number of works it covers, and so it makes sense to consider first what instructors actually do (and might) assign. We thus begin, simply and appropriately, with what teachers—in a wide range of courses, departments, and educational institutions—ask their students to read. I include the hard data, gleaned from an unscientific survey, because the results both confirm the most popular plays' status and generate surprise at the next levels. Through accidents of history there are far more extant dramas by Euripides than by the other two great Athenian tragedians, Aeschylus and Sophocles. Euripides first entered the tragic competitions in 455 BCE, launching a career that lasted roughly a half-century. The scholars of Alexandria in the third to second centuries BCE attributed ninety-two plays to him. Four of these were regarded then as spurious, and of the remainder seventy-eight survived intact to Alexandria to be gathered as the collected works. Nineteen plays (eighteen if, as is commonly thought at present, *Rhesus* belongs to a now anonymous fourth-century playwright) have outlasted the dangers of existence on papyrus, parchment, and paper. Thirty-four teachers responded to the question of which plays they assign. Interestingly, all eighteen texts receive some support. One instructor indicated that he teaches all the plays in a three-year cycle, so I have omitted him from the following figures, which indicate the total number of teachers out of thirty-three and a percentage:

The Bacchae, 26, 79%
Hippolytus, 23, 70%
Medea, 22, 66%
Alcestis, 15, 45%
Helen, 11, 33%
Electra, 10, 30%
The Trojan Women, 9, 27%
Iphigenia at Tauris, 8, 24%
Iphigenia at Aulis, 8, 24%
Ion, 7, 21%
Hecuba, 7, 21%
Heracles, 6, 18%
Orestes, 5, 15%
Cyclops, 5, 15%
Andromache, 3, 10%
The Heraclids, 3, 10%
The Suppliant Women, 3, 10%
The Phoenician Women, 2, 6%

The frequency of the assignment of particular dramas seems to arise from a combination of the absolute interest in these works and more practical matters such as with which other dramas they are bundled in collections of translations. *The Bacchae*'s predominance comes as little surprise, nor does the high number of teachers who assign *Hippolytus* and *Medea*. These three dramas frequently appear in translation and on the stage, and their typically Euripidean interest in gender, psychology, and the gods corresponds to the qualities of Euripides's plays that survey respondents almost universally feel are most important about this playwright's work and to which students respond, often with excitement. The order of the next tier, however, is unexpected, for one would expect *The Trojan Women* to come fourth overall, given its concern with the horrors of war and the effects of war on women, both of which topics have resonated strongly in the modern world. This is not to diminish the importance of *Alcestis*—a wonderful drama that always sparks debate in the classroom—but the wide gap between *Alcestis* and *The Trojan Women* indicates that something has shifted in the reception of Euripides, at least in the university. *Helen*'s ranking is even more surprising, since it is relatively obscure, as a late play loosely assigned the category of "romance," and, moreover, it is bundled with other less-favored plays in the popular University of Chicago Press series; instructors who choose to teach Euripides's *Helen* thus are making a very deliberate choice. For the sake of comparison, we should note that part of the popularity of *Alcestis* might arise from its presence in the first volume of the Chicago Euripides with *Hippolytus* and *Medea*, though nobody should discount as reasons for its frequent selection the presence of the hero Heracles and the importance of Alcestis herself for understanding women in Greek drama and society. Otherwise, the relative popularity of the Euripidean dramas comes as expected, with the middle primarily dominated by Euripides's engagement with the legacy of Aeschylus's *Oresteia* (the two Iphigenia plays and *Electra*). And it similarly comes as no surprise that the likes of *The Heraclids* and *The Suppliant Women* bring up the rear, since the former remains the province of specialists and the latter is now of concern mostly to students of Athenian democracy.

The work of Euripides, however, is so marvelously diverse in style, perspective, and subject that teachers can enrich their classes by including some of the lesser-known yet exciting plays. The least-frequently read play, *The Phoenician Women*, begins a list of dramas that instructors curious to venture out of the "big three" might consider. This tragedy, while certainly not of the first rank in plot construction and characterization, is nonetheless a fascinating reexamination of the story of Oedipus's family that crams in virtually every aspect of the Oedipus legend and thus offers much for mythologically bent students to discover. *Heracles*, arguably the work of highest literary quality in the third tier in frequency of assignment, presents the student with a provocative and disturbing study of heroism and the gods in Euripides, while *Orestes*, a late play, should be of interest to any instructor concerned with Euripidean psychology, the relation between Athenian politics and drama, and cultural reactions to the

Oresteia. In courses on Greek drama where Aeschylus's trilogy is read, students delight in the extremely different take on the Oresteian myth offered by the two Iphigenia plays. *Hecuba*'s depiction of women, violence, and revenge makes it a powerful and controversial text for the classroom, whereas many students may find the virtues of *Ion* somewhat difficult to grasp without an especially capable instructor.

Texts: Greek, Bilingual, and English Translation

Perhaps no decision is as crucial to the teaching of Greek drama as the selection of a translation. Unfortunately, the quality of the translation itself is often not the only determining factor in the instructor's decision, since the price, the accompanying essays and notes, and the other texts bundled with a particular desired play can also influence the decision. With an ancient text, especially one intended for performance, the situation becomes even more complicated, and the often ironic tone of Euripides's dramas presents added difficulties for the modern reader who does not know Greek. Translators make important, often controversial interpretive decisions, and the unwary instructor may be the victim—or the beneficiary—of those decisions. Moreover, to render any Greek drama into an English version that is accurate and interesting to read, the translator must distinguish between the meters of the main dialogue scenes in iambic trimeter (the meter most closely approximating normal speech in ancient Greek poetry) and the lyrical choral odes. Translators may choose to forgo any attempt at poetic equivalency and produce a prose English edition, or they can struggle with English poetry and hope not to produce a drama that sounds stilted and unintelligible.

The current state of Euripidean translations into English is fluid, since a number of editions have recently been published and other important new versions are forthcoming. Indeed, the spate of new translations of ancient texts testifies further to the enduring popularity of these works. The essay by Deborah Roberts in part 2 of this volume describes how difficult translating Euripides can be, so I limit my remarks here to the more practical considerations of selecting a translation. Our discussion benefits from the detailed responses of the seasoned teachers in the MLA survey, whose choices have been based on classroom success and often on knowledge of the original. While the choice of translation is one of the most personal decisions an informed teacher can make, nonetheless several important trends emerged from the survey.

Most survey respondents recommend, for those who read Greek, the edition of Euripides edited by James Diggle in the series Oxford Classical Texts. These volumes present all the extant plays, accompanied only by a critical apparatus. Oxford and Cambridge University Presses have ongoing series of editions of individual plays accompanied by detailed commentaries, which can be of great use to instructors; for the most popular plays, the teachers in the survey recommended the Oxford commentaries by E. R. Dodds on *The Bacchae* and by

W. S. Barrett on *Hippolytus*. These better-known commentaries from Oxford and Cambridge lack translations, thus limiting their use for those without a knowledge of the Greek language. Instructors who have learned some Greek but not enough to read texts unassisted can now turn to the Harvard Loeb editions edited by David Kovacs or to a less widely available series published by Aris and Phillips. Each of these collections offers facing pages of Greek with English translations. The Greek texts of both reflect current scholarly consensus on manuscript variants and have fairly literal translations. The Loeb series offers several plays in each volume with limited notes, while each Aris book contains a single text but with copious commentary by a leading scholar, which, combined with the translation, makes these volumes valuable for instructors with limited language skills who would like a detailed commentary. Among the more widely read dramas, the ongoing Aris series now includes *The Bacchae* (Seaford), *Alcestis* (Conacher), *Electra* (Cropp), *Trojan Women* (Barlow), *Hecuba* (Collard), and *Hippolytus* (Halleran). Instructors and ambitious students now also have the option of using the *Perseus Project* Web site (www.perseus.tufts.edu; see also the computer resources section in this volume) to move back and forth between a translation of Greek and (if the correct font is installed on the user's computer) the original text or (if the correct font is not installed) even a transliteration of the Greek into Roman script with links to a dictionary and information on morphology and syntax. *Perseus* has now begun to revise its texts of Euripides with the new Loeb edition edited by Kovacs.

One of the ironies of the modern history of publishing is that the Internet makes Greek texts available to the widest public possible at the very moment when that public might have the smallest number of Greek readers in it. In addition to *Perseus*, *Diotima* has an expanding roster of quality translations for texts portraying women in the ancient world (www.stoa.org/diotima/anthology .html). We can add here that decent, though dated, translations of Euripides are also available over the Web from MIT's *Internet Classics Archive* (classics.mit.edu/ index.html).

While the editions already discussed can be valuable resources for the instructor, they would likely be cumbersome and perhaps insufficiently lively for the average undergraduate class, and thus we turn to the question of English editions for undergraduate courses. Translators must walk a fine line between often conflicting fidelities to the letter and to the spirit of the original text, and few things can stifle a class like a dull translation. An excessively lively rendering, however, can betray the excessive intervention of the translator, and such translations may not come with sufficient notes to provide the background lacked by most current students. The survey respondents expressed personal as well as professional struggles over the choice of English editions. While it is a truism to observe that there is no perfect translation, most instructors seem frustrated by what is available.

Nonetheless, the survey participants' overwhelming favorites for classroom use are the translations from the famous University of Chicago series The

Complete Greek Tragedies, edited by David Grene and Richmond Lattimore, though the reasons for their dominance are not always the most ideal. The Chicago series includes translations of all Euripides's extant plays by twelve different translators in five economical volumes, the advantage of which becomes even stronger through the sheer ubiquity of used copies. One survey respondent's comments typify the consensus: "standard, cheap, easily found but not especially good translations." Mary-Kay Gamel further observes, "The widespread use of the Chicago series in classrooms is unfortunate. This series was cobbled together in the late 1950s: Wyckoff's *Antigone* dates from 1954. Only a few of these translations were very good to begin with, and they have now all passed the life span of a translation, traditionally twenty-five years. The rapid changes in contemporary speech and cultural norms have probably shortened that life span considerably." But the availability and low price of these editions weigh heavily in the decisions of many teachers, while others are more enthusiastic about their essential quality. Froma Zeitlin, for example, reports that she uses the Chicago translations because she values their correspondence with line numbers in the Greek, their closeness to the Greek in meaning, and their overall poetic merit. In general, the translations for this series by William Arrowsmith were singled out for special praise for their vigor and relative accuracy. Other dramas do not fare so well in this edition, with the translation of *Hippolytus* by David Grene frequently cited in the survey for its inaccuracies and datedness. The most common complaint about the Chicago translations concerns their inadequate support materials, an absence many found especially perplexing given that Chicago recently reissued these works. Survey respondents almost invariably criticized both the aged introductions, which also do not situate the dramas in fifth-century Athens, and the general lack of notes. An example of the interpretive problems the support materials can cause can be seen in Rex Warner's introduction to his translation of *Medea*, which asserts a unitary Medea myth used by Euripides and known by the audience. The assumption that the audience would thus know the exact nature of Medea's revenge (the killing of her children) flies in the face of the great pains Euripides takes to make this decision as shocking, and thus as new, as possible (see Knox, "*Medea*"). These deficiencies present a real dilemma for teachers. A beginning instructor or one who is not well-grounded in studies of Greek culture would need to supplement the Chicago translations with study guides or secondary readings, but such an instructor might not be in the position to do so. The unpleasant alternatives are to use other editions, which, as we shall see shortly, often present their own particular problems, or to increase the book costs to the students or simply to overlook these deficiencies. After almost a half-century of dominance by the Chicago translations, it might be time for newer ones to move into greater prominence.

So what other choices are available? Euripides translations of varying usefulness and cost can be found from a variety of sources, including Oxford University Press (multiple versions), Penguin (multiple versions), Focus Publishing,

Hackett Press, and the University of Pennsylvania Press. What follows is a summary, based on the comments of survey respondents, of these editions' strengths and weaknesses. The need to base discussion on the real experiences of teachers and the relative availability of translations force me to exclude some editions from consideration. Because of the previously mentioned current explosion of new translations, I am supplementing this discussion with comments solicited from colleagues after the survey as well as my own observations. While the relative novelty of some of these translations prevents a full assessment of their utility for the classroom, initial reactions, taken in the context of trends evident in the survey, can provide a useful guide.

Oxford publishes translations in two different series. The first, Greek Tragedy in New Translation, founded by Arrowsmith and now edited by Peter Burian and Alan Shapiro, aims to offer eventually all the extant tragedies and thus far includes ten by Euripides. The translators in this series are either poets knowledgeable of Greek, classicists with some poetic talent, or teams of scholars and poets. These editions are of very high quality, focusing on a single text in each volume, with often excellent supporting materials, but most teachers find the cost of these individual books too much for their students. Peter Burian has, however, reported to me that Oxford will begin bundling the plays when the series is complete. But Oxford has not completely priced itself out of the present undergraduate market. Two editions in the economical current series Oxford World Classics offer a translation and copious notes for eight dramas (*Medea*, *Hippolytus*, *Electra*, and *Helen* in one, and *Bacchae*, *Iphigenia among the Taurians*, *Iphigenia at Aulis*, and *Rhesus* in the other) by a classicist with broad literary interests, James Morwood, along with an introduction by a distinguished scholar of Greek tragedy, Edith Hall. The dialogue sections here are prose, which might bother some, but the translations are otherwise generally accurate. The inclusion of the fascinating "romance" *Helen* along with three of the most popular tragedies might make this an appealing choice for teachers desiring to broaden their students' understanding of Euripides's artistic range.

Through its various subsidiaries, Penguin offers versions by no less than five different translators, including *The Bacchae* (Meridian Classics), by Michael Cacoyannis—better known for his Euripidean films—and *Three Great Plays of Euripides* (also Meridian), by Rex Warner, which includes *Medea*, *Hippolytus*, and *Helen*. While economical, the strengths of these editions do not compare with those of similarly priced competitors. More recently, Penguin's Signet line has published Paul Roche's translations in *Euripides: Ten Plays*, which, given its scope (the three most popular plays, plus *Alcestis*, *Ion*, *Electra*, *Iphigenia at Aulis*, *Iphigenia among the Taurians*, *The Trojan Women*, and *The Cyclops*, the only extant satyr play), its poetic value, and its very low cost, seems an attractive alternative for instructors concerned about book prices but who also wish their students to read a wider range of plays. I have found that, when assigning some plays from this edition, students often begin reading others from the same volume, with convenience abetting their curiosity; this tendency is by my standards no small argument for using Roche's volume. Roche's somewhat heavy-handed prefaces, however, need to be handled with care, and his stage directions often project a strong interpretive line that is not necessarily justified by the text; see, for example, his direction in *The Bacchae* that Pentheus should be "shaken" by the Stranger's (Dionysus's) assertion that he does not understand who Pentheus is (416). Roche's volume also does not stand up well if an instructor uses editions of dramas by other Greek tragedians with more elaborate translations; students can be very astute at spotting when low price does not justify inclusion. Penguin's more prominent translations, by Philip Vellacott, of seventeen Euripidean dramas in four volumes were cited by survey participants for their low cost and availability, but many also argued that their often tendentious introductions and occasional textual decisions of questionable logic (e.g., his omission of part of Phaedra's crucial speech on knowledge and virtue in *Hippolytus*) can also prove very misleading for generalists or beginners. Penguin seems to be gradually replacing the Vellacott translations with new ones by John Davie, with supporting materials by Richard Rutherford; the first two volumes published have won praise by no less a translator of Greek than Robert Fagles.

Another recent entry into this field comes from the University of Pennsylvania Press. Under series editors David Slavitt and Palmer Bovie, the Penn Greek Drama Series offers the first translation of all extant Greek drama from a single source in over fifty years. This series presents translations primarily by prominent writers and poets, often working with a minimal knowledge of ancient Greek but aided by professional classicists (though not to the same extent as in the Oxford series), so it has aimed more at the spirit than the letter of the original texts. Euripides's plays, each assigned to a different translator, are bundled into several volumes, and as is inevitable with such enterprises, the results are often mixed. The translations are of an unfailingly high literary quality with often beautiful and exciting poetry, but a reader has to be careful with translations sometimes so far removed from the original texts. Moreover, aside from a glossary at the end of each volume and a brief translator's preface before each play, novice readers and teachers receive little information about historical and literary contexts, which is somewhat puzzling since this omission has been a widely perceived shortcoming of the Chicago series. The instructor thus could find these editions valuable for engaging students with lively, contemporary poetry. For example, Marilyn Nelson, in her translation of *Hecuba*, compares the plight of Hecuba with that of African American slave women and imaginatively interpolates part of the spiritual "Nobody Knows the Trouble I've Seen" into Euripides's text. Overall, however, the series is currently still too new to assess the actual extent of its success in the classroom.

The Penn series contrasts strongly with ones produced by two smaller, independent presses, Focus Publishing and Hackett, both of which offer contemporary translations, by classicists, of individual plays with notes and introductions. The real strength of the Focus Classical Library lies in the support its translators give to their readers at a relatively low cost. The Focus series is still under development, and it currently consists of *The Bacchae* (Esposito), *Heracles* (Halleran), *Medea* (Podlecki), and *Hippolytus* (Halleran), so it already covers the four most widely read dramas. Survey respondents frequently identified the Focus editions as useful for students and teachers; several commented that students are "grateful" for the copious and clear notes, the introductions, and the current bibliographies. The Focus texts are not as widely available as most of the competing editions, but no other group of translations was so uniformly praised. When, in 2002, Focus bundles its Euripidean texts into a single, more economical volume, it will offer an extremely attractive option for a wide range of instructors. Hackett, an increasingly active publisher of distinguished translations of Greek texts, published in 1998 a single edition of *The Bacchae*, by Paul Woodruff, and plans to produce more translations in future years. Thus instructors dissatisfied with the Chicago series should keep their eyes open to developments at Hackett and Focus.

Required and Recommended Student Readings

Most instructors, when asked which works they require undergraduate students to read, quickly agree about the best resources, though the nature of these works does vary with the type of course being conducted. The overwhelming majority of respondents to the survey indicated that, for understanding Euripides, the best secondary reading is often another primary text, whether that text is one of the Homeric epics (for myth and traditional values), a tragedy by Sophocles or Aeschylus on a similar subject or myth (especially since Euripidean drama often seems to react to such predecessors), a comedy by Aristophanes in which Euripides appears as a character, or Thucydides's *History of the Peloponnesian War*, for its depiction of the degenerating moral and political climate during which most of the extant dramas were composed. Most students gain from seeing the sophistic Thucydidean politicians resonate in their Euripidean counterparts and from understanding that the savagery depicted in dramas such as *The Trojan Women* and *Hecuba* did not just emerge from the poet's imagination. Most of the surveyed teachers made similar recommendations about required readings in Greek culture in general and Euripides in particular, and here we will work from the general to the specific.

For understanding the historical setting of Greek drama and the issues it engages, two books emerged as clear favorites, with others close behind. The course book produced by the British Joint Association of Classical Teachers (JACT), *The World of Athens*, offers a concise general overview of fifth-century Athens aimed at students. Since the role of women in Greek tragedy is one most students find compelling, many teachers require background reading on that complex subject; most frequently recommended is *Women in the Classical World*, edited by Elaine Fantham et al. Similarly, many require Helene

Foley's essay "The Conception of Women in Athenian Drama." Some teachers assign the relevant sections of reference works such as the *Oxford History of Greece and the Hellenistic World* (Boardman, Griffin, and Murray) or the *Oxford Classical Dictionary* (Hornblower and Spawforth). Highly regarded for student use now is a new survey text, *Ancient Greece: A Political, Social, and Cultural History*, edited by Sarah Pomeroy et al. Students also generally find useful as a clear short guide to the function of Greek drama in Athens a chapter in Simon Goldhill's *Aeschylus: The* Oresteia, "Drama and the City of Athens."

Mythology also dominates any discussion of required student readings because of its importance to drama, the prevalence of drama as a source for myth in Western culture, and the decline of general knowledge in this subject among students. Grappling with the often dense networks of mythological allusions in Greek tragedy is perhaps the greatest challenge for the modern student. Instructors thus often assign students readings in collections of and textbooks on Greek mythology. Survey respondents frequently cited three such books that are both widely available and regularly updated in improved editions: Mark Morford and Robert Lenardon's *Classical Mythology*, Barry Powell's *Classical Myth*, and Stephen Harris and Gloria Platzner's *Classical Mythology: Images and Insights*. The last of these might be of more use to literature instructors since it includes entire texts of dramas (for Euripides, *The Bacchae* and *Medea*) rather than the customary selection of extracts. Some prefer Pierre Grimal's *Penguin Dictionary of Classical Mythology* and Michael Grant's *Myths of the Greeks and Romans*, since the latter discusses important mythological characters partially in terms of their depiction in fifth-century dramas. As handbooks these two volumes help students navigate the complexities of Greek mythology, and their relatively low price makes them attractive as required or recommended purchases. Instructors pointing students to important variants in mythology sometimes require Timothy Gantz's more advanced sourcebook, *Early Greek Myth*. Influenced by French scholars working from a structuralist perspective, the scholarly study of Greek tragedy is also dominated by myth, and college teachers thus frequently recommend or require the seminal work of Jean-Pierre Vernant and Pierre Vidal-Naquet, widely available in the collection *Tragedy and Myth in Ancient Greece*. Vernant and Vidal-Naquet have had an enormous effect on other scholars whose work is frequently assigned to students and recommended to other teachers; Helene Foley, Simon Goldhill, Charles Segal, and Froma Zeitlin feature prominently here.

This leaves us with recommended student readings for Greek tragedy in general and Euripides in particular. For the readings in Greek tragedy, at least, there is again clear consensus. Most experienced teachers believe that students need to appreciate what it was like for a fifth-century Athenian to see a play by Euripides in the Theater of Dionysus. The surveyed instructors believe that two books are particularly invaluable for helping students understand Greek drama as performed in ancient Athens. Oliver Taplin's *Greek Tragedy in Action* provides an extremely approachable introduction to Greek tragedy as a performed art, covering matters such as gestures, entrances, and exits in chapters keyed to the most commonly read plays. Since Taplin uses for this book the widely read Chicago translations, this study can serve as a quite handy course companion and could help overcome some of that series's deficiencies as discussed earlier. From the Euripidean corpus, Taplin studies *Hippolytus*, *Ion*, and *The Bacchae*. To help students understand the historical situation of Greek drama and the mechanics of its staging, many instructors require Graham Ley's *A Short Introduction to the Ancient Greek Theater*. Both of these texts are concise, well-written, widely available, and relatively economical. Since the completion of the survey, David Wiles has written a valuable guide, *Greek Theatre Performance*, that introduces students to Greek performance practice in its historical context. Often required are also Bernard Knox's "Myth and Attic Tragedy," in his *Word and Action*; Albin Lesky's "What Is Tragedy?," the first chapter in his *Greek Tragedy*; Simon Goldhill's *Reading Greek Tragedy*; and Rush Rehm's *Greek Tragic Theatre*. More-ambitious teachers assign chapters from *Nothing to Do with Dionysos?*, edited by John Winkler and Froma Zeitlin, a volume that brings together many important essays on resituating Greek drama in its historical and cultural contexts. *The Context of Ancient Drama*, by Eric Csapo and William Slater, goes much further than Ley in delineating its subject, mainly through copious selections of primary texts, and has proved a valuable supplement for many undergraduates and their instructors. *The Cambridge Companion to Greek Tragedy* (Easterling) presents accessible essays by important scholars on a range of subjects, including a surprisingly lengthy segment on reception, especially of productions of tragedy on the theatrical and operatic stage and in film over the past four hundred years. Teachers interested in having their students read approaches from a feminist perspective generally assign selections from Froma Zeitlin's *Playing the Other* and Nicole Loraux's *Tragic Ways of Killing a Woman*, both of which contain substantial examinations of Euripidean drama. The subject of required readings on Euripides in particular is more complex, since many of the seminal studies are confusing for undergraduates (particularly Greek-less ones) and since here one quickly encounters the sharp divides among scholars of Euripides (see below). Most instructors in general courses do not assign specific studies, but those who do favor William Arrowsmith's seminal essay, "A Greek Theater of Ideas," R. P. Winnington-Ingram's "Euripides: *Poietes Sophos*," and the relevant essays in *Oxford Readings in Greek Tragedy*, edited by Erich Segal. The more general books cited above provide ample sections specifically on Euripides, as do the works discussed below in "The Instructor's Library."

I should stress here that the selection of secondary readings for an undergraduate class is further limited, aside from the specialized, often technical pitch of much scholarship, by the widespread scholarly use of untranslated ancient Greek, as well as a heavy reliance on French and German scholarship, which is also often quoted without translation into English.

Aids to Teaching: Audiovisual and Computer-Based Resources

As with previous sections, the following discussion is based on the responses of the survey participants, but here it is supplemented by information culled from the journal *Classical World*, which regularly issues special volumes with updated listings of such resources for teaching. This information, continuously updated, can now be accessed over the Internet (www.drjclassics.com). I examine audiovisual aids first, followed by computer resources. Films for the Humanities offers four films on Greek tragedy in general, ranging from twenty to forty-five minutes in length: *The Rise of Greek Tragedy, The Role of the Theater in Ancient Greece, Staging Classical Tragedy*, and *Theatrical Devices in Classical Theater*. While these videos all share the goal of helping students understand ancient theater through visiting extant theaters such as the one at Epidauros or demonstrating characteristics such as theatrical masks, instructors do not uniformly find them stimulating for their students, despite generally recommending these films as introductions. Many teachers prefer to handle such topics themselves through slides and computer projections, combined with showing performances of entire plays.

Films often prove invaluable in connecting the words on the page to students' experiences and imaginations. Adele Haft comments, "Films are a wonderful way to help students visualize the plays and to show them how individual each director's vision can be." Some plays have been served on film much better than others, with, as would be expected, mainly films of the most popular plays available. That said, it is surprising that there is no video version of *The Bacchae*, especially since it is performed in theaters regularly. Many respondents expressed the desire for films of more dramas. I defer further discussion of the available films since they are well covered by the essays in part 2 of this volume by Marianne McDonald and Mary-Kay Gamel.

Many instructors find that using movies with themes similar to those of the ancient Greek plays can prove a powerful catalyst in bridging the gulf between modern students and ancient Greek tragedy. Again, Marianne McDonald reports on her own experience in this vein, but in assembling the survey results I was struck by how pervasive this practice is, whether it takes the form of watching films with students in class or comparing dramas under study with films the students might know. Dale Grote, who often uses *Pennies from Heaven* in this light, observes, "The indispensable idiom or medium for shared emotional experience is film. Not films about ancient plays or even based on them, but films that capture something of the motifs explored in the plays." For example, several of the instructors in the survey compare *The Bacchae* (again, a drama lacking a film version per se) to the Rolling Stones' *Gimme Shelter* for the interplay of personal liberation, crowds, and violence. To further illuminate *The Bacchae* others use Peter Weir's *Picnic at Hanging Rock* or Jean Genet's *The Blacks*. Because American films and Greek drama share a tendency to use trial scenes to crystallize and amplify important social themes and tensions, movies built around courtrooms can prove especially telling. A teacher with a more diverse student group might thus discuss Euripides's *Hecuba* alongside Steven Spielberg's *Amistad*, two stories about slave rebellions and their consequences that trials attempt to resolve. This resource is as limitless as the instructor's imagination.

Assessing computer-based resources in a book such as this is somewhat precarious, given the speed with which the field changes, but some general parameters can be drawn. Technology has greatly enriched the teaching of Greek drama at every level, and this trend only stands to increase as the tools improve. The collection of texts and contextual materials, combined with appropriate search features, allows the modern reader's understanding of Euripides to become significantly broader and deeper. The backbone of the computer-enhanced study of Greek drama has been the *Perseus Project*. *Perseus* is a multimedia interactive digital library that contains Greek literature (in ancient Greek and English translation), history, art, and archaeology. All its databases are hyperlinked, so that highlighting, for example, the word *Delphi* in Euripides's *Ion* and then clicking on the Atlas function will locate Delphi on a map, while clicking on Encyclopedia will give a full entry on the site, and clicking on Sites will lead the user to images and plans of and information about this important place for Greek myth and literature. *Perseus* enriches the knowledge of instructors at all levels and helps students navigate the complexities of Greek culture through self-guided access to primary materials. Instructors who would like to show their students different Greek theaters or contemporary paintings of the sacrifice of Iphigenia or of the death of Heracles now have easy access to such representations. Many specialized teachers of classical literature have made their Perseus-based lessons available through the *Perseus* Web site. *Perseus* was designed initially for the Macintosh operating system, with the *Hypercard* application running four CD-ROMs that contain all the databases, but because its designers set up the databases independent of *Hypercard*, they have been able to easily transfer these materials to the *Perseus* Web site (www.perseus.tufts.edu). A platform-independent version of the CD-ROMs has now been released, with engines that can access the databases locally on the CDs or over the Internet, thereby allowing instructors to tailor their use to the appropriate teaching environment. Thus, the question arises of which version of *Perseus* to use. The advantages of the CD-ROM version are that the material is local and therefore not subject to the vagaries of traffic on the Internet and that it can display text and image together on the screen as the user chooses, whereas the Web restricts the user to the available window. The interface of the CD-ROM version is also much more intelligible for an undergraduate than the increasingly complex Web site. Moreover, the CD-ROM databases are more thoroughly interconnected, and all images are available, whereas with the Web version copyright requirements can restrict the availability of some images to users from institutions with site licenses. But the vast majority of materials in *Perseus* are free over the Internet, and the Web edition of *Perseus* is continually expanded and updated, both of which factors might weigh heavily in the Web version's favor. *Perseus* can also help overcome the often large gaps in student knowledge of mythology; I add here that the mythology textbooks by Powell and by Morford and Lenardon each have their own interactive Web sites for study (cw.prenhall.com/powell; www.oup-usa/xx/0195143388) .

The Internet offers a steadily increasing amount of teaching materials produced by faculty members who are often excellent scholars as well. One advantage of these resources is that their authors are often easily accessible for further advice through e-mail. But because such resources can also be ephemeral, with links subject to migration to new servers and even new university addresses, one must be careful with recommendations, so the selections here in most cases must meet the criteria of strong institutional support and independence from an excessive reliance on the efforts of a single person. These sites all take advantage of the interconnectivity of the Web and refer the users to smaller related sites; there is as yet no single Web site specifically constructed for the study of Euripidean drama, though I am making available a companion Web site for this volume (www.temple.edu/classics/euripides.html) that will regularly update Internet resources for the study and teaching of Euripidean drama. Aside from *Perseus*, the Web site for the principal North American professional organization for the study of the ancient world, the American Philological Association (www.apaclassics.org), can be a good starting point, for it offers links to all the other major sites for studying Greek literature (including online scholarly journals) and online abstracts for papers on Euripides delivered at recent APA annual meetings. Readers of Euripides who use the Internet but are frustrated by the lack of selectivity in commercial search engines can turn to *Argos* (argos.evansville.edu), a peer-reviewed, limited-area search engine for Internet resources on the ancient and medieval worlds. *The Stoa: A Consortium for Electronic Publication in the Humanities* (www.stoa.org) features tools for the study of antiquity, especially online scholarly publication designed for a wide audience; it serves as a stable, permanent clearinghouse for important yet potentially ephemeral materials. *The Stoa* also features QuickTime VR movies of several Greek theaters; these movies allow the user to move around the theaters and to follow relevant links to the *Perseus* Web site (www.stoa.org/metis). Because gender and the status of women in Euripidean drama are such important concerns for students and teachers, an extremely useful site is *Diotima: Materials for the Study of Women and Gender in the Ancient World* (www.stoa.org/diotima/). Aside from *Perseus*, this is the Web site most frequently praised by instructors in the survey. It present links to course materials, bibliographies geared to the representation of women in Euripides, and related anthologies of primary texts to help readers better understand the role of women in Greek drama. *Diotima* also offers unique scholarly resources, such as a catalog of suicidal females in Greek and Roman mythology and a series of electronic reprints of articles on gender in antiquity by an important scholar, David Konstan. Translations of Greek texts with commentaries figure to be an increasingly important resource in *Diotima*; thus far it includes such important texts for teaching Euripides as the *Homeric Hymn to Demeter* (see Foley, "*Anodos* Drama") in a translation by Gregory Nagy and even a full English text with notes to Euripides's *Alcestis*. The Archive of Performances of Greek and Roman Drama at the University of Oxford (www.classics.ox.ac.uk/apgrd/index.html) provides valuable information about Greek drama and the performance of classical plays since the Renaissance. Teachers seeking online reviews of current scholarship will appreciate the second oldest electronic journal in the humanities, *Bryn Mawr Classical Review* (ccat.sas.upenn.edu/bmcr), which publishes timely reviews of current scholarly work in the field of classical studies (including archaeology) and provides search engines keyed to authors and subjects. A judicious use of these resources by instructors and students can greatly enrich their educational experience.

The Instructor's Library

This section addresses primarily the nonspecialist teacher of Euripides in survey and general literature courses, though it also affords the more specialized classicist an overview of the most important scholarly resources in English for research on Euripides. While certainly throughout the last century scholars working in virtually all the major European languages made important contributions to the study of Euripides, I include here only works published in English, since they are the most pertinent for our intended audience. Moreover, the works of many of the most important French scholars of the past quarter century, such as Marcel Detienne, Nicole Loraux, Jean-Pierre Vernant, and Pierre Vidal-Naquet, have now been translated into English, so they can enter our consideration. And while many of the key works of German scholarship on Greek drama have not been so fortunate, they have nonetheless exerted enough influence on Anglo-American academics to make their presence felt here.

Bibliographies

Most specialized printed bibliographies on Euripidean drama are now somewhat dated, and others are of limited use to the generalist searching for important recent work applicable to the classroom. For the French journal *Métis* Suzanne Saïd edited a worthy annotated bibliography on Greek tragedy encompassing publications between 1900 and 1988, though its utility is limited to teachers with some ability to read French. Somewhat older, though still very valuable, is the short list in Christopher Collard's introductory edition, *Euripides*. The considerably harder to find journal *Lustrum* periodically publishes bibliographies on Euripides, while the easily obtainable journal *Classical World* assembles every few years a special survey issue on books for teaching classics in English, with bibliographies on Greek history and literature, as well as on specific authors. Teachers will likely find these bibliographies the most productive resource; the most recent survey is from 1995. Excellent bibliographies can also be found in *The Oxford Classical Dictionary* (Hornblower and Spawforth) and *The Cambridge History of Classical Literature* (Easterling and Knox 64–87, 184–88). The 1985 bibliography for *Directions in Euripidean Criticism*, edited by Peter Burian, would also be useful for North American teachers of Euripides. A more thorough (at times, for a student, overwhelmingly so) source is *L'année philologique*, an international bibliography of classical studies; users can now access its resources electronically through software of the *Database of Classical Bibliography*. Searching can be done through nineteen indexes, including a full word list for subject searching (e.g., "altar" in Euripides), an ancient Greek word list, and an index of modern languages (e.g., "Euripides" in Japanese). In addition to traditional Boolean searching within and between indexes, the database offers range searching (e.g., "Euripides" 1976–80), a choice of three output formats (Chicago, MLA, and tagged), and facilities for copying, downloading, printing, and revisiting results. Information on the database can be obtained from the American Philological Association Web site (www.apaclassics.org).

Print bibliographies will likely become of limited value, since the Internet allows the motivated teacher to discover constantly updated, often searchable bibliographies pitched to a variety of needs. At the *Perseus Project* Web site David Kovacs provides a bibliography appended to a biography of Euripides, though the biography probably aids teachers more than the bibliography, which is selected from the author's own, fairly strongly held but unacknowledged point of view, and important names such as Charles Segal and Froma Zeitlin do not appear. The bibliography from *Euripides and Tragic Theatre in the Late Fifth Century*, edited by Martin Cropp, Kevin Lee, and David Sansone, is available online (www.classics.uiuc.edu/dsansone/banff_bibliography. htm). Since this volume consists of essays from an important 1999 conference, its bibliography is comprehensive. *Diotima* contains bibliographies on particular topics as well as on authors, and they serve both specialists and generalists; as with other aspects of this Web site, these bibliographies are oriented to modern critical approaches and issues of gender. *Diotima* also offers a very easy to use set of search engines interfacing with other, often more specialized, online bibliographies such as *TOCS-IN* (*Tables of Contents of Journals of Interest to Classicists*: www.chass.utoronto.ca:8080/amphoras/tocs.html). *Diotima* and *TOCS-IN* are regularly updated by appropriate scholars.

Journals

Many journals of classical studies tend to concentrate on examinations of a level of specialization inappropriate for the generalist teacher, yet a number do frequently publish studies on Euripides and Greek tragedy in general that reach out to larger constituencies. *Arethusa* primarily devotes itself to disseminating scholarship using modern critical methodologies and invariably translates all Greek passages. Through *Project Muse* of the Johns Hopkins University Press, it is now available over the World Wide Web, along with the more traditional (though of increasing accessibility to generalists) *American Journal of Philology*. Web-based journals will certainly become more important in future years, and generalists should consult the APA Web site for a current list. Other journals publishing Euripidean studies that should prove helpful to generalist and novice teachers are *Arion, Classical Antiquity, Greece and Rome, Helios, Ramus*, and two journals of regional North American associations of classicists, *Classical Journal* and *Classical World*. The availability of *Bryn Mawr Classical Review* over the Internet easily allows the generalist to keep abreast of current major work on Greek literature (ccat.sas. upenn. edu/bmcr/).

Reference Works and Background Studies

Greek History and Culture

Certainly, the secondary reading in the section above on required and recommended student readings would serve for the teacher, especially a novice one, as introductions. There is a further veritable embarrassment of riches for the teacher needing to become better acquainted with Greek history and culture, for in recent years the major academic presses have published a number of excellent reference and background works, including *The Cambridge Illustrated History of Ancient Greece*, edited by Paul Cartledge; *Ancient Greece: A Political, Social, and Cultural History*, edited by Sarah Pomeroy et al.; and *The Oxford Classical Dictionary*, edited by Simon Hornblower and Anthony Spawforth. While there have been a number of recent excellent studies of ancient Greek history, many classicists recommend Nancy Demand's *A History of Ancient Greece*, and Thomas Martin's *Overview of Archaic and Classical Greek History* is especially notable because it was developed in conjunction with the *Perseus Project*, which offers an abbreviated online version of Martin's work (www.perseus.tufts.edu/cgi-bin/text?lookup=trm+ov+toc/), along with an abundance of links to primary works for each section, including one on the development of Greek drama in Athens.

For books on specific subjects I incorporate the recommendations of the survey respondents. Those seeking background information on women in the time of Euripides will find an excellent introduction in the collections of essays

Reflections of Women in Antiquity, edited by Helene Foley; *Women in the Classical World: Image and Text*, edited by Elaine Fantham et al.; and Sue Blundell's *Women in Ancient Greece*. Page Dubois's *Centaurs and Amazons: Women and the Pre-history of the Great Chain of Being* was recommended by many survey respondents for its feminist insights into how women were represented and imagined in classical Athens. Walter Burkert's *Greek Religion* offers a fairly comprehensive and readable background work for a subject vital to understanding Greek drama, as does *Athenian Religion: A History*, by Robert Parker. Ethical debates are at the heart of many tragedies. To learn more about the Greek ethics, consult *Merit and Responsibility*, by Arthur Adkins; Martha Nussbaum's *The Fragility of Goodness: Luck and Ethics in Greek Tragedy and Philosophy* (a rich, wide-ranging study that culminates in a reading of Euripides's *Hecuba*); and *Shame and Necessity*, by Bernard Williams, a philosopher who boldly and brilliantly takes the rather unfashionable stance that we have much in common with the Greeks. To further appreciate the intellectual ferment of the fifth century that enabled the "tragic moment" and informed much Euripidean drama, teachers are advised to read virtually any book by G. E. R. Lloyd; *The Greeks and the Irrational*, by E. R. Dodds; Friedrich Solmsen's *Intellectual Experiments of the Greek Enlightenment*; and, by Jean-Pierre Vernant, *The Origins of Greek Thought, Myth and Thought among the Greeks*, and *Myth and Society in Ancient Greece*.

Several outstanding reference works on Greek literature and drama were highly praised by many survey respondents. Aside from the articles on Greek tragedy and the three major tragedians in *The Oxford Classical Dictionary* (Hornblower and Spawforth), the recent second edition of *The Oxford Companion to Classical Literature*, edited by M. C. Howatson, received several recommendations, as did the articles on the tragedians in T. James Luce's *Ancient Writers: Greece and Rome*; the essay by Christian Wolff on Euripides in *Ancient Writers* garnered numerous testimonials from survey respondents. No teacher of Greek literature should lack access to the outstanding *Cambridge History of Classical Literature* (vol. 1, *Greek Drama*), edited by Patricia Easterling and Bernard Knox, for this volume should answer virtually every question an instructor might have about Greek literature and its authors. Those requiring a less comprehensive, slightly more digestible compilation should consult *Ancient Greek Literature*, edited by Kenneth Dover. Several scholars have attempted to cover the complex history of Greek literature single-handedly, including Jacqueline de Romilly, in *A Short History of Greek Literature*, and Albin Lesky, in his monumental study *A History of Greek Literature*.

Greek Drama and Theater

General Context and Background   The novice instructor or generalist seeking more background on Greek tragedy need not look far for help. In addition to his general history of Greek literature, Albin Lesky has also assembled one of the benchmark resources for teaching and research on Greek tragedy, the appropriately titled *Greek Tragedy*. Lesky's work provides an overview of both the extant and the lost dramas of all the major playwrights, and along with the more recent *Cambridge Companion to Greek Tragedy*, edited by Patricia Easterling, it is the most valuable reference work specifically designed for the study of Greek tragedy. Easterling's volume focuses more on making interpretive sense of Greek drama as a whole and as a creature of the fifth-century Athenian polis. For an understanding of the context of the City (or Great) Dionysian Festival during which the tragedies were performed, the standard reference work is Arthur Pickard-Cambridge's *The Dramatic Festivals of Athens*, in the second edition revised by John Gould and David Lewis. If generalists find this work a bit overwhelming but are still interested in original sources in the context of dramatic productions, they should consult *The Context of Ancient Drama*, by Eric Csapo and William Slater. Indispensable for appreciating the visual aspect of Greek tragedy is A. D. Trendall and T. B. L. Webster's *Illustrations of Greek Drama*, accompanied by the more recent *Images of the Greek Theatre*, edited by Richard Green and Eric Handley.

Performance: Theater, Actors, and Chorus   Aside from the brief volumes by Simon Goldhill, Graham Ley, Rush Rehm, Oliver Taplin, and David Wiles mentioned in the recommendations for students, there are a number of very good general introductions to Greek tragedy and its performance, almost all of them by British scholars. Erika Simon's *The Ancient Greek Theatre* (a translated German work) was praised by several survey respondents, as was David Wiles's *Tragedy in Athens: Performance Space and Theatrical Meaning*. For those interested in performance, the already cited books by Taplin and Wiles head the field, building on the older work of Peter Arnott in two books, *Introduction to the Greek Theatre* and *Greek Scenic Conventions in the Fifth Century B.C.*. J. Michael Walton has contributed two fine books on this topic that also serve as worthy general introductions to Greek drama, *Greek Theatre Practice* and *The Greek Sense of Theatre: Tragedy Reviewed*. On modern performances of Greek tragedy, see Marianne McDonald's *Ancient Sun, Modern Light*, Fiona Macintosh's "Tragedy in Performance," and Helene Foley's "Modern Performance and Adaptation of Greek Tragedy."

Because of the prominence of the chorus in Greek drama and the difficulty many teachers have in explaining its function to students (who have even greater difficulty understanding it), the chorus must feature in any discussion of teaching Greek drama. Modern pedagogical discomfiture with the chorus might stem, given the widespread reliance on Aristotle's *Poetics*, from Aristotle's silence on the matter. A good starting point is Easterling's essay "Form and Performance," which traces conventions for the number of actors and shows the historical development of the chorus through choral lyric poetry. Easterling uses several Euripidean dramas, especially *Medea* and, in more detail, *The Trojan Women*, to show the role of the chorus in a drama's rhythm and structure. From there, one might move to John Gould's essay "Tragedy and the Collective Experi-ence," accompanied by Simon Goldhill's response, "Collectivity and Otherness." Gould challenges the argument by Jean-Pierre Vernant and Pierre Vidal- Naquet that the chorus represents the experience of the collective citizen body of Athens. More specialized, though fascinating and controversial, is John Winkler's essay in *Nothing to Do with Dionysos?*, which contends that the chorus was composed of adolescents in military training and that their choral dances were based on group military movements ("Ephebe's Song"). I should also note here that the journal *Arion*, which is dedicated to publishing articles for a wide audience, devoted two special issues (Golder and Scully) to essays on the ancient Greek chorus. These papers, originally given at a conference in Boston in 1992, feature excellent gen-eral articles on choruses in Greek culture, as well as two on the Euripidean cho-rus (Rehm, "Performing the Chorus;" Scully).

Other Topics in Greek Drama   There are now excellent books covering vir-tually every aspect of Greek drama and theater. H. D. F. Kitto's two volumes, *Greek Tragedy* and *Form and Meaning in Drama*, are dated but still service-able. Goldhill's *Reading Greek Tragedy* serves as an enlightening introduction for instructors interested in using modern critical theory to examine this field. *Towards Greek Tragedy*, by Brian Vickers, presents a large, somewhat prob-lematic though at times exhilarating perspective on Greek tragedy as a whole. Peter Walcot's *Greek Drama in Its Theatrical and Social Context* is a handy, brief overview of a complex topic. W. B. Stanford's *Greek Tragedy and the Emotions* offers a concise, approachable look at the affective power tragedy likely had on its original audience. Two considerations of the elusive relation between Greek tragedy and Shakespeare offer contrasting views of the appro-priate role of such comparisons. John Jones's classic account, *On Aristotle and Greek Tragedy*, attempts to move the study of Greek drama away from the character-based assessments typical of Shakespearean scholarship earlier in the century and toward a more plot-centered perspective guided by Aristotle's *Po-etics*. In addition to its general critical contribution to the field, this work also provides brief studies of many important dramas. Roughly two decades later, Adrian Poole tried to resurrect comparative study with a more historically in-formed, though still somewhat romantic, approach in *Tragedy: Shakespeare and the Greek Example*. Teachers interested in current scholarship on the re-lation between Aristotle and Greek tragedy should consult the collection of es-says edited by Amélie Rorty, *Essays on Aristotle's Poetics*, and Elizabeth Belfiore's *Tragic Pleasures* and *Murder among Friends: Violations of Philia in Greek Tragedy*. The latter contains a wealth of insights into using Aristotle to study Euripides. Greek drama did not arise from a poetic vacuum but built on earlier forms of poetry, so to get a sense of the relation of Greek drama to other forms of Greek poetry, teachers can consult *The Varieties of Enchantment: Early Greek Views of the Nature and Function of Poetry*, by George Walsh (two chapters on Euripides), and *Poetry into Drama: Early Tragedy and the*

Greek Poetic Tradition, by C. J. Herington. Focusing on the relation between literature and society, Richard Seaford, in *Reciprocity and Ritual: Homer and Tragedy in the Developing City-State*, attempts to give a Marxist spin to the development of tragedy in Athens by arguing that the Dionysian cult and mysteries promoted civic unity in the polis, as opposed to the Nietzschean idea of Dionysus as a symbol of disorder and "anti-structure" (Seaford, *Reciprocity* 363–67); the *Bacchae* naturally looms large in this argument. Seaford provides a powerful, yet often one-sided, counterweight to the approach to Euripides's last tragedy as represented by Charles Segal's *Dionysiac Poetics*. Indeed, Segal and Seaford engaged in an extensive debate on the relative merits of their perspectives in *Bryn Mawr Classical Review* in 1998 (98.3.10; 98.5.2.6; 1998.07.01: ccat.sas.upenn.edu/bmcr/1998) that would prove instructive and thought-provoking to any serious reader of Greek drama.

Modern Adaptations of Euripides

While Euripides has not spawned the same quantity of modern imitations as Sophocles, the quality of his offspring has been fairly high, with musical versions outnumbering the purely theatrical (in the modern sense). Using these plays in the classroom can illuminate the original dramas by helping students see that the ancient playwrights, like the moderns, were making definite choices about plots and characterizations and that deciphering these choices is an important part of coming to understand the text. Martin Mueller's *Children of Oedipus* offers a thoughtful overview of modern versions of Greek tragedy from 1500 to 1800, providing a more detailed base than Peter Burian's briefer, though more current (and probably more useful for undergraduate teachers) essay "Tragedy Adapted." In the seventeenth century, Racine contributed no fewer than three tragedies modeled on Euripides: *Andromaque*, *Iphigénie*, and, most notably, *Phèdre*, an adaptation of Euripides's *Hippolytus*. *Phèdre* also incorporates elements from other ancient treatments of this myth and focuses more on the psychology and experience of the central female character than on the adolescent son of Theseus (Mueller 46–63). If students have properly understood the uniqueness of the virginity of the Euripidean Hippolytus, Racine's introduction of a secret girlfriend into his play will be quite instructive. Racine's *Iphigénie*, in turn, is based on *Iphigenia at Aulis*. In the next century Goethe followed with Euripides's other drama on Iphigenia, but Goethe built into his play large sections of the Electra story, thus placing the matricide and Orestes's release from it more centrally in his play than did Euripides. Goethe and Racine may not fare particularly well in the curricula of North American universities in the twenty-first century, but a more recent transformation of Euripides's *Bacchae*, by the Nigerian Nobel laureate Wole Soyinka, holds much potential for reaching the diverse student audiences of this era. Soyinka forges a rich synthesis of Greek, Christian, and African mythologies that provide much fodder for student discussion, particularly if the play is read alongside the Euripidean original. Among survey participants Soyinka's work seems to be the modern version of a Euripidean drama most frequently taught today. Of similarly greater interest in America now are the poet HD's versions of *Ion* and a more extensive reworking of *Hippolytus*, called *Hippolytus Temporizes*, in addition to lyrics from several other plays. Eugene O'Neill's *Desire under the Elms* evokes the situation of Euripides's *Hippolytus* wherein the younger wife prefers the son. Also of possible interest to more advanced classes where students have knowledge of German are two plays on which Hugo von Hofmannsthal later collaborated operatically with Richard Strauss: *Elektra* and *The Egyptian Helen* (1928). *Elektra*, on the surface, strives to be Sophoclean, yet its morbidity, its sheer wildness, and its capacity to mix horror with stunningly beautiful moments resemble Euripides more. *The Egyptian Helen* is the Viennese reworking of Euripides's drama *Helen*. Other transformations of Greek tragedy in the twentieth century that might seem to evoke Euripides, such as O'Neill's *Mourning Becomes Electra* or Sartre's *Flies*, actually connect more significantly to the *Oresteia* of Aeschylus (Burian, "Tragedy Adapted"). Sartre, I might add here, did author a *Trojan Women* (see Roberts's essay in this volume).

In addition to Strauss's Hellenizing operas, Euripidean drama has been a regular source for the musical stage, especially in France with Jean-Baptiste Lully's *Alceste* (1674) and Marc-Antoine Charpentier's *Medea* (1693). Jean-Philippe Rameau's *Hippolyte et Aricie* (1733), as its title suggests, takes its lead more from Racine than from Euripides. Christoph Gluck in turn in the late eighteenth century wrote another *Alceste* and operas based on both of Euripides's *Iphigenia* dramas. Shortly after, Luigi Cherubini composed *Médée*, a role Maria Callas famously portrayed (Kerrigan) and one of the more successful operatic adaptations of Euripides. In the twentieth century there were two powerful operatic versions of *The Bacchae*: one, by Hans Werner Henze, *The Bassarids* (1966, libretto by W. H. Auden), and the other, *King Roger* (1926), by the Polish composer Karol Szymanowski. Last but not least, *The Bacchae* is an important subtext to Benjamin Britten's *Death in Venice*, based on Thomas Mann's novella of the same title, which is itself perhaps the most important and profound reworking of a Euripidean drama in the modern world.

Scholarship on Greek Drama and Euripides

Collections of Essays on Greek Drama

This section has two parts: first, collections with multiple authors organized topically or thematically and, second, otherwise unrelated articles by individual authors published as a single volume. All these works should prove useful and interesting to teachers of Euripides. *Oxford Readings in Greek Tragedy*, edited by Erich Segal, preserves from the middle fifty years of the twentieth century a number of articles that have been fundamental to understanding various topics and specific dramas. Roughly one-third of these essays focus on Euripides. More recently, *Greek Tragedy*, an assortment of articles culled by Ian McAuslan and Peter Walcot from issues of the Oxford journal *Greece and Rome* between 1972 and 1989, presents a particularly agonistic article by Simon Goldhill against an increasingly key mode of investigation, "Reading Performance Criticism," and a variety of articles by other British scholars on particular plays and topics, including seven on Euripidean drama. Better known is the influential collection edited by John Winkler and Froma Zeitlin, *Nothing to Do with Dionysos? Athenian Drama in Its Social Context*, a group of diverse and innovative essays aimed at restoring the social context of ancient Greek drama through understanding the theatrical productions as civic events. While these essays, most of them originally published in specialist journals, generally do not work through readings of specific texts, few readers will come away from this book without a much greater appreciation for the role of drama in the Athenian polis. The vast majority of survey respondents felt that this was one recent critical work on Greek drama with which most teachers of Euripides should be acquainted. Also frequently recommended was a collection of papers edited by M. S. Silk, *Tragedy and the Tragic: Greek Theatre and Beyond*, which encompasses a wide range of topics (including comparative ones) from an even broader range of perspectives. Taken together, these two collections will give teachers an excellent grounding in contemporary approaches to Greek drama. Instructors interested in political theory and Greek tragedy can consult the collection of essays edited by J. Peter Euben, *Greek Tragedy and Political Theory*.

Since, with notable exceptions, most publishing on classical texts occurs in journals, not monographs, the generalist might often miss some of the more important work done on particular topics or specific dramas. Fortunately, aside from collections such as *Nothing to Do with Dionysos?*, several of the leading scholars on Greek tragedy have occasionally collected their writings into individual volumes providing ready access to work of great significance; all these selections include general articles on Greek drama and society, as well as on specific dramas by Euripides. Anyone remotely acquainted with scholarship on Greek literature will not be surprised that this list is headed by Bernard Knox, whose articles on tragedy have remained cogent and timely decades after their original publication. In *Word and Action*, Knox assembled a range of essays, including a lucid general account, "Myth and Attic Tragedy," and articles on the three tragedians, including classic treatments of *Hippolytus* and *Medea* that still must enter into any informed discussion of these dramas. It is also difficult to discuss the study of Greek drama without mentioning Charles Segal and Froma Zeitlin, both of whom have issued collections of insightful, often groundbreaking articles on tragedy. Segal and Zeitlin were some of the first scholars in America to bring structuralist theory (among other modern approaches) to bear on Greek literature with great success. Segal's selection of published essays, *Interpreting Greek Tragedy: Myth, Poetry, Text*, begins with two key treatments of Greek drama and structuralism and also presents influential treatments of Euripides's *Hippolytus*, *Helen*, and *Bacchae* from a variety of critical perspectives. The publication of Zeitlin's collection, *Playing the Other: Gender and Society in Classical Greek Literature*, was especially propitious for generalists since Zeitlin has often preferred the long essay over the book for expressing her thoughts, a practice that might otherwise leave underexposed some of the most compelling critical work done on Euripides in recent years. Among a range of essays on Greek literature and culture, *Playing the Other* offers perspicuous studies on Euripides's *Hecuba*, *Hippolytus*, and *Ion*. Teachers of Euripides would also benefit from studying *Tragedy and Myth in Ancient Greece*, by the Frenchmen Jean-Pierre Vernant and Pierre Vidal-Naquet, a collection of essays of enormous influence on these two American scholars, as well as on others. Survey respondents frequently cited this volume, which helped bring structuralism to classical studies, as a key component in the library of a teacher of Greek drama.

Collections of Essays on Euripides

There have been three approachable, relatively recent essay collections in English concerning Euripidean drama. The first and oldest of these, *Euripides: A Collection of Critical Essays*, edited by Erich Segal, comes praised by many survey respondents as indispensable and features such classic examinations as William Arrowsmith's "A Greek Theater of Ideas," perhaps the single essay most frequently recommended in the survey. The other three collections arose from conferences on Euripides. *Directions in Euripidean Criticism*, edited by Peter Burian, offers several vital essays typical of modern scholarship on commonly read dramas; teachers in particular will gain from Bernard Knox's lucid introduction, "Euripides: The Poet as Prophet"; Froma Zeitlin's piece on *Hippolytus* ("The Power of Aphrodite"); and Charles Segal's "The *Bacchae* as Metatragedy," which offers in a more concise form many of the insights from his large monograph *Dionysiac Poetics*. Generally considered less successful is another conference-based collection of essays edited by Anton Powell, *Euripides, Women, and Sexuality*, certainly a topic of great central interest to teachers of Euripides, and the *Medea*, *Hippolytus*, and *Bacchae* receive a good deal of attention, though the book suffers from a somewhat loose organization and a lack of focus. Still it provides a useful starting point for those exploring the subject. Yet another conference assembled most of the important Euripidean scholars in 1999. The volume of their collected papers, *Euripides and Tragic Theatre in the Late Fifth Century* (Cropp, Lee, and Sansone), presents a wide, diverse range of critical approaches to Euripides.

Book-Length Studies of Euripidean Drama in General

Monographs on Euripides have appeared frequently over the past two decades in particular and from a wide, often conflicting, range of perspectives. Ann

Michelini's essay later in this volume provides an introduction to the history of the controversies over how to read Euripidean drama, as well as an overview of major books written recently on Euripides; a fuller treatment of these issues can be found in her valuable 1987 study, *Euripides and the Tragic Tradition*. Here I shall integrate consideration of other books with results from the survey of teachers. As noted by Michelini, the three works written during the 1960s and 1970s in English that contributed the most to understanding diverse and often neglected aspects of Euripides's plays were D. J. Conacher's *Euripidean Drama*, Anne Burnett's *Catastrophe Survived*, and Cedric Whitman's *Euripides and the Full Circle of Myth*; all these works were cited with varying levels of enthusiasm by survey respondents. This list is not intended to slight the contemporary T. B. L. Webster's *The Tragedies of Euripides*, which functions more as a handbook, imparting, among other matters, valuable information about chronology and what is known about the last plays. Christopher Collard's brief 1981 introduction in the Greece and Rome supplement series, simply titled *Euripides*, received frequent praise in the survey. With the rise of structuralism and other critical methodologies, the 1980s and 1990s saw some of the most insightful and groundbreaking books written on Euripidean drama, along with the development of a fairly sharp schism among scholars into two camps, which we can loosely, perhaps too much so, designate as Kovacs-Gregory and Foley-Segal-Zeitlin, a phenomenon discussed by Michelini later in this volume. From the general works on Euripides by these scholars, survey respondents frequently urged teachers to consult Justina Gregory's *Euripides and the Instruction of the Athenians*; Charles Segal's *Euripides and the Poetics of Sorrow* (a collection of previously published articles); and Helene Foley's *Ritual Irony: Poetry and Sacrifice in Euripides*, an important study of religion in Euripides employing modern anthropological theory. Other general books on Euripides but with particular focuses that have been published recently and were recommended by survey participants are Francis Dunn, *Tragedy's End: Closure and Innovation in Euripidean Drama*; Michael Halleran, *The Stagecraft in Euripides*; and the single most extensive feminist analysis of Euripides, *Anxiety Veiled: Euripides and the Traffic in Women*, by Nancy Rabinowitz. On this last study, however, generalists need to be advised that there is a diversity of approaches among Euripidean scholars working under the general rubric of feminism, and reviews have not been universally enthusiastic. Froma Zeitlin's appraisal, available over the Web (ccat.sas.upenn.edu/bmcr/1994/94. 11.03.html), should be read alongside this provocative, rich, and passionate book. I return to *Anxiety Veiled* in the later section on women and Greek tragedy. Halleran's book follows the lead set by Oliver Taplin in *The Stagecraft of Aeschylus*, dissecting matters such as entrances and exits to develop a "scenic grammar" that Halleran applies in particular to *Heracles*, *The Trojan Women*, and *Ion*. One final study commendable to all serious students of Euripides (and particularly praised by Zeitlin) is Shirley Barlow's *The Imagery of Euripides*. Originally published in 1971 and reissued with additions in 1986, this book offers the reader an informative account of Euripides's imaginative powers as a poet. Although its primary audience is the professional classicist, all the Greek is translated and Barlow's prose is readable and lively. Another more specialized book that also might serve some teachers well is *Narrative in Drama: The Art of the Euripidean Messenger-Speech*, by Irene de Jong, which studies, from the perspective of narrative theory, an aspect of Greek tragedy that often confuses generalists. *The Gorgon's Severed Head: Studies of* Alcestis, Electra, *and* Phoenissae, by C. A. E. Luschnig, is a loose collection of essays on the three cited plays. Thus teachers of Euripides can now consult sound works of scholarship on Euripidean drama from a variety of perspectives and on a range of particular topics.

Books and Independent Chapters on Specific Plays

Here I restrict attention to the most popular plays. Where no book-length treatment is available in English I refer to chapters in other books previously cited. As observed in the previous section, Ann Michelini's essay in part 2 can help put some of these studies in the appropriate intellectual context. Most survey respondents did not recommend books on specific plays, so here I am relying more on my sense of the field and correspondence with colleagues in the discipline. The second tier of the most commonly studied dramas by Euripides generally, but with notable exceptions, lacks book-length treatments, and for these dramas, teachers should consult Michelini's essay later in this volume; readers needing further treatments of the less frequently read dramas should consult the bibliographies cited earlier and keep abreast of reviews at the *Bryn Mawr Classical Review* Web site.

The Bacchae, unsurprisingly, has received some of the most generous treatments, beginning with R. P. Winnington-Ingram's brief but masterly examination of Euripides's attitude toward the god of tragedy, *Euripides and Dionysus*. Because of *The Bacchae*'s interest in the power of illusion and the presence of Dionysus, the god of tragic theater, scholars have increasingly focused on the role of metatheater in the play's meaning, with Foley's essay *"The Bacchae"* likely influencing Charles Segal's ambitious, richly multifaceted, though perhaps overly long *Dionysiac Poetics and Euripides'* Bacchae, itself reissued in 1997 in an even longer edition in order to incorporate the continued critical interest in this drama over the previous fifteen years. *The Bacchae* also weaves its way in and out of Zeitlin's "Playing the Other" and "Thebes" and *Nothing to Do with Dionysos?* (Winkler and Zeitlin). Teachers interested in the larger issue of Dionysus in Greek culture can also consult *Masks of Dionysus*, edited by Thomas Carpenter and Christopher Faraone, which presents essays by distinguished scholars of Greek drama and religion, many of which engage Euripides's tragedy.

Medea also has been the subject of much fertile discussion, beginning with Bernard Knox's groundbreaking essay "The *Medea* of Euripides," which is available in *Word and Action*, and continuing through various parts of Nancy Rabinowitz's *Anxiety Veiled*. Along the way, Emily McDermott wrote a very readable monograph, *Euripides'* Medea: *The Incarnation of Disorder*, which should prove valuable to generalists, and Pietro Pucci produced *The Violence of Pity in Euripides'* Medea, a work written from various theoretical perspectives, though its insistent deconstructionist tack and often opaque style have sometimes left even informed specialists somewhat bewildered. Foley's seminal article "Medea's Divided Self" is available in her book *Female Acts*. In his study *Persuasion in Greek Tragedy* R. G. Buxton devotes a chapter to *Medea*. The rich history of *Medea* on the modern stage is examined in Medea *in Performance, 1500–2000*, edited by Edith Hall, Fiona Macintosh, and Oliver Taplin. Teachers interested in the larger myth of Medea should consult the collection of essays on Medea edited by James Clauss and Sarah Johnston, which contains a probing yet concise examination of Euripides's drama by Deborah Boedeker. John Kerrigan's essay "Medea Studies: Euripides to Pasolini" provocatively examines Medea's career in modernity.

Hippolytus may have generated more scholarship per line than any other play by Euripides over the past two decades, with no fewer than four monographs devoted to it in addition to an abundance of articles. Zeitlin and Segal, as previously noted, have made valuable contributions from a range of perspectives that have become available in the volumes of their collected essays. Knox's classic essay on this play, "The *Hippolytus* of Euripides," has influenced most subsequent examinations. *The Character of the Euripidean Hippolytos*, by George Devereux, develops the psychoanalytical perspective sketched by Segal's essay "Pentheus and Hippolytus on the Couch and on the Grid." Celia Luschnig and Barbara Goff have each written volumes engaging the play's complex systems of imagery; Goff's study employs a range of theoretical perspectives, building on Zeitlin's important essay on eros and the self, "The Power of Aphrodite." Most recently, Hanna Roisman, in *Nothing Is as It Seems: The Tragedy of the Implicit in Euripides'* Hippolytus, argues, against accepted critical consensus, that Phaedra is a "master rhetorician" who manipulates all around her and who is not a victim of Aphrodite and a misogynistic Hippolytus. This is a nuanced, bracing account of the drama that many teachers might find problematic (not least because it builds on the excessively subtle, overly ironic theories of Philip Vellacott) but that also should provide much food for thought. A teacher who wants to challenge students' immediate conceptions of this play (not to mention scholarly consensus) and provoke discussion could couple Nancy Rabinowitz's readings with Roisman's ideas.

While there has been no single book-length treatment of *Alcestis*, there is a 1968 collection in the Twentieth Century Interpretations series, *Twentieth Century Interpretations of Euripides'* Alcestis: *A Collection of Critical Essays*, edited by John R. Wilson. These essays are of course now dated but are still valuable as long as they are supplemented by the more recent work in the books of Segal (chapters in *Euripides and the Poetics of Sorrow*), Gregory, and

Rabinowitz; indeed virtually every recent book-length study of Euripidean drama contains a chapter on *Alcestis*. Another pertinent supplement is Helene Foley's "*Anodos* Drama," which studies how Euripides in *Alcestis* (and *Helen*) deploys the myth of Demeter and Persephone "to set up a complex dialogue between the Athenian past and the Athenian present that both challenges and in the end subtly confirms contemporary ideology on a large range of topics" (134). Written for a generalist audience, this essay is valuable both for readers of this drama and for those wanting an approach through myth to the larger subject of women in Euripidean drama, to which we turn now for a more detailed examination.

Epilogue: Women and Greek Tragedy

For both the novice and the experienced reader (not to mention spectator) few aspects of the Greek theater are as intriguing and problematic as the role of women, and Euripidean drama increases the complexity of this subject by presenting female characters acting outside the social norm while still often retaining some level of sympathy. The parts of female characters in Greek tragedy were written by men, played by men, and performed largely for men, yet they are some of the most compelling portrayals of women in the history of world theater. Few bodies of theatrical literature, even Shakespeare's, contain such vibrant roles for women, especially older ones, a primary reason for the continuing strength of Greek drama on the modern stage. Euripides's interest in women and their status is one of the facets that makes his work so compelling to students in the classroom; it is almost impossible to teach *Medea*, for example, without students falling into sharply divided camps, for and against the title character. Yet how could a culture that so thoroughly restricted the lives of women have produced such a remarkable set of roles that seem to rebel against these very restrictions? Later in this volume, Laurel Bowman tackles this question with respect to *Medea*, and here I try to provide a bibliographical framework for the teacher. We can divide the general question of women and Greek tragedy into two parts: women in the theater audience and the representation of women in drama itself. The two questions are obviously related, since one wonders what an Athenian woman would have made of Medea's great speech on the unfairness of marriage or Phaedra's passion for her stepson. Moreover, even if women were present in the theater, would the intended, or "notional," audience of the dramas still have been the body of male citizens there?

Whether women were actually in the audience has recently become a subject of great scholarly interest and controversy. Women were generally kept confined to the house and appeared in public almost exclusively for religious ceremonies, and the tragedies were produced as a part of a festival honoring the god Dionysus. If, as many scholars now believe, tragedy was an expression of the (male) ideology of the polis, then how could women be part of the work's intended meaning or of its notional audience? The evidence for their attending the theater, such as it is, is decidedly mixed, but on the basis of this evidence Eric Csapo and William Slater (286–87) have decided that women were present in the audience. Anthony Podlecki's article "Could Women Attend the Theater in Ancient Athens?" presents an excellent summary of the evidence, and Jeffrey Henderson, in "Women and the Athenian Dramatic Festivals," sets the evidence in the contexts of comparative studies and the more anthropologically informed work of Froma Zeitlin on the dramatic representation of women, and thus Henderson concurs that women were part of the "real" and "notional" audiences. Simon Goldhill, however, a staunch advocate of the "polis ideology" approach to Athenian tragedy, rebuts these argument not once, but twice ("Representing Democracy"; "Audience"). Goldhill's second statement sums up much of his work on the role of drama in the political life of Athens. If Athenian tragedy was embedded in "the special context of democracy and its institutions, where to be in an audience is above all to play the role of democratic citizen" ("Audience" 54), then how could a restricted and noncitizen group such as women participate? Goldhill's arguments are compelling, but he also does load the dice by limiting the nature and function of drama to a purely sociopolitical realm wherein it either supports or problematizes the ideology of the polis. (For an argument against that approach see Griffin, "Social Function," though Seaford's "Social Function" responds cogently.)

Whether or not women were present, it still stands that they almost certainly were not there in great numbers and that the culture of ancient Greece was, at best, patriarchal, so how and why Greek drama used women as it did remains open to question. The French scholar Nicole Loraux, whose work has increasingly become available in translation, has had an enormous influence on American feminist classicists (among others). A collection of her essays, *The Children of Athena: Athenian Ideas about Citizenship and the Division between the Sexes*, includes treatments of Aristophanes's *Lysistrata* and Euripides's *Ion*. The generally accepted starting point for discussing this topic is Helene Foley's essay "The Conception of Women in Athenian Drama," which points out the difficulties in simpler psychological and structuralist-influenced approaches to this subject for the tragic stage. Foley is more concerned with how the crises enacted in drama negate polarities, such as male-public versus female-private, and how they expose social contradictions. Setting parameters for further study rather than driving home a single thesis, Foley closes by pointing to a line of inquiry that she and Zeitlin (leading others) have pursued in subsequent years: how "the relatively more limited and defined role in which the female is confined by Athenian culture can be used to define the more inclusive male role by contrast" (162). After two decades of publishing articles on the representation of women in Greek tragedy that extended and developed the argument of her initial essay, Foley presented her mature position on the subject in the Martin Classical Lectures at Oberlin College. Foley has collected these lectures along with her more important articles in the form of the book *Female Acts in Greek Tragedy*, whose final three chapters focus on women in Euripidean drama. Students and teachers interested in the rich and complex problem of women in Greek tragedy should start with *Female Acts* and Zeitlin's *Playing the Other* and then move on to the radically different argument of Nancy Sorkin Rabinowitz in *Anxiety Veiled*.

Zeitlin has explored the appropriation and representation of the female by Greek literature throughout her career, in essays such as those conveniently assembled in *Playing the Other*, which, taken together, offer the thesis that tragedy "plays the other" because it is an inherently feminine genre by the social constructions of Greek culture. "From the outset," Zeitlin argues,

> it is essential to understand that in the Greek theater, as in Shakespearean theater, the self that is really at stake is to be identified with the male, while the woman is assigned the role of the radical other.
>
> (*Playing* 346)

Thus, male-authored dramas represent the female as a means of speculating about gender roles and exploring the masculine, appropriating the female to create the male. Zeitlin's arguments are multifaceted and resist easy summary, so generalists are urged to explore these essays for themselves.

As already noted, Nancy Sorkin Rabinowitz's *Anxiety Veiled: Euripides and the Traffic in Women* is a powerful, insightful examination that has sparked controversy even among other feminists. Borrowing her subtitle from an article written in 1975 by Gayle Rubin, which itself grew into a foundational text of feminist literary and anthropological theory of women and exchange, Rabinowitz makes no bones about her frequent discomfiture with the texts she studies. Relying on a range of Marxist and Freudian thought, as well as on Freud-based feminist film criticism, Rabinowitz's examination of the cultural practice of Euripidean tragedy argues that tragedy, victimizing and fetishizing women, is "comforting to men" (168). In an interesting twist on the controversy over women's participation in the tragic festival, Rabinowitz argues that their presence was virtually required by the polis ideology of tragedy. Euripides's plays, she contends,

> set forth codes of behavior giving women in the audience reason to participate in the culture; on the other hand, they reinforce men's need and right to continue to control women. Women in the ancient audience may have, like many later readers, resisted this structure proposed to them, by focusing on the power and the women's community behind the text.
>
> (14)

Women thus would only have been included in order to be marginalized. Like Zeitlin's work, Rabinowitz's work deserves to be read on its own terms, if for no other reason than the great insights it often yields when it engages specific passages in dramas. A more recent work by Laura McClure, *Spoken like a Woman:*

Speech and Gender in Athenian Drama, astutely examines the paradox of the female who speaks powerfully onstage in a culture that expects silence in a woman. McClure attempts to situate the language of female dramatic characters within the sociohistorical context of fifth-century Athens, examining, in addition to the *Oresteia* and Aristophanes, Euripides's *Hippolytus* and *Andromache*. Thus, the subject of women in the Greek theater (in both senses) and feminist approaches to it are complex and diverse realms of inquiry and doubtless will continue to be so in the future.

APPROACHES

Introduction

Part 2 of this volume consists of essays on teaching Euripides. Before presenting an overview of these essays, I need to clarify two issues. The first concerns
what initially seems to be an issue so simple, spelling, that it needs no comment, yet to avoid confusion I must address the potential problems that can
arise in the English spelling of Greek names. Ancient and modern Greek use
different alphabets than other European languages, so the representation of
the same sounds is not necessarily uniform worldwide or throughout history.
For most of Western history, we have spelled Greek names according to the
practice of the ancient Romans, somewhat anglicized. Thus the Greek name
for the hero of the *Iliad*, transliterated as *Akhilleus*, becomes, through the
Romans, *Achilles*, the name with which most speakers of English, including
me, feel most comfortable. The vast majority of shifts are instantly recognizable: for example, *Hippolytus* and *Hippolytos* and *Bacchae* and *Bakchai*. Others, such as the transliterated *Hekabe* for *Hecuba*, require a little more
thought. Sometimes students need reassuring that the names *Herakles, Heracles*, and *Hercules* refer to the same figure. Those needing further assistance
should consult the reference works cited in part 1, and the popular mythology
textbooks discussed there all have presentations on transliterated and Roman
spellings of Greek names. Please be aware that I have allowed contributors to
choose the spelling system with which they are most comfortable, so Greek
names will not be consistent throughout the essays but will be so inside each
one. The second issue concerns translations. Since the translations of Euripides in the Chicago series remain by far the most commonly used, contributors
to part 2 refer to those editions unless otherwise noted. Some contributors provide their own translations of select passages, and such changes are acknowledged inside the particular essay, but no confusion shall arise since the line
numbers in the Chicago translation correspond closely enough to the original
Greek. One notable exception here is the essay on *The Bacchae* by Stephen
Esposito, who uses the translation from his own fine edition of the play.

Part 2 is subdivided into four sections, headed by two essays dealing with
basic considerations for teaching Euripides. Deborah Roberts provides an
overview of the vexed problem of translating Euripides, including a survey of
the history of Euripidean translation, the issues confronting the teacher selecting a translation, and a comparative discussion of some select passages. Ann
Michelini outlines scholarship on Euripides over the past century as a history
of reception, to help the teacher see how we have come to think about Euripides as we do and to identify the basic critical issues confronting the teacher of
Euripides today.

The second section of part 2 involves performance, studied from three different angles. Marianne McDonald, who has published extensively on Greek
drama and film, offers us insights into the use of filmed versions of Euripidean

drama (as well as other movies) in the classroom. Mary-Kay Gamel, an experienced teacher and director of Greek drama, follows with a discussion on a subject of growing pedagogical importance: performance in the classroom and, specifically, the use of student performances to increase the students' engagement and understanding of Euripides. Michael Halleran concludes this section with an essay on ancient performance practice, a topic that should have a central role in the undergraduate classroom. Halleran shows how imagining the original performances helps students comprehend key textual issues.

The third section concerns pragmatic issues and activities for Euripides in the classroom. Adele Haft shows that encouraging students to write their own Greek dramas is a sure route to enjoyable enlightenment; Haft generously provides detailed instructions. Gary Meltzer's classroom exercise on debate in *Medea* similarly encourages active student engagement with the material, but from a forensic angle, allowing the students' own work to help them see the role of the Sophists in the culture of Euripides (and ours). Paul Allen Miller wraps up this practical group by explaining the role of Euripidean drama in his large Introduction to Mythology course; Miller traces the way Euripides revises the *Oresteia* legend to show how myth functioned in fifth-century Athenian society, always a popular subject with students.

Part 2 concludes with a group of essays examining critical approaches to specific issues and plays. Dale Grote leads off with a quick overview of how to use Aristotle's ideas in the classroom with Euripidean drama and follows with an amusing and provocative explanation by Aristotle himself about what he really meant in that murky and elliptical little book we have come to know as Aristotle's *Poetics*. Since Aristotle's ideas still exert a powerful, but often misguided, influence on the teaching of Greek drama, this essay is invaluable. Laura McClure's essay discusses another source of popular (mis)perceptions of Euripides, Aristophanic comedy, wherein Euripides appears several times as a character. McClure shows how Aristophanes can help teachers explain the nature and role of Euripidean drama in his own time. The essays of Mark Padilla and Monica Cyrino describe the ways myth (Padilla) and folktale (Cyrino) function in two dramas featuring the popular hero Heracles. These essays shift this section into more extended treatments of individual plays. Laurel Bowman's treatment of women in *Medea* cuts against the traditional scholarly emphasis on the sacred marriage oaths between Jason and Medea, stressing instead that a fifth-century Athenian would have seen Medea not as a legitimate wife but as a concubine. This argument might prove controversial in the classroom, but few things about this play are simple or uncontroversial. Justina Gregory's examination of another play about female revenge further restores the position of a powerful tragedy, *Hecuba*, that has recently become more popular after years of neglect. Gregory focuses on yet another complex issue for teaching Euripidean drama: its relation to contemporary Athenian politics. The volume concludes with detailed studies of important issues confronting the teacher of two very popular dramas, *Hippolytus*, led by Ian Storey (with Martin Boyne and Arlene Allan), and *The Bacchae*, with Stephen Esposito. Storey and Esposito take us through the central controversies and problems facing students of these two tragedies today.

By the end of part 2, readers of this volume should thus have a sense of the current study of Euripides, important issues confronting the teacher, and specific recommendations for improving the teaching of Euripidean drama in the North American classroom. Having lived with drafts of these essays for a while now, I can vouch for their effectiveness, as they have enriched my own teaching of the dramas of Euripides.

PRACTICAL AND THEORETICAL
CONSIDERATIONS: AN OVERVIEW

Euripides in Translation

Deborah H. Roberts

In the early decades of the twentieth century, English-speaking readers and audiences were likely to encounter the plays of Euripides in Gilbert Murray's popular and widely performed translations, in the older versions reprinted in the Everyman's Library edition, or perhaps in Arthur S. Way's Loeb Classical Library translations, with the Greek on the facing page. None of these are much read today, except by scholars with an interest in the history of translation, in Murray's work, or in the poetry of Shelley, whose rendering of Euripides's satyr play *Cyclops* appeared in the Everyman edition. The history of Euripidean translation does not present us with any earlier version that has significantly outlasted its own period, like Chapman's Homer or Pope's. This fact is perhaps not surprising, since translations are notoriously short-lived, but early renderings of Euripides have failed to win even the kind of respect sometimes given to versions notable in their own day.

In Robert Browning's versions of *Alcestis* and *Heracles*, the plays themselves are curiously denied an independent identity; they are embedded in longer narrative poems (*Balaustion's Adventure*; *Aristophanes' Apology*), as if in some kind of evasion or absorption of the world of the theater in which Browning's own plays had met with failure. Indeed, the *Alcestis* in *Balaustion's Adventure* takes the form of a Greek spectator's retelling of the play, with remembered dialogue, descriptions of action, and occasional commentary. Browning's narrator (a young Greek woman) repeatedly praises the poet but at one point engages in something like a correction of the chorus: she tells us first what she wishes they had said and then what they did say (line 1520).

Discomfort with Euripidean choruses, and especially with the choral odes originally performed in song and dance, is of long standing among translators; the convention of the chorus, with its music lost and its rhythms all but inaccessible in translation, is one of the features of Greek drama most alien to later readers and audiences. Such discomfort is evident in the oldest extant translations of Euripides in English (both sixteenth century), George Gascoigne and Francis Kinwelmersh's *Jocasta*, a version of an Italian adaptation of *Phoenician Women*, and the young Lady Jane Lumley's rendering of *Iphigenia at Aulis*, found among the family's private papers. Lumley simply omits choral odes entirely, perhaps as too difficult; Gascoigne and Kinwelmersh follow their Italian source in rewriting the odes extensively, omitting most of the more abstruse mythological material and adding to the moral reflections.

Certainly one of the difficulties of Euripidean choral odes lies in their glancing allusions to people and places in myths that may be unfamiliar to modern readers and audiences. When the chorus of the *Hippolytus* wish they could escape the pitiable events unfolding before them, they sing:

> And may I fly high over the sea waves of the Adrian coast and the water of the Eridanus, where the unhappy girls drip amber-gleaming tears into the dark-colored swell in lamentation over Phaethon.
>
> (Halleran, Aris ed., lines 735–41)

Phaethon, mortal son of the sun god, lost control of his father's chariot team and was killed by Zeus to save the earth from burning up; his sisters, lamenting him, turned to poplar trees, their tears to amber. Although the explicit function of this mythical allusion is simply to evoke a faraway place, the reference to the sisters' lamentation clearly anticipates the chorus's own mourning for Phaedra, who is about to kill herself. For an audience familiar with the myth, however, the reference to Phaethon also indirectly foreshadows Hippolytus's loss of control over his horses and his resulting death. A modern translator cannot presume that his or her audience knows this story. Some twentieth-century versions leave this difficulty unresolved in the text and provide explanatory footnotes; others omit the footnotes and make it the reader's responsibility (or the teacher's) to discover the mythical context. Translators in a third group add to Euripides's words to provide more information; they don't tell the whole story— a strategy quite alien to lyric, whose narrative mode tends to be elliptical— but instead provide what might be called hints. So, for example, David Grene gives us:

> Into that deep-blue tide,
> where their father, the Sun, goes down,
> the unhappy maidens weep
> tears from their amber-gleaming eyes
> in pity for Phaethon.   (738–41)

And Robert Bagg writes:

> [. . .] the river Eridanos,
> by whose black current
> live black poplars, sisters endlessly tearful,
> echoing in exquisite deliquescence
> the plunge of Phaethon their brother [. . .].   (lines 1128–32)

By allusions to other elements in the myth (the Sun, the sisters' transformation into poplars, Phaethon's plunge), these translators appear to remind their readers of a story once known and partly forgotten. (Phaethon? Oh, yes, that's the one who . . .)

If, however, obscure choral references to myth present a challenge to the translator of Euripides, this challenge is hardly peculiar to Euripides; it is one he shares with Aeschylus and Sophocles, as he also in places shares with them the challenges posed by lyric's density of metaphor and its sometimes enigmatic brevity. The particular difficulty of Euripidean choruses seems to me (speaking both as a translator and as a teacher of Euripides in translation) rather to lie in the passages in which Euripidean lyric conveys its wealth of impressions and ideas in language that is both elaborate and somehow ordinary. In many of Euripides's choral odes and other songs, such as the monodies and duets especially common in his later works, he prefers relatively straightforward similes to metaphors, and much of his imagery is richly descriptive rather than figurative; moreover, imagery often gives way to brief narratives of events and direct expressions of wishes, fears, and thoughts. Euripidean odes are in some ways easier to understand than the odes of Aeschylus, but this doesn't make them easy to translate, and what is difficult about them is often a matter of tone: we see what's being said but not how it is meant.

The problem of what we might call Euripides's tone of voice is not limited to lyric; his stylistic register in spoken iambics as well is hard to grasp and harder to convey. It is in general difficult to know what level of diction to choose in translating Greek tragic dialogue, which was written in an idiom for which there is no obvious correlative in current English. Bernard Knox has memorably described the translator as having to make his or her way between "Pinion and Grab," that is, between a high-flown, perhaps archaic style, and current colloquial speech (Rev. of *Aeschylus* 59). Euripides himself was identified in antiquity with an everyday diction (at least, everyday by contrast with the sublimely startling constructions of Aeschylus) that matched his particular brand of realism. In Aristophanes's *Frogs* he is described as having put tragic diction on a reducing diet (939–43), and Aristotle speaks of his concealing artifice by choosing words from ordinary speech (*Rhetoric* 3.2.5).

What seems to trouble many translators of Euripides is his very plainness, felt perhaps (in spite of its lyrical and rhetorical power) as insufficiently "poetic" when turned into English. T. S. Eliot famously reproached Gilbert Murray for the images he had added to Euripides: "So, here are two striking phrases which we owe to Mr. Murray; it is he who has sapped our soul and shattered the cup of all life for Euripides" (48). In the lines to which Eliot refers, Euripides's straightforward "I am lost, I have forfeited all joy in living, my friends, and I want to die" (Morwood, *Medea*, lines 225–27) is rendered by Murray as "I dazzle where I stand, / The cup of all life shattered in my hand." This passage is taken from a speech, but lyric instances are easy to find; when (for example) the chorus of *Alcestis* speaks of Apollo as "providing remedies for poor suffering mortals" (Conacher, lines 971–72, a fairly literal translation), Murray calls these "Pale herbs of comfort in the bowl / Of man's wide sorrow" (54).

Modern translators continue to make such additions, both in choral odes and elsewhere. Where Euripides writes, "I have found nothing stronger than Necessity" (Conacher, *Alcestis*, lines 965–66). William Arrowsmith gives us "Necessity is stone" (1238). Where Euripides writes, "Circling in their round came troubles and a fate more harsh than these" (Kovacs, *Hecuba*, lines 639–40), Kenneth McLeish has "Now misery, now pain, / swarms on us, surrounds us" (91), perhaps evoking clouds of insects, and Marilyn Nelson renders the same lines as "Now grief, and worse than that, destiny / holds me in its unbreakable embrace" (lines 834–45).

Arrowsmith, McLeish, and Nelson may all be read as engaging in what Michael Riffaterre has called "transposing presuppositions." A literary translation, as Riffaterre puts it, "must translate what the text only implies" (217), and when direct translation fails to convey the implications and presuppositions of the original, these must be suggested elsewhere or otherwise. The English word *necessity* is close to the Greek here but lacks the power of the Greek word; the translator compensates by evoking the inalterable solidity of stone. In the passage from *Hecuba*, the word translated as *sufferings* occurs twice in the first line, divided only by two conjunctions; this juxtaposition, and the implied multiplication of troubles, can't be replicated easily in English syntax, and McLeish's "swarms" reaches for the same effect. Nelson's "unbreakable embrace," like Arrowsmith's "stone," reinforces for English-speaking readers the inescapability of fate.

I suspect, however, that these translators are also responding, as Murray did, to Euripides's relative plainspokenness. Those who describe their versions as "freely translated" go even further; in Robert Meagher's version of *Hecuba* (*Hekabe*), the lines quoted above have been replaced by something vividly metaphorical and unrecognizable as Euripides: "Our avalanche of ruin began / With one small slip of soul" (26). The strongest argument for such additions in choral odes and other lyric passages might be that with the loss of Euripides's music—including the musical innovation that seems to have marked his late plays—we need something in its place to convey and effect a heightened emotion. But some translators seem to feel a similar lack in literal renderings of spoken dialogue. In the introduction to her recent translation of *Medea*, Eleanor Wilner declares that she has "added metaphor to more fully embody and thereby evoke meaning" (9), and this is true of dialogue as well as of lyric. We find a contrasting means used toward a similar end when HD tries to achieve the "emotional tension" of the Greek in the dialogue passages of her *Ion* ("a play after Euripides") not by expansion but by "concentrating and translating sometimes, ten words, with two" (32).

If some translators work to supplement or otherwise intensify what they experience as Euripides's plainness of style, others set themselves the task of capturing that plainness, that is, of conveying in English Euripides's evocation of the way people actually talk. John Davie, the author of the new Penguin version, justifies his choice of prose as making possible a translation that "conforms far more to how people speak" (xlv), and it could indeed be argued that for a contemporary English-speaking audience only prose can adequately hide its artifice and seem like ordinary speech. What Euripides gives us, however, is not ordinary speech itself but poetic diction (in metrical verse) that imitates or enacts ordinary speech; we thus find many other recent translators choosing verse, more or less formal or free, as a medium and following something like Robert Bagg's strategy: "I have tried to approach colloquial American speech as closely as the decorum of a passage permitted" (*Hippolytos* 11–12).

Both Davie and Bagg, different as their translations are in other respects, declare themselves to be aiming for something that resembles or represents ordinary speech. They are also alike in stressing the importance not only of striking the right note in general but also of conveying the range and variety of Euripidean tragic discourse (a concern that appears regularly in the introductions to recent translations). This variety is partly a matter of character and of occasion, but it has to do as well with Euripides's use of certain conventions, such as the explanatory prologue, the debate with two speakers, and the messenger's account of offstage action, each with its own sort of rhetoric and all largely alien to the experience of modern English-speaking readers and audiences. Such conventions are not limited to Euripides, but (judging from Aristophanes's parodies in *Frogs*, lines 1198–248) he seems to have made more frequent and more standardized use of the prologue than anyone else, and his debates reflect the increasing interest in rhetorical display in late-fifth-century Athens. It is probably easier for a translator to convey the pathos of Andromache, the anger of Medea, or the prurient hostility of Pentheus than to bring to life fifty lines of background information, which may give modern English-speaking readers both more and less than meets their expectations, and to engage those readers' interest in rhetorical debate. (Ronald Duncan, author of an English adaptation of Sartre's adaptation of *Trojan Woman*, tells us that he has made further cuts in part because "with Racine in the background, the French have still an appetite for rhetoric which a contemporary English-speaking audience will not swallow" [xvi].)

What is most difficult of all, perhaps, is to do justice to the many scenes and passages in Euripides in which there are elements or hints of irony, parody, or humor. It is the very subtlety of these modes in Euripides that makes them hard to represent in translation. Euripides's comedy is never broad, and his ironies are often less than obvious; scholars regularly disagree about whether a particular passage or speech is indeed to be understood as ironic, or as comic, and to what effect.

Even where there is general agreement that a passage is in some way comic or ironic, it isn't always clear how to translate that passage. In *Alcestis* (to take one example), Heracles makes a drunken speech, thus evoking the gluttonous excesses attributed to the hero in comedy. We know that Heracles is drunk: a disgusted slave has just told us so, and there are also a number of stylistic hints (see Conacher's commentary on the peremptory and the owlish in this speech). But these are subtle hints, and straightforward translation generally fails to make Heracles's condition clear. Here are three examples of the speech's opening from recent versions (the first in continuous prose, the second in prose with line divisions, the third in metrical verse):

> You there, why do you look so grave and careworn? A servant ought not to scowl at the guest but welcome him with an affable air.
> (Kovacs, lines 773–75)

> You there, why do you look so solemn and thoughtful?
> It is not right for a servant to glower at a guest
> but rather, he should receive him with an easygoing temper.
> (Rabinowitz, lines 773–75)

> Say, man, what makes you look so deadly sober?
> A servant's supposed to cheer the guest with smiles,
> not frown upon him.   (Chappell, lines 755–57)

Here the expression of Heracles's drunkenness is left largely up to the actor or to the reader's imagination. But what if a translator wants to assist that imagination by conveying in English what is evidently suggested by the Greek? A few try to give the sort of subtle indication we find in Euripides; thus Conacher (in prose) italicizes words to suggest a drunken emphasis ("Servants shouldn't *scowl* at guests" [line 774]), and Dudley Fitts and Robert Fitzgerald (in verse) seem to be evoking the overcareful utterance of the drinker ("Hello there. Why so / Solemn? Why do you look so / Grim?" [57–58]). Several translators express the resemblance between Heracles's speech and the sentiments to be found in drinking songs by turning one section or another of his lines into a formally distinct song, further marked by italics or quotation marks, and giving a stage direction that has the drunken hero sing.

> *All men have to die, and that's a fact:*
> *There isn't one who knows when he'll get sacked.*
> *Death isn't visible before he comes:*
> *You can't predict your death by doing sums.*
> (Fitts and Fitzgerald 58)

"Bottoms up!
Give every day an easy chance
And leave the rest to circumstance." (Chappell, lines 769–71)

Only one translator, as far as I have been able to find, makes Heracles's drunkenness blatant; this is William Arrowsmith, who does so by translating the entire speech into the English of the stage drunk:

Hey, you there!
Yeah, I mean you, with the big frown on your face!
What'sh your problem, sourpuss?
Butler'sh oughtta be polite, goddamit.
Servish with a smile.   (lines 968–72)

We may perhaps read Arrowsmith's particular choice of idiom here in the light of his argument elsewhere that in Greek comedy "dialectal humor should always be translated by convention rather than realistically"—that is, with a recognizably conventional comic dialect such as "minstrel-Southern" or "variety-hall Yiddish" ("Lively Conventions" 133, 134). (He does not address what now seem obvious problems in the use of such conventions, with their deployment of broad caricature and often demeaning stereotypes.) By giving Heracles the conventionally slurred speech of the drunk, Arrowsmith is doing in *Alcestis*—a play with many comedic elements—something very like what he recommends for comedy. He recognizes in a footnote that "Herakles' Greek is more correct and 'sober' than my translation" but argues that this is a matter of ancient convention, which left more up to the actor (114). He thus represents himself as merely making explicit what Euripides suggests—but in so doing, he clearly makes a significant change in his original, precisely because he makes explicit what Euripides merely suggests.

The passages I have cited exemplify something of the range of translations of Euripides in the second half of the twentieth century, a range whose extremes common usage still describes by the terms "literal" and "free," with imitation or adaptation as a move into something beyond translation and "word for word" as a kind of impossible vanishing point of the literal. Translators at the one end tend to speak of accuracy, of being true to the meaning, or of staying close to the Greek, even sometimes at the expense of English idiom; at the other end, they are more likely to dwell on the need to make the play available to modern readers and audiences or to cite a double allegiance to the demands of poetry in English and to Euripides's text.

When translators suggest a primary commitment either to the original at the expense of English idiom or to English idiom and the English-speaking reader at the expense of what is in the Greek, they locate themselves not only along the spectrum from literal to free translation but also in relation to a somewhat different opposition, articulated by earlier theorists and recently given new prominence. As Friedrich Schleiermacher describes this opposition, "Either the translator leaves the writer alone as much as possible and moves the reader toward the writer, or he leaves the reader alone as much as possible and moves the writer toward the reader" (42). The first sort of translator, for Schleiermacher, tries insofar as is possible to enable readers to understand a text that will, however, remain foreign to them; this translation will always seem like a translation. The second sort tries to make the author speak as if he or she were a native speaker of the language of the translation; this translation will seem like an original text in the new language. An explicitly politicized version of Schleiermacher's opposition has recently become prominent in translation studies, especially through the work of Lawrence Venuti, who sets what he calls "foreignizing" translation against domestication. The agenda of Venuti's foreignizing translation is both to make more visible the act of translation in its own right and to avoid the assimilation of the translated work and its culture to the language and culture of the translation.

We can trace in earlier translations of Greek tragedy a tradition that consciously seeks to avoid such assimilation; Browning, for example, tries to translate *Agamemnon* "in as Greek a fashion as English will bear" (ix). No translator of Euripides—at least to my knowledge—has gone as far as Browning does in his *Agamemnon* in the direction of replicating Greek syntax and vocabulary in English. But some recent translations reflect an agenda similar to Venuti's; Ruby Blondell, for example, notes in the introduction to her recent translation of *Medea* that she has "tried not to erase the Otherness of the text and culture" (168). Her fellow translators in the volume *Women on the Edge* (an anthology of four Euripidean tragedies) share this aim, and their general introduction criticizes earlier translators such as Rex Warner for disguising cultural difference.

For Venuti, the translator must reveal that difference not so much by seeking accurately to represent it—an impossibility, he holds—as by "disrupting the cultural codes that prevail in the target language." In translations of an ancient text, this may mean the use either of archaic English or of English that is in some other way nonstandard (perhaps "marginal") to "stage an alien reading experience" (20). There is, of course, a long tradition of archaizing in translations of Greek tragedy; Way's Loeb Classical Library versions of Euripides are full of such English survivals (long out of ordinary use in his own day) as "unholpen," "guest-fain," and "quotha," but this practice is now out of fashion. What's more, there is an inescapable paradox in the use of any particular identifiable marginal discourse, which is that it tends at once, in Venuti's terms, to "domesticate" and to "foreignize." Derek Mahon's version of *The Bacchae* includes such comic-book sound effects as "Whoosh!" and "pow!" and disrupts our expectations with slang, anachronistic description, and allusions to modern texts and contexts. The reader of such a translation is reminded that the work is a translation (after all, Euripides couldn't have quoted from *Casablanca*) but also experiences the assimilation of Euripides's story and culture to ours.

Such a double effect is not surprising, and many translators refuse the choice Schleiermacher and his heirs declare they must make. In his general preface to the series Greek Tragedy in New Translations, Arrowsmith speaks first as if he were on the side of domestication: "Our most urgent present need is for a re-creation of these plays—as though they had been written, freshly and greatly, by masters fully at home in the English of our own times." To achieve this end, he tells us, the translators must themselves be poets. But he goes on to argue for a collaboration between poet and scholar that will resist assimilation of the original text: "Clearly, few contemporary poets possess enough Greek to undertake the complex and formidable task of transplanting a Greek play without also 'colonializing' it or stripping it of its deep cultural difference, its remoteness from us" (*Euripides:* Alcestis vii).

That these two concerns are balanced in Arrowsmith's preface reflects in part his desire both to meet the needs of the "general reader or student" and to produce versions that can be acted. In general, translators who stress literalness or accuracy and see themselves, in Schleiermacher's terms, as bringing the reader to the writer are writing primarily for readers (including teachers and students), while those who stress the accessibility of the translation in English and wish to bring the writer to the reader are often writing for performance of some kind or other. One of the obvious reasons that translations for production tend to deal more fully in equivalents, supplements, and expansion is that the audience cannot be assisted by explanatory commentary as the reader can.

A translator's practice may of course be affected by other differences in the circumstances of the intended reader and in the proposed function or context of use of the translation. Is the reader expected to know the original language or not? Is the reader a student or Arrowsmith's "general reader," an adult or a child? What should the reader get from the translation? The same considerations obviously enter into a reader's choice of translation. What particular concerns, then, should govern the choice of a translation of Euripides specifically for use in undergraduate or graduate classes, and what might a translation designed for teaching look like?

The translators in the Aris and Phillips series, designed explicitly for students and teachers at a variety of levels, try to be (in the words of the general editor, Christopher Collard) "both accurate and idiomatic" (Conacher, *Euripides:* Alcestis vi). Paul Woodruff, whose version of *The Bacchae* is "intended primarily for classroom use," describes himself as aiming "first of all at being clear and true to the basic meaning of the text" and then as trying to convey "the beauty of poetry given the chorus as well as the rhetorical power and cleverness of the dialogue and speeches" (vii). The assumption in both instances is that a text for teaching should give priority to what Woodruff calls "basic meaning," and in fact, anyone who has taught literature in translation knows the risks of using a translation that alters or interprets the original freely. The student—or teacher—who bases a reading on a particular cluster of images, or who draws conclusions about Athenian culture from a striking formulation of the position of women, may feel both let down and barred from further independent interpretation when informed that the words in question do not actually appear in the Greek. But there are obvious risks as well in the use of a translation that is as accurate as possible but gives little sense of Euripides as poet and dramatist. Students who may in any case be prepared to dislike ancient literature—because of its cultural and chronological distance, because of its canonical "greatness"—will be even less likely to give Euripides a chance if they encounter his plays in a form that makes it unclear what anyone ever saw in them.

The most widely used translations for the last few decades have been those in the Chicago series edited by David Grene and Richmond Lattimore, and for good reason. They are fairly close to the Greek, sometimes elaborating slightly by way of explication but not radically expanding or cutting the original. Their avoidance, by and large, of both archaism and colloquialism has made them reasonably accessible to several generations of students. Finally, they aim at poetic effect as well as accuracy, and at their best (here I would cite especially Arrowsmith's *Bacchae*) they do give some sense of the dramatic and poetic vigor of the originals.

Despite these virtues, however, the series is not altogether satisfying. Some of the translations are on the flat side, and they can be (and have been) criticized both by those who want a more exact representation of the Greek and by those who want stronger poetry. These versions also lack explanatory footnotes, which may present a difficulty both for students and for teachers who are themselves not classicists, although I have always liked the brevity of their introductions, which leave class discussion relatively unencumbered by authoritative interpretation.

There are numerous alternatives currently available, from the deliberately literal to the self-consciously literary; I have mentioned some of these above. I am not convinced that in the case of Euripides (unlike Sophocles, for whose Theban plays I would recommend the Fagles translation) any more-recent series deserves to displace the Chicago series for classroom use. But it makes sense to experiment with other translations for particular plays—or for particular purposes. What seems to me especially worth noting is that not every course in which Euripides is taught calls for the same sort of translation. In a course that is centrally concerned (for example) with tragedy in its fifth-century cultural context, with the representation of women in Greek literature, or with fifth-century intellectual history, a translation that gives students the closest possible idea of the vocabulary, phrasing, and cultural resonance of Euripides's language will be most useful. In a course on the tragic tradition in Western literature or a course on drama in performance, it may be more important for students to read translations whose poetic and dramatic effectiveness will keep them from underestimating the plays or being baffled by claims of their theatrical power and historical influence.

Euripides's *Medea* is one of the most frequently taught and frequently translated of his tragedies and is quite well rendered in the Chicago series by Rex

Warner. But for those who want to teach the play in a course on women in antiquity or on fifth-century Athens, I would recommend the new version by Ruby Blondell in the anthology *Women on the Edge*, whose translators seek to help the reader "locate these plays within their original social, cultural, and performance contexts" (xiii). Blondell's introduction and notes are extensive and thorough, and her translation is attentive to the distinctive cultural signif- icance of various linguistic usages. She translates metaphors "more rather than less literally" (168), and, like her fellow translators in this volume, deliberately retains in English the repetition of thematically important words in the Greek (a feature of a number of Euripidean tragedies): *sophos*, for example, which might with perfect semantic accuracy—and thus literally—be rendered in dif- ferent contexts as *wise, clever,* or *skillful,* always appears as *clever,* "even though this sometimes sounds rather odd in English" (168). Blondell also takes pains to distinguish Greek words that are sometimes rendered by a single word in English; thus, she avoids using *love* for both *philia* (friendship, familial bond, belonging) and *eros* (erotic desire, passion).

Blondell's translation, unlike the others in the volume, is metrical, and though she "would not call it poetry" (168) it is by and large an effective ren- dering, even if her other concerns do occasionally lead to awkwardness or odd- ity (something we should perhaps welcome, with Venuti, as a reminder of difference).

For those who would prefer to teach *Medea* in a translation attentive above all to "poetic necessities" (Wilner 12) and to the play as drama, I would suggest (rather than the older adaptation by Robinson Jeffers, which cuts and alters the original quite drastically) Eleanor Wilner's new version (with Inés Azar) in the Penn Greek Drama series. Wilner, as I noted above, adds metaphor freely and sometimes elaborates where she feels explanation is called for, but plot and cho- ruses are intact, and the translator's avowed "shamelessness" (12) arises partly from her respect for the rhetorical force of Euripidean lyric and dialogue.

A brief passage illustrates the contrast between the three translations. About a third of the way through the play, the chorus sing an ode that moves from general reflections on men's and women's behavior and its treatment in poetry to the particular circumstances that inspired these reflections, Medea's exile from her home and betrayal by her husband, Jason. Warner's translation of the first strophe reads as follows:

> Flow backward to your sources, sacred rivers,
> And let the world's great order be reversed.
> It is the thoughts of *men* that are deceitful,
> *Their* pledges that are loose.
> Story shall now turn my condition to a fair one,
> Women are paid their due.
> No more shall evil-sounding fame be theirs.
>   (lines 410–20)

Warner inexplicably renders the indicative verbs of the first two lines as imperatives but otherwise follows the Greek quite closely, making a few slight changes apparently to point up the contrast between men and women. In fact, however, his translation—although a perfectly reasonable rendering of the Greek—has disguised certain things that Blondell's version reveals.

> Streams of sacred rivers are flowing uphill;
> all things are twisted backward, even justice;
> it is men whose plans are full of guile;
> pledges made in the name of the gods
> no longer stand secure.
> The stories that they tell
> will twist my life around,
> bestow on it a glorious reputation.
> Honor is coming to the female race
> No longer will malicious stories
> hold women in their grasp.   (lines 410–20)

Blondell shows us that Euripides uses the same verb (which she renders as "twist") both to describe an unheard-of reversal in the order of nature and to predict a reversal in the reputation of women; she also shows that he uses the same noun (which she renders as "stories") for the source of women's future glory and their former ill-fame. Finally, in retaining the expression "female race"—odd to the ears of English speakers—she reminds us by her translation, as she does in a footnote, that Greek literature sometimes describes women as if they were in fact a distinct kind of being with a distinct origin.

Wilner's version, in contrast, is little concerned with details of wording; here we can see exemplified what I described at the start of this essay as an effort to intensify Euripides's plain speech—or to re-create an intensity lost in the plain translation of his speech—by the addition of metaphor:

> Backward flow the rivers,
> uphill to their source,
> justice and the order
> of the universe
> reversed; the god-sworn
> oaths that held men
> to their word are torn
> like rotted rope.
> Now will the feet
> of sense tread air, and
> thought stand on its head.
> Now will men admire
> our women's ways, and give

us sway; no more will they
insult and slander us; honor
shall be our daily bread. (lines 438–53)

Whatever version of a play is required, it is worth making others available to students. I would recommend that those who teach Warner's or Wilner's *Medea* put Blondell's on reserve—and vice versa. The student who reads Arrowsmith's *Bacchae* (still my first choice, with Woodruff's as runner-up) might compare with it some of the many other recent translations across the spectrum from Richard Seaford to C. K. Williams and might look as well at such transformations as Mahon's The Bacchae: *After Euripides* and Wole Soyinka's The Bacchae *of Euripides: A Communion Rite*. None of these is Euripides's play, but students can find aspects of Euripides reflected or refracted in all of them. What's more, such comparisons may lead students to engage more self-consciously in the process of reading in translation and perhaps to escape the passivity Schleiermacher seems to ascribe to the reader of translations, who must either be brought to the writer or be left to await the writer's arrival. Euripides's own texts consistently provoke the reader to active engagement and resist any simple or consistent line of interpretation; it may do them a kind of justice to read them as variously interpreted by different translators.

Modern Views of Euripides

Ann N. Michelini

This essay contains three sections. The first deals with earlier work on Euripides through the middle 1970s and the genesis of critical attitudes that persist today.[1] The second section, on scholarship in the last two decades, addresses changes and developments in the modern view of Euripides. The third offers bibliographical information on special topics and discussions of some individual plays.

A Tradition of Euripidean Scholarship

The modern view of Euripides was formed at a crucial moment near the turn of the nineteenth century, when German intellectuals, including Johann Winckelmann, popularizer of classical art; the brothers August and Friedrich Schlegel, lecturers on world literature; and the great poets of the day, Schiller and Goethe, rediscovered the Athens of the fifth century BCE. For them, this brilliant era held out the promise that a culture, even their own modern German one, might be regenerated and transfigured by artistic achievement.

These intellectuals saw in Greek art a balance and serenity that was lacking in the contemporary artistic scene, with its taste for the grotesque and its emphasis on a tormented, self-questioning interior life. As the sculptures of the Parthenon exemplified "classic" visual art, the plays of Sophocles stood as the major emblem of literary achievement in the Periclean decades between mid-century and the outbreak of the Peloponnesian War (431 BCE). But the moment of cultural triumph was perceived as fleeting: Athens's decline into "degeneracy" during the war years was thought to be portrayed both in the satiric comedies of Aristophanes and in the sober historical narrative of Thucydides. Thus the study of this Athenian "classical" period also provided a warning against the danger of decay and loss, a danger posed precisely by modern literary tendencies (Michelini, *Euripides* 3–6).

This story of triumph and collapse, however, had some difficulty in assimilating the work of Euripides, a poet who for almost a half-century (455–06 BCE) was the contemporary and rival of Sophocles and whose work had a dangerously modern flavor. The solution for the theorists of the early Romantic era, and for many who have followed them, has been to ignore the essentially coeval careers of these two poets and to place Euripides in the later and "decadent" period to which his work seemed to belong.

The characteristics of Euripidean drama that made it so disturbing are well known. Vigorous debates (agons) in the plays present in provocative terms the controversies of an age of intellectual ferment (Michelini, *Euripides* 64–65, 74–92). Slaves, the elderly, and women are prominent, active, and vocal, and their interventions often have the effect of puncturing the heroic pretensions of dominant males. Equally disturbing is the fluidity of moral and intellectual values. Euripidean plays frequently defeat any attempt to identify certain characters as sympathetic or in the right: apparently likable figures turn unlikable (Admetus) or even bloodthirsty (Ion and Creusa in *Ion*, the protagonist in *Hekabe*), and villains emerge as curiously sympathetic (Eurystheus in *Children of Heracles*, Clytemnestra in *Electra*). Euripides's most famous character, Medea, seems to vibrate between emotional appeal and chilling evil not just scene by scene but almost line by line. The instability of Euripidean psychology in turn affects the impact of the ideas that his characters present with such topical vividness (Michelini, *Euripides* 86–87, 211; see also Gibert) .

The multiform volatility of the Euripidean theater undermines even the dramatic illusion of reality; the plays are "stagey," commenting metatheatrically on their own status as artifacts. Other features enhance this effect: the patently artificial prologue, in which a character seems to address the audience directly, filling in the background of the plot; the formally staged debates between two characters and the insertion of speculative and intellectualized arguments into these debates; and the deus ex machina endings, in which a divine figure descends to resolve the plot (see Michelini, *Euripides* 95–116). This is a drama that denies its audience the pleasures of rest and harmony and that thrives on dissonance. No wonder Euripides for two centuries has seemed so irretrievably modern.

Criticism of Euripides through the first half of the twentieth century continued to vibrate between the horns of the dilemma that the early critics had set up: Euripides was often "defended" as a dramatist whose work exemplified traditional Hellenic values, or he was (at least from the viewpoint of the defenders) "attacked" as a rebellious poet, who introduced "melodramatic" themes and characters into the lofty genre of tragedy. The attitude of defense has naturally been more appealing, since scholars tend to glorify the texts to which their lives' work has been devoted. But the attempt to rehabilitate Euripides has often led to partial and limited views of an author who usually fails to fit the assigned model of the "serious" or the "tragic."

The amazing books of A. W. Verrall are a striking instance of the defense technique. A respected English scholar, Verrall proposed to cure apparent defects in the plays by assuming that the plays had encoded secret meanings for the Athenian intelligentsia, who would, for instance, understand that any mythical wonders or divine apparitions should be disregarded. More-successful early English-speaking critics were Gilbert Murray and H. D. F. Kitto. Although they sometimes questioned whether Euripides was primarily a tragic artist, rather than a satirist or propagandist, these scholars took a sympathetic view of Euripides's modern quality, noting his use of irony and topical themes and associating him for better or for worse with the intellectual theater of Ibsen or Shaw. Of course, for scholars who saw Euripides as necessarily "classic, " this approach impugned the value of his work.

In 1967, Desmond J. Conacher published *Euripidean Drama*, a comprehensive book on Euripides that, while it avoided theory and generalizations, did include perceptive interpretations of all the plays, demonstrating the amazing versatility and inventiveness of this playwright. Shortly after, Anne Pippin Burnett's book *Catastrophe Survived*, which drew on a rich German scholarly tradition in the structural analysis of tragedy (see discussion of this work in Michelini, *Euripides* 19–22, 30–34), examined Euripidean variations on the theme of danger and reversal. But Burnett's demonstrations of Euripides's skillful theatrical technique were balanced by an attempt to seek "deeper" meaning in the plays by means almost as extreme as those of Verrall. Burnett's conclusion that certain characters were punished because of their "lack of faith" (121, 162) had little support in the text and depended on Christian notions of redemptive divine love that are alien to Greek religion.

Three plays, *Ion*, *Iphigenia among the Taurians*, and *Helen*, seemed to represent an extreme of tendencies frequently noted in Euripides, toward a lighter, more comedic or "melodramatic" style. Throughout the 1960s a number of European scholars studied these plays, and Burnett had made them the centerpiece of her analysis of plot variation. In 1974, Cedric H. Whitman used the categories of literary development proposed by Northrop Frye to argue that Euripidean drama produced "a kind of deliberate polytonality, as if tragedy were being written in two keys at once" (*Euripides* 113). By adopting a critical system that allowed validity to a variety of artistic modes, Whitman offered a way out of the cycle of apology and rehabilitation. Yet Whitman preferred the lighter dramas he chose, because he felt that in them extraneous elements were subjected to a "larger, controlling vision" (*Euripides* 139). He paid less attention to the air of charm and comedic insubstantiality that pervades these plays and that has led some critics to argue that they do not belong to the tragic genre at all. If a sensation of "wholeness" can be found only in these exceptional dramas, then it may be that wholeness, like the serene beauty that the early critics missed in Euripides, is not central to his work.

The modern view of Euripidean drama began with a conundrum: how can such an artist fit into the picture of an era of ideal and balanced perfection? My response is that the costs of maintaining this picture are too high, since it excludes not only the work of Euripides but also much of the creative ferment that emerged from the fragmented and contentious cultures of Greece and that reached its peak in the second half of the Athenian fifth century. The jagged, confrontational, artificial, and disturbing drama of Euripides is as much a part of the story of the fifth century as are the outrageous ideas of Parmenides, Zeno, and Anaxagoras or the sculptures of the Parthenon. Euripidean drama does not permit us the luxury of separating off a "classical" period immune to the "disease" of modernity: this artist, whose plays fascinated his contemporaries while failing to win Athenian dramatic contests, to a surprising extent evokes the alienated and even hostile relations between artist and public that often characterized the modern period of the past two centuries. While it would be a gross error to treat as identical two periods so remote in culture, social systems, and economy, it is not unfair to say that, in reading Euripides, modern readers often found uncomfortable reminders of the cultural dilemmas of their own time.

Recent Work on Euripides

The interpretation of Euripides continues to be haunted by repetitive gestures of rehabilitation, assimilating the refractory artist to reassuringly traditional models of ancient Greek culture and art. David Kovacs, assuming ironic style to be an invention of the late modern era (*Heroic Muse* 9), made a bold attempt to read Euripides "absolutely 'straight,'" an approach that the author hoped could deal effectively with "the puzzling or unattractive features which a correct interpretation ought to explain" (*Heroic Muse* 21, 11). Kovacs's approach was to some extent replicated and extended by Justina Gregory, who saw Euripidean drama as a series of "lessons to the Athenians" (12; see discussion in Michelini, "Euripides: Conformist").

The considerable contemporary evidence that Athenian audiences found Euripidean drama both fascinating and disturbing (see Michelini, *Euripides* 70–94) may have little appeal, even to scholars who take a more theoretically informed view of Euripidean drama: emphasis on the discontinuities between Euripides and his tradition still seems to carry the implication that the artist's work is being devalued. I would, however, again point to the curious double standard according to which contemporary works are conventionally praised as challenging, disturbing, or even shocking, while the issue of dissonance in "classical" drama continues to be shunned. Instead, recent critics have successfully emphasized the ways in which tragedy in general challenged and problematized traditional Greek ideology. From this viewpoint, it no longer becomes necessary to take Euripides "straight" in order to see his plays as homogeneous with their tradition.

Especially important has been the work of Charles Segal. In his book on Sophocles, *Tragedy and Civilization*, Segal sees the tragic hero as a "liminal" figure, on the borders where nature and culture are "at a point of fluid interchange." Tragic drama, he argues, disrupts social and linguistic norms, permitting the audience to "experiment with other modes of grasping the world" (47–48; see also Segal, *Interpreting* 24–25). Segal's approach is a valid one and not essentially in conflict with the idea that Euripides may have pushed this tragic tendency to an extreme. Segal's work on Euripides is well represented by two recent collections: *Euripides and the Poetics of Sorrow* revised and expanded a number of important articles (see my review "Euripides: Conformist"), while others were reprinted in *Interpreting Greek Tragedy*. Among other themes, *Poetics of Sorrow* explores Euripides's use of gender concepts as they affect tragic drama's commemoration of the end of a heroic life. Male heroic death occurs in a public context, while women's deaths are private and domestic. In Segal's view, plays such as *Alcestis* simultaneously express and repress the grieving of women.

Equally vital to the newest approaches to Euripides has been the work of Froma I. Zeitlin. With John Winkler, Zeitlin published *Nothing to Do with Dionysus?*, a collection of articles that does much to situate tragic performance in its social milieu (see esp. Goldhill, "Great Dionysia"; Zeitlin, "Thebes"). Several of Zeitlin's most important articles on drama have recently appeared in revised form in *Playing the Other*, a collection focused on explorations of male and female gendered roles in tragic drama (see my review "Replaying"; on *Ion* and *Hippolytus*, see the last section of this essay). Zeitlin's approach, even more than Segal's, is strongly influenced by the work of French scholars, such as Marcel Detienne and Jean-Pierre Vernant, who brought structuralist and anthropological approaches to classical studies. Zeitlin argues that women, although largely excluded from the public sphere, provided an important category of otherness that was well suited to the subversive explorations of tragedy.

Euripides's subversive stance and his challenging approach to the contemporary audience were well suited to the issue of women's roles, which remained highly restricted in Athenian society, at a time when relations among male citizens approached an extreme of democratization. His plays, though to a much more restricted extent, also explored the role of slaves and non-Greeks. Influential on both Zeitlin and Segal has been the work of Helene P. Foley, a Euripidean scholar whose pioneering emphasis on gender has led her to focus on literary reflections of social and ideological systems (*Ritual Irony* 17–64; see also the last section of this essay). Foley's treatment of *Iphigenia at Aulis* shows the connections between marriage rituals and Iphigenia's sacrificial death (*Ritual Irony*, ch. 2). Nancy Sorkin Rabinowitz (*Anxiety*) has placed a contrasting emphasis on conservative elements in Euripidean treatments of gender, arguing that, while plays like *Hippolytus* and *Alcestis* seem to offer an opening to female agency and personhood, these openings are fleeting, and male dominance is eventually reinstated (see my review "Euripides: Conformist" and the discussion on *Alcestis* below).

An approach to Euripides that does justice to the full impact of his drama would supplement the emphasis placed by Charles Segal and others on the interplay of imagery in a system of structuralist oppositions with considerations such as audience response and authorial persona; dramatic technique, including motivation and dramatic character; and the manipulation of ideological and moral values. John Gibert's *Change of Mind in Greek Tragedy* (Greek in the text is not translated) offers a counterweight; see also Francis Dunn; Harvey Yunis; and Foley (*Ritual Irony*).

Both for modern critics and for the ancients, Euripides's failure to offer works that can be seen as modeling traditional values sets this playwright apart from his predecessors. This oppositional stance is a definitive marker of Euripidean style. It resonates with a familiarity that can lead modern readers to a double awareness, both of the essential strangeness of the Athenian fifth century and of its analogies to our own time. As the Greeks may have been the first to realize, the recognition of similarity in the alien inevitably becomes a process of self-discovery and a source of new perspectives.

Works on Individual Plays and Special Topics

This section does not deal with all of the nineteen plays in the Euripidean corpus but offers some bibliographical information on several of the most intriguing, most popular, and inevitably most controversial tragedies, as well as on a few specialized topics.

Alcestis, the first extant play, has proved endlessly provocative. Alcestis, in sacrificing herself for her husband, places the survivor spouse in a difficult position that is resolved only when the hero, Heracles, brings Alcestis back from the dead. The ending of the play centers on a joke by Heracles, who presents a silent and veiled Alcestis as a potential concubine for the bereaved husband. Admetus first resists, faithful to his deathbed promises to Alcestis, but eventually he succumbs, only to discover that, like the Count in *The Marriage of Figaro*, he has broken his vow with his own wife. The comic tone and apparently happy ending may match the play's presentation in place of a satyr play or comedy. (For background, see Michelini, *Euripides*, app. 2, 325–29. For discussion of gender issues, see C. Segal, *Euripides and the Poetics*, and Rabinowitz, *Anxiety*.) Nancy Rabinowitz's gendered reading of *Alcestis* succeeds beyond any other in finding unity in the play, through explicating the final scene between Heracles and Admetus. Others have pointed out that Alcestis's sacrifice threatens to damage Admetus's status as a man, since it places him in the position, usually given to women, of accepting protection against the threat of death. Rabinowitz has shown that, through his friendship with Heracles, Admetus reestablishes his status in the world of men, especially since the two conduct an exchange in which Alcestis is reduced to a more normal female role, as a silent token or intermediary between men.

Perhaps the quintessential Euripidean drama is *Medea*, a play that challenges gender norms as it does audience expectations, repeatedly evoking conflicting responses to its remarkable protagonist, who questions the oppressive circumstances of women's lives while she pursues an annihilating revenge that is congruent with a male heroic ethic of pride and honor, a course that eventually leads her to murder the children whom she loves. The best treatment of gender issues may be Foley's "Medea's Divided Self." (For a contrasting view, see Rabinowitz, *Anxiety*). Other important works are Bernard Knox's "The *Medea* of Euripides," Emily McDermott's *Euripides' Medea: The Incarnation of Disorder*, and Deborah Boedeker's essay, as well as the sophisticated theoretical approach of Pietro Pucci. Almost a companion play to *Medea* and apparently produced only a few years later is *Hekabe*. Assailed by not one but two deaths of children on a single day, the aged and enslaved Queen of Troy takes terrible revenge on her tormentor. The play contrasts the idealism of youth with the cynical desperation of age, constructing a tragic hero out of most refractory material, an old woman who eventually triumphs by influencing Agamemnon, the slave-master of her sole surviving daughter, to connive at her revenge. Formerly neglected, the play has recently received much attention (see Reckford; Nussbaum, *Fragility*; Michelini, *Euripides*; Zeitlin, *Playing*; and C. Segal, *Euripides*. For conservative views, see Kovacs, *Heroic Muse*; Gregory; and a fuller treatment in Mossman).

Produced only three years after *Medea*, *Hippolytus* is a striking contrast. As I have suggested, modern critical fascination with this play may stem from its exceptionalism, in that it somewhat mutes the ironic dissonance typical of Euripides (*Euripides* 277–97). Charles Segal's work on *Hippolytus* extends from the 1970s through the 1990s (see *Interpreting* and *Euripides*), and he has done much to illuminate the intricate strands of imagery that lace through this complex play. Besides Segal, there are Barbara Goff's study of the intersection between speech and the metaphor of knotting, *The Noose of Words*; a monograph by C. A. E. Luschnig, *Time Holds the Mirror*; and a long article by Zeitlin ("Power"), as well as a chapter in Rabinowitz's *Anxiety Veiled*. Segal has already made much in his *Alcestis* chapters of the dichotomy between inside and outside as equivalent to female and male worlds, respectively (see *Euripides*, esp. ch. 5). The same patterns appear in *Hippolytus* but with much more complexity. As Zeitlin and others (Knox, "*Hippolytus*"; Frischer) have shown, Phaedra and Hippolytus, kept apart throughout the play and placed in opposing relations to sexuality, are, like the two opposed goddesses Aphrodite and Artemis, paralleled and associated in imagery and in dramatic experience. Zeitlin also focuses on the experience of Hippolytus's painful transition, which parallels that of the protagonist of *Ion*, from the tranquil and idealized world of youth into the complexities of maturity ("Power"; "Mysteries").

Bacchae, one of Euripides's last plays, has also been one of the most popular. In it Euripides returns to a more old-fashioned form of tragic drama in which the active chorus of Bacchantes and its magnificent choral songs are of major importance. But the return to the archaic, as usual, serves only to put in question not only traditional heroic norms but also the very concept of tragic drama itself. Because the play deals with Dionysus, patron god of the theater, it has obvious metatheatrical aspects. In addition, the complex and contradictory role of the god, who is the numinous embodiment of a sacred, ecstatic, and murderous cult, raises issues of religion and piety that cut to the core, both of tragic experience and of Greek religion. The fullest treatment is by Charles Segal, *Dionysiac Poetics and Euripides' Bacchae*, an ambitious exploration of the play from a number of modern critical viewpoints (see also Foley, *Ritual Irony*). Segal shows how the overlapping roles for Dionysus, who is both actor in the drama and deus ex machina, create self-referential overtones throughout. Further, when the "tragic hero" of the play, Pentheus, driven to madness by Dionysus, assumes female attire as a Bacchante, his transvestism powerfully evokes the gender issues prevalent in Euripidean drama, as well as metatheatrical

themes of costume, also played on by the later appearance of Pentheus's severed head, which, Segal argues, must be identical with the tragic full-head
mask ("Metatragedy").

Trojan Women, a popular Euripidean play for production that focuses powerfully on the grief and suffering of captive women, has received extensive discussion by N. T. Croally; his approach is a conservative one, in that, like
Gregory, he believes that the poet instructs by exploring ambiguities and oppositions in traditional ideologies. Among the less well known plays, *Iphigenia at
Aulis*, set at the time of the Greek embarkation for Troy, has recently received
attention (see Foley, *Ritual Irony*; see also Luschnig, *Tragic Aporia*; Gibert;
and Michelini, "Expansion"). Produced posthumously and perhaps completed
from an unfinished version, the play is a fascinating evocation of romantic
themes that were to come to fruition in the family comedies of Menander. It
also modernizes epic by connecting the Trojan saga to a theme of Panhellenic
aggression that became prevalent in the fourth century and eventually served
to support the conquests of Alexander the Great. *Orestes* is a particularly disturbing play, in which the hero, who has murdered his mother, attempts to save
himself by a series of violent plots that seem to merge the heroic and the criminal. (Porter, aimed primarily at classicists, has useful general material in the
first two chapters; but note the seminal article by Zeitlin, "Closet.") The tightly
knit action climaxes in a paradoxical appearance by Apollo, who reconciles the
characters by insisting on a marriage between Orestes and his cousin
Hermione, at that moment a hostage with Orestes's sword at her throat!

Electra and *Heracles*, still not much discussed, each receive a chapter in my
Euripides and the Tragic Tradition (on *Electra*, see also Burnett, *Revenge*; on
Heracles, see Foley, *Ritual Irony*). *Electra* retells the familiar story of the
revenge against Clytemnestra in a particularly unheroic version: the heroine
has been married off to a respectable but poor farmer, with the result that her
revenge, taken out of its traditional heroic context, appears more culpable.
Heracles, a remarkable tragedy that breaks many rules of dramatic structure,
begins with a stereotyped rescue drama that turns to tragedy when the maddened hero slaughters the family he has just saved. The manifest cruelty of this
reversal is made vivid for audience members by their own shock at the dramatic shape of the play, and the close constitutes one of Euripides's most daring challenges to the religious concepts traditionally embodied in tragic drama.

I discussed the tragicomedies in the second section of this essay; on *Ion*, see
also Nicole Loraux ("Kreousa"), who studied the play's relation to Athenian
patriotic ideology and the role of citizen women; on *Helen*, a deft exploration of
illusion and reality, see Charles Segal ("Two Worlds"). Along with *Children of
Heracles* (Burnett, *Revenge*; Falkner), *Suppliants* is a fascinating example of a
Euripidean play on civic or patriotic themes (Michelini, "Political Themes").
The playwright readapts myths popular in Athenian public oratory, obliterating
the gap noted by Zeitlin between Athens, the triumphant solver of tragic problems, and Thebes or Argos, sites of grisly tragic events ("Thebes"). With his

Athenian plays, Euripides brings tragedy home to its native polis, problematizing the very myths used to support the self-image of the imperialist fifth-century democracy.

Fragments of plays that have not survived provide useful information on the wide range of Euripidean drama (e.g., the amazing speech from *Cretans* in which a queen defends her sexual liaison with a bull). The lost plays are reconstructed in T. B. L. Webster's *The Tragedies of Euripides*, and translations and discussions of some plays appear in Christopher Collard, Martin Cropp, and Kevin Lee's *Euripides*. Specialized topics are covered by the following, some of whom are also mentioned above: Shirley A. Barlow (imagery), Francis Dunn (endings of plays), John Gibert (dramatic character), Michael Halleran (dramatic technique), Michael Lloyd (the agon, or verbal contest), Marianne McDonald (filmed versions), Harvey Yunis (religion; see also Foley, *Ritual Irony*).

NOTE

[1]For a detailed history of Euripidean scholarship through the middle 1970s, see the first chapter of my book *Euripides and the Tragic Tradition*.

Moving Icons: Teaching Euripides in Film
Marianne McDonald

Classics are not museum pieces but living icons for understanding the present. In my undergraduate courses on Greek drama, classics, and mythology, which all include Euripides, films help convey the originals. Maria Wyke rightly claims, "Incorporating feature films, especially the works of acknowledged filmmakers, into classical course offerings need not represent a 'selling out' to the lowest common denominator or a trivialization of the tradition of Western Culture; rather, it is an effective means to make antiquity more readily accessible and to throw light on our own age as well" (127). One informs the other, and both can be great works of art. Nevertheless, we should also not be ashamed to point out the superiority of the classics when that is the case. They are always relevant and have important political and social messages.

I ask that students read the original texts, mainly in translation, and then I show a film. Lectures and discussions are based not only on the classic but also on the film. I generally follow the Aristotelian model of analyzing both from the standpoints of plot, characterization, thought, language, music, and spectacle. We compare the relevance of both the film and the ancient classic to modern times and our new multicultural society. Both ancient and modern contexts are investigated, and I think both are enriched by the mixture.

I point out how plays and films differ. There is an immediacy and a danger in live performance that a movie shown in a movie house cannot replicate. A film, with its technological capabilities, can collapse time and space; a character can enter past and future and fly in a jet to remote countries. The close-up also adds emotional commentary. The camera is a new director and sometimes fills the role of the chorus: what it sees can elucidate the text. The actor in a play delivers a new performance every time the play is staged; in film, the acting performance is frozen. The audience views it in a room with a large screen, and each individual is alone with his or her own private thoughts and the screen. In film, what is to be viewed is chosen in advance by the camera, whereas a person who sees a play chooses what part of the stage to look at, whose face to concentrate on. A play is more of a social event; that was certainly true in ancient Athens at the Greater Dionysia, the dramatic festival that marked the new year and the opening of the seas to travel. In fifth-century Athens, theater was designed as much to impress allies as to educate and amuse the citizens (Gregory).

Euripides has exciting things to say that still apply to many current issues. He depicts political corruption with devastating accuracy; his pungent criticism alienated his fellow citizens, and he spent the last years of his life in Macedonia. We know that he won few prizes in competition. Nevertheless, he speaks directly to us moderns. He can accurately be called not only the first psychologist but the first feminist as well. In Euripides the new heroes are more often heroines; slaves and children also now have their say. Euripides understands the victim and communicates the power of the oppressed.

It is not only because we have more plays by Euripides (19) than we do by Aeschylus (7) and Sophocles (7) that he is the most popular of the three as a model for modern films. The pathology and the passions that he investigates are so much a part of our modern life. In addition, tragedy lets both ancient and modern citizens investigate vital issues: What is the price of vengeance? What war is worth the death of the young? Does a responsible citizen owe more to family or to country?

Michael Cacoyannis based his filmed Trojan Trilogy on three plays by Euripides: *Elektra*, *Trojan Women*, and *Iphigenia*. Each film, in its own way, brilliantly translates the play into cinema. In the *Elektra*, Cacoyannis was still learning how to use a chorus effectively. He also rewrote Euripides's play and made it more Sophoclean. Whereas Euripides shows Electra and Orestes to be neurotics, Cacoyannis shows them as heroes; this was also what Sophocles did in his version. Euripides questions the act of matricide and Apollo's oracle that commanded it. In Euripides's play, Orestes wonders if an avenging fiend (979) had spoken in Apollo's place. But Cacoyannis eliminates the gods and adds scenes that show how Clytemnestra and Aegisthus are wastrels abusing both children and country. These differences from the original contribute to lively class discussion.

On a formal basis, one can find fault with some of Euripides's plays but never with the emotional impact that they deliver. *Trojan Women* is perhaps the greatest antiwar play ever written, and it shows why Aristotle called Euripides "the most tragic of the tragedians" (*Poetics* 1453a13). Cacoyannis in his film of this play uses the moving translation by Edith Hamilton. In the prologue, he calls Euripides's play a "timeless indictment of the horror and futility of all wars." He concludes it by saying, "We who have made this film dedicate it to all those who fearlessly oppose the oppression of man by man." The film was made during the years of the military occupation by a junta in Greece (1967–74). Cacoyannis spent those years in exile and made the film in Spain with an international cast, in contrast to *Elektra* and *Iphigenia*, which had Greek casts and were filmed in Greece.

Cacoyannis suggests a Marxist message: wars are fought for profit. In the film he adds lines that say that Helen was just an excuse for the Trojan War; the real motive was gold. His additions bring the play up to modern times, but he retains the power of the ancient text. Katharine Hepburn is moving as the aged Hecuba, mourning her grandson, hurled from the battlements of Troy because the Greeks had "found out ways to torture that were not Greek" and feared a little boy: "A little child, all innocent of wrong—you wish to kill him" (Hamilton 64–65).

Aristotle may criticize Iphigenia's change of mind in *Iphigenia at Aulis*, but by the end of the play it is not the logic that affects us but the emotions: the pity that we feel for Iphigenia and the fear that what happened to her might happen to our child, as indeed, if our child was a soldier, it could. The naive young are frequently sacrificed by old people in power who vote for war.

Cacoyannis's *Iphigenia* has been called a four-handkerchief film (Knox, *Word* 351), and no one is dry-eyed by the end. Cacoyannis follows Euripides closely, but one can see the parallels with modern Greece. At the time the film was made, Greece had just recovered from being occupied by the junta. The church, angered by the state's appropriation of its property, supported some of the junta's conservative agenda because of financial accommodation. In the film this corruption comes out in the way Calchas, the seer, is depicted. He clearly rigs the oracle and takes his vengeance on Agamemnon by exacting the life of his daughter in return for the life of the sacred deer that Agamemnon killed. Power struggles that typify Greek politics are unmasked in the sordid exchange between Menelaus and his brother. The message of Euripides's play and this film applies not only to Greece but universally—whenever and wherever a war is fought for personal gain.

Cacoyannis stresses the human elements over the supernatural ones. Artemis does not substitute a deer for Iphigenia as the interpolated end of Euripides's play suggests (Diggle). Now we see Iphigenia's death in Agamemnon's agonized eyes. Cacoyannis also adds a love interest between Iphigenia and Achilles (McDonald and MacKinnon 231–32).

The abuse of the weak is once again a theme. Cacoyannis uses clever cinematic devices—namely, an extended prologue and scenes that show the hunt for the deer and the later hunt for Iphigenia—to allow the viewer to see parallels between them: both are victims of a power-mad army. The final shot of Clytemnestra shows her staring at the fleet with blazing eyes, her hair blowing across her face, from the wind that was purchased by her daughter's life. Vengeance is in her eyes, conveyed by a silent stare. The cinema illustrates the text and makes it more vivid. A close-up silently conveys the internal life of a character in a film.

The classics are vitally modern and should be taught in a way that retains their excitement. In a class I taught on Greek tragedy and film in 1990, my students read Euripides's play and saw Cacoyannis's *Iphigenia*. Several of these students were going off to fight in the Gulf War: the class identified with Iphigenia and performed this play as their final project. It was staged outdoors, and jets flew over our heads during the performance. We, the audience, saw our children being sent off to fight a war that did not concern many of us but concerned rather our leaders in Washington who sought power. We were all Clytemnestra, and we wept.

I have shown some films in connection with Euripides's *Iphigenia at Aulis* because I detect a similarity in theme and plot. Jean-Pierre Jeunet's *Alien Resurrection* shows Ripley as a parent with Agamemnon's terrible dilemma: she knows she must kill her child for the communal good. *Ulee's Gold* highlights the relationship between a father and a daughter-in-law, and in a reversal of Euripides's play, the daughter is saved. The father chooses to commit a crime to save his family.

In 1998 I gave a miniseries of films based on Irish history and linked them with the classics. I compared Terry George's *Some Mother's Son* with Euripides's *Trojan Women*, and the topic of my lecture was mothers and war. This film shows two women, in a national war between Ireland and Britain, faced with their sons' being taken prisoner, which in the Irish context means being sent to prison (if you're lucky). The contrast between the two women is rather like the contrast between Hecuba and Andromache. Hecuba urges hope where Andromache despairs, but by the end of the play Hecuba joins Andromache in her lament: suffering and the loss of a child bring the women together. It also unites the audience in outrage against war and the victimization of the powerless by the powerful.

Euripides's tragedies were performed with music, and many modern renditions eliminate this essential element. I have used a video of Berlioz's *Les Troyens* to offer what might be considered a modern *Trojan Women* with music. The plot is varied and expanded: Cassandra is a heroine who balances Dido in the second half of the opera. Opera is also very useful for teaching the classics and was born as a revival of Greek tragedy. In both Euripides's play and this opera one understands the suffering of women during a war, and this is the key message of both.

Now I elucidate at greater length how I compare an ancient play and modern film, using Euripides's *Bacchae* as a parallel to Neil Jordan's *The Crying Game*. I call the talk for my class "Transformation, Liminality, and Gender." Both the film and the play involve cross-dressing and the education of a man who does not allow Dionysus into his heart. In *The Crying Game* the god is less vindictive.

Both the play and the film deal with what constitutes theatricality and identity. When does the persona (the Latin name for "mask") become the person? Dionysus-Bacchus is the god of the theater and the god of wine. He is called a god most fierce and most gentle; his nature has both aspects. He is the god of transformation, leader of the dance, and croupier for *The Crying Game*.

The plots of the play and the film both center on vengeance and the discovery of one's own nature. Jody, a black man serving in the English army, is taken hostage by the IRA. His vengeance is to seduce his guard by stimulating the guard's own passion. Jody has several guards, but he chooses the most vulnerable and humane, a man who is called Fergus. He shows Fergus a picture of his "special friend," the beautiful Dil, and asks Fergus to find her if he is killed, to tell her he was thinking of her, and to see how she is doing.

Fergus and Jody are similar: they are both subject to prejudice (Irish in one case, black in the other); both are doing their duty. Jody, a Dionysus parallel along with his "girlfriend" Dil, gradually seduces Fergus, a Pentheus stand-in. Jody is victimized just as Dionysus was at the beginning of the *Bacchae*; he is taken prisoner, and he exacts his vengeance.

Fergus is told to execute Jody, but as Jody tries to escape he runs into a British Saracen tank and is killed. The IRA hiding place is destroyed, and Fergus escapes to London. He gets involved with Dil but is horrified to discover that he/she is a man.

Jude, a brutal IRA agent with whom Fergus had been sleeping and who had seduced Jody so that he could be captured, finds Fergus and tries to involve him in another operation. Jude and Dil have a shoot-out, in which Jude is killed. Fergus goes to prison for Dil.

Just as Dionysus takes vengeance on the Thebans, so Jody takes vengeance on Fergus. Dionysus seduces the king, Pentheus, into dressing up like a woman and leads him to the mountains where, after being discovered to be a man, he is dismembered by his mother and other bacchantes. Dil, like Pentheus, is looked on with horror when he is discovered to be a man.

Jody symbolically dismembers Fergus by forcing him to question his own identity as a white man, as a nationalist, as a heterosexual, and as a human being. By the end of the film nothing will be as Fergus thought it was at the beginning: all his ideological constructs are deconstructed. His myths are shattered. He has escaped Dionysus.

Dil speaks about Fergus in the third person to Col the bartender as a way of communicating with Fergus: the third person is another disguise, and it functions as a type of mask. This also makes Fergus into an object and empowers Dil. The opening scene at the fair, the site of illusion and play, is the first round in this game of discovery: what is behind the mask. The illusion provides insight into multivalent truth: theater likewise is a source of Aristotelian anagnorisis, or "recognition."

Dil/Dionysus is at home in his/her body and identity, whereas Fergus doesn't know either his body or his identity. Fergus forces Dil to disguise herself, but disguising "her" is hopeless, and he/she returns as soon as possible to his norm of assuming the feminine gender while being comfortable with "her" masculine sex (Singer, *Androgyny*).

Jody returns as a god, not the deus ex machina, but the ghost in the machine of Fergus's memory, returning at inopportune times and forcing Fergus to make connections. Fergus lets Dil make oral love to him. At the point of his climax, Fergus is looking at a picture of Jody. This transforms into a vision of Jody playing cricket: both breathe heavily. When Fergus discovers that Dil is a man, and is repulsed to the point of vomiting, he sees Jody running and smiling, again dressed in his cricket clothes. Jody has won this round of the game of vengeance. Dionysus likewise reappears as the smiling god at the end of the *Bacchae*, when he gloats over his vengeance.

At the beginning of the *Bacchae*, Pentheus is repelled by the idea of an effeminate creature like Dionysus, but he gradually "becomes" Dionysus and shares his desires. At the end Pentheus is elevated above the other women, appearing in a tree just as Dionysus will also be elevated at the end of the play. He is shown to be a doublet of Dionysus and his erotic partner. In a staging I saw in Sicily, Dionysus seduced Pentheus in a bed in front of the audience before dressing him as a woman. It is this same discovery of desire that Jody awakes in Fergus. He is as effectively seduced by Jody/Dil as Pentheus was by Dionysus.

This film is powerful, exactly as is the *Bacchae* from the fifth century BC, because we interpret it in the light of our own myths. Just as history is created by both the historian and the reader, or a play by the playwright, director, and audience, so is the film created by the director as well as the viewer. *The Crying Game* understands the game and has many willing players. Dionysus would make us all winners.

Many other modern films suit the Bacchic theme. The film of John Guare's *Six Degrees of Separation* shows a stranger entering a household, disrupting it, and transforming it forever. Luchino Visconti's *Death in Venice*, based on Thomas Mann's story, illustrates the destructive power of the advent of passion into a person who was regarded as a proper and sober member of society. Joseph Mankiewicz's film of Tennessee Williams's *Suddenly Last Summer* tells of a *sparagmos*, indirectly caused by an indulgent and controlling mother (Katharine Hepburn once again). Even when the original text and the film are not closely related, it is worthwhile looking at the parallels.

I taught Barry Levinson's film *Sleepers* in connection with Aeschylus's *Eumenides*, Sophocles's *Antigone*, and Euripides's *Orestes* and called my talk "Rigged Trials." Both Euripides's play and this film show how arbitrary justice can be and how it can be manipulated. I also taught *Orestes* along with Quentin Tarantino's *Pulp Fiction*. Both show the desperate acts that can result from alliances between criminals. The "friends" in this film mirror the deadly factions with which Euripides was familiar toward the end of the Peloponnesian War. The date of the play is 408 BC, and the war ended in 404 BC. These "friends" seized power in the democracy and led Athens down a fatal path; Orestes, Electra, and Pylades are all criminals bent on destroying what they can as long as it can benefit them. This play ironically reworks a theme that is typical of Euripides: in a hostile universe with gods as corrupt as human beings, the only thing one can count on is a friend. As Heracles says after he has been unjustly forced to kill his own children, "He who would prefer wealth and power over good friends is mad" (*Heracles Furens* 1425–26). The *Orestes* abounds in statements such as the line about how one friend is better than ten thousand relatives. But some friends can be as irrational and unethical as the gods or the universe, and it is this moral chaos that Euripides presents so well in *Orestes* and that also occurs in *Pulp Fiction*. In both works we have sympathy for the racist and murderous criminals. Euripides's *Orestes* also suits Peter Fonda's *Wild Angels* or *The Hired Hand* with their amoral criminal behavior of "friends."

To show the disastrous relationship between brothers in Euripides's *Phoenissae*, I have shown Gérard Corbiau's *Farinelli* and also Athol Fugard's *Blood Knot*. One might add Martin Scorsese's *Raging Bull*, a film that also parallels Sophocles's *Ajax*. Each of these films shows confrontations that are based on the stubbornness of the protagonists, a situation fundamental to much of Greek tragedy.

Medea is another favorite that has often been filmed, whether simply as a play, directed by Peter Steadman in the original Greek (New York Greek Drama Company, 1986), or with Judith Anderson (1959 production) or Zoe Caldwell (1982 production) in Robinson Jeffers's translation. It has also been rewritten as a modern myth for Paolo Pasolini's film with Maria Callas, and it inspired a modern adaptation, Jules Dassin's *Dream of Passion*.

The filmed plays lack the cinematic freedom provided by an original film script. Pasolini, in his *Medea* (1970), uses framed pictures that remind us of Renaissance paintings. He cast Maria Callas in the title role, a performer as well known as—if not better known than—Medea herself. Pasolini transforms Medea into the witch that we find in Apollonius Rhodius and Seneca. There is little of Euripides's psychologizing. Medea here is a primitive earth mother who contrasts with the volatile, civilized Jason who betrays her. Just as she is a source of life, she can also take life away. We understand her boasting at the end as she stands apart from Jason, separated only by fire, the fire of her passion and anger. She claims then, "Nothing is possible any more." Jason has rejected his mythical childhood (which takes the symbolic form of a centaur) and become a man without gods. He is also a man without honor who is violently punished for his wrongs. Pasolini keeps the essential plot, extending it by adding the search for the Golden Fleece from Apollonius's epic. He begins by showing the fairy-tale life of a child, and then he shows the mature, calculating reality that follows —and ultimately destroys—that mythical past. He does not have Euripides's acute characterization, but he does understand the nature of myth.

Jules Dassin in his *Dream of Passion* tells the story of Medea in a new way. Melina Mercouri plays a professional actress who is cast in Euripides's play. She meets a woman, Brenda Collins (played by Ellen Burstyn), who is in prison for killing her children out of jealousy because her husband was having an affair. This woman educates Mercouri in the passion that gave her the strength to carry out her bloody vengeance. Mercouri gains insights into herself that help her deliver a realistic performance in the stage production enacted in the film. This film concentrates on psychological nuances more than Pasolini's does, and it never reaches the heights, or the depths, of Euripides's play. It is hard to conceive of a woman like Brenda who would kill her children merely out of jealousy; Euripides's Medea certainly did not. Brenda had a mother who was abandoned by her father, so she has a history of resentment against men, and we see signs of mental illness. This is not Medea. Euripides's heroine kills like a Homeric hero, for her honor (Knox, "*Medea*" 224). She was a princess who saved Jason but was rejected and about to go into exile, having lost everything after she had delivered everything to her husband. She knew exactly what she was doing. Her vengeance is extreme but believable, and it is hardly due simply to thwarted love. No one reason can be given for Medea's actions. Showing the differences between the film and Euripides's play highlights his genius. Brenda is trivial when compared with Medea.

One can also use Medea in connection with films that deal with women who protest against society when they are oppressed and who may commit violent crimes as a result. *Thelma and Louise* suits this purpose well. Medea escapes in a dragon-drawn chariot, but Thelma and Louise drive off a cliff. We do not see them crash, but we can imagine it as their dragon-drawn chariot carrying them to a freedom that at least is their choice over a humiliating life in prison. They, like Medea, make grim choices to save their honor.

I have also used Athol Fugard's filmed play *Boesman and Lena* alongside *Medea*. It shows the abuse by a man of a woman who then uses stratagems for her vengeance. Her fighting back becomes an existential gesture that allows the relationship to continue and that shows the proximity of love to hate. In Euripides's *Medea* the Greek term *thumos* is used throughout the play to convey the changing of Medea's love to hate and to anger, a violent anger that overcomes her reason. Fugard's film shows this transformation well.

Euripides's *Hippolytus* has inspired many films. Dassin's *Phaedra* is loosely based on Euripides's play. Dassin adds Marxist messages, showing how capitalists exploit the worker. His Theseus (Raf Vallone) is a mogul of an international shipping corporation. Hippolytus (Anthony Perkins) is his son by an English woman (to suggest an Amazon, his mythical mother?). Phaedra (Melina Mercouri) is a spoiled woman interested only in her love affairs. Hippolytus goes to his death when his automobile is forced off the road by a truck (the bull from the capitalist company?); his fragile but fast Aston Martin sails into the ocean (horsepower instead of horses). Dassin again delivers melodrama instead of tragedy, and at times this film becomes domestic farce. It may be soap opera, but it allows a comparison with the original rich text left us by Euripides. Euripides's play shows us that people can act with generosity and love and that in doing so are better than the fickle and cruel gods. Hippolytus forgives his father, whereas the two warring goddesses of this play are incapable of forgiveness. As is typical of many film directors who rework the classics, Dassin eliminates the gods and the supernatural. This modernization loses some of the mythic quality. A better film is Delbert Mann's *Desire under the Elms*, which is based on Eugene O'Neill's play and which features the theme of a young wife preferring the son to the father. This film also stars Anthony Perkins, possibly because with his boyish innocence he is such an ideal Hippolytus figure.

Each year more films are made that can be used to elucidate Euripides. Films are constantly reworking the ancient themes, and in this way the ancient texts achieve a new relevance. The reciprocity leads to new interpretations even of the classics. These films help with the teaching of the plays even when they are not faithful to or inspired by the Euripidean original. Love, hate, war, vengeance, passion, anger, defeat, and victory all feature in the plays of Euripides. Film, with its close-ups and silent sequences, illustrates the original text, and we find that Euripides has come to life in modern times. Euripides, the modernist who was criticized for his innovations by Aristophanes (*Frogs*), would probably be the first to embrace the new media. The psychological "I" has been well translated by the camera's eye.

Filmography

Berlioz, Hector. *Les Troyens*. Bel Canto, 1983.

Cacoyannis, Michael, dir. *Elektra*. Lopert, 1961.

———, dir. *Iphigenia*. Videocassette. Columbia Tristar Home Video, 1977.

———, dir. *Trojan Women*. Videocassette. USA Home Video, 1971.

Corbiau, Gérard, dir. *Farinelli*. Sony, 1995.

Dassin, Jules, dir. *A Dream of Passion*. Videocassette. New Line Home Video, 1978.

———, dir. *Phaedra*. Perf. Melina Mercouri and Anthony Perkins. Lopert, 1961.

Fonda, Peter, dir. *The Hired Hand*. Universal, 1971.

———, perf. *The Wild Angels*. Dir. Roger Corman. American International, 1966.

Fugard, Athol, perf. *Blood Knot*. 1964. Creative Arts Television Archive, 1996.

———, perf. *Boesman and Lena*. Dir. Ross Devenish. New Yorker Films, 1974.

George, Terry, dir. *Some Mother's Son*. Columbia, 1996.

Guare, John, screenwriter. *Six Degrees of Separation*. Dir. Fred Schepisi. MGM, 1993.

Jeunet, Jean-Pierre, dir. *Alien Resurrection*. Twentieth Century Fox, 1997.

Jordan, Neil, dir. *The Crying Game*. Miramax, 1992.

Levinson, Barry, dir. *Sleepers*. Warner, 1997.

Mankiewicz, Joseph, dir. *Suddenly Last Summer*. Adapt. Tennessee Williams. Columbia, 1959.

Mann, Delbert, dir. *Desire under the Elms*. Perf. Anthony Perkins. Paramount, 1957.

Medea. Dir. Wes Kenney and José Quintero. Perf. Judith Anderson. WNTA-TV, 1959.

Medea. Perf. Zoe Caldwell. Ivy Classics Video, 1989. Films for the Humanities.

Pasolini, Paolo Pier, dir. *Medea*. Perf. Maria Callas. Janus, 1970.

Scorsese, Martin, dir. *Raging Bull*. United Artists, 1980.

Steadman, Peter, dir. *Medea*. New York Greek Drama Company, 1986. Films for the Humanities.

Tarantino, Quentin, dir. *Pulp Fiction*. Miramax, 1994.

Thelma and Louise. Dir. Ridley Scott. MGM, 1991.

Ulee's Gold. Dir. Victor Nunez. Perf. Peter Fonda. Orion, 1997.

Visconti, Luchino. *Death in Venice*. Warner, 1971.

Performing Euripides

Mary-Kay Gamel

Texts originally intended for performance are often taught with the same assumptions and techniques as those designed for silent reading. The last few years, however, have seen the rise of "performance studies" and approaches that take into account the very different circumstances of production, presentation, and consumption of performance texts. "Performance teaching" can help students explore the frequently ignored performance dimension of such texts with exciting results. Performance offers an active mode of learning that involves the body and the emotions as well as the mind. Performance—even of a short scene, even at the most rudimentary level—requires a number of decisions, each of which illuminates different issues in a text. A student performing a speech in character, for example, must understand the kind of language the character uses and must decide which words to emphasize, what tone of voice to use, and how to stand or move. A dialogue between characters requires performers to investigate the characters' relationships to each other in terms of psychology, status, history. In such hands-on—or, rather, "bodies-on"—learning, students learn by doing rather than by hearing or reading. Understanding the variety of possible meanings in every text helps students create their own readings. Finally, performance teaching is a communal experience in which students learn together, getting insights from one another as well as from the teacher.

Paying attention to performance offers significant insights into ancient Athenian culture:

> When an actor takes his place on a stage, even in the most apparently trivial vehicle, and his audience begins to respond to his performance, together they concentrate the complex values of a culture with an intensity that less immediate transactions cannot rival. They embody its shared language of spoken words and expressive gestures, its social expectations and psychological commonplaces, its conventions of truth and beauty, its nuances of prejudice and fear, its erotic fascinations, and frequently its sense of humor. [. . .] The theater exists at the center of civilized life, not at its peripheries. (Roach 11-12)

Using performance techniques to teach Athenian drama is especially appropriate given its original conditions of production and consumption. In Athens, theater was a communal experience with didactic as well as aesthetic aims. The plays presented at the Theater of Dionysos were not antiquarian "classics" but dramas that raised issues of immediate import to their audiences—social and political issues, as well as intellectual and philosophical ones. Tragedies, which draw their characters and situations from myth, address these questions less directly than do comedies, but it is clear that Athenian audiences examined performances in both genres for their topical meanings (see, e.g., Podlecki; Euben; Vickers; Winkler and Zeitlin).

Live performance is always connected to a particular time and place. Although thinking about a script's meaning for its original audience can expand students' understanding of the past, we "cannot avoid seeing the past with the eyes of the present," so "subsequent performances" of older scripts always raise questions about cultural and artistic differences (Miller 51). In performing ancient Greek plays students must confront a culture very different from their own—a confrontation that offers the chance for rich discoveries. Performance teaching also suits contemporary American students, who are usually experienced, sophisticated viewers of film and video. Performance can thus help teachers exploit rather than fight the current turn away from print culture, raising students' awareness of how performances are created and of the cognitive, intellectual, and artistic dimensions of various media. Performance involves a range of abilities, so students can contribute and succeed in different areas. Learning through performance is pleasurable, as the joy of playing suffuses the serious work going on. And the artistic results can be quite extraordinary; of the many *Hamlets* I have seen, the best was a college production. Dionysos, god of theater, is generous and democratic; he does not reserve his blessing for professional work.

Euripides

Drama handbooks that try to sum up "the Greeks" in a few paragraphs often read Aristotle's *Poetics* uncritically and take Sophocles as the model of "Greek tragedy" (for concise but good discussions, see Brockett; Brown). Euripides's plays do not fit conventional assumptions about "classical" drama as lofty, measured, consistent. Characters can change abruptly from one moment to the next, as do Medea (*Medea* 1021–55) and Agamemnon (*Iphigenia at Aulis* 278–542) while debating whether to kill their children. (Line numbers given in this essay refer to the Greek text.) In their speech, motivation, and action, some Euripidean characters seem to be "psychologized," rounded individuals, while others are pointedly artificial figures, and sometimes a character is portrayed in different ways in the same script. Euripides's plots include both linear, logical development (as in *Trojan Women*) and event-filled, surprising, episodic structures (as in *Helen*). They include revisions of traditional events and characters, false conclusions, and abrupt, obviously mechanical resolutions (see *Iphigenia among the Taurians*; *Electra*). Aristocratic ideals such as self-validation, military prowess, and desire for fame jostle "common" values such as contentment, cooperation, and peace. Conflicts between the genders are frequent.

Euripides's dramaturgy includes both naturalistic interactions and ostentatious uses of tragic conventions such as expositions, recognition scenes, and messenger speeches. The language of the plays ranges from colloquial dialogue to self-conscious rhetoric to gorgeous lyrics. Although the tragedies are set in the mythic Bronze Age, anachronisms can suggest implications for the contemporary Athens in which they were performed. And abrupt changes of focus and tone—from seriousness to comedy and vice versa—disrupt "organic" classical form. Discontinuities in *Medea*, for example, include the artificiality of the Nurse's exposition (which the Tutor points out by asking, "Why are you standing all alone before the gates, loudly bewailing evil tidings to yourself?" 50–51); the slave Nurse's criticisms of aristocratic values and behavior (119–30); the contrast between the woman heard screaming inside the house and the cool, self-possessed Medea who then appears (214); Medea's anachronistic references to Athenian laws and customs regarding women in her appeal to the female chorus (230–51); the unexpected appearance of Aigeus, who offers Medea a way out of Corinth (663); and more.

Such discontinuities have often been taken as signs of Euripides's failure as a dramatist. Even in his own time, Euripides's plays were regarded as unusual in both form and content. In Aristophanes's *Frogs*, Euripides is criticized for various innovations such as dressing aristocratic characters in rags and the use of solo arias; he responds proudly that he encourages audiences to think:

> I turn everything inside out
> looking for new solutions
> to the problems of today,
> always critical, giving
> suggestions for gracious living
> and they come away from seeing a play
> in a questioning mood, with "where are we at?"
> and "who's got my this?" and "who took my that?"
> (Lattimore, *Four Comedies* 62; 971–79)

In the *Poetics* (written a century after the original productions of the tragedies that have come down to us) Aristotle criticizes Euripides more than he does any other dramatist. He especially dislikes episodic structures ("the worst kind" [*Poetics* 1451b]), shifts in character (e.g., Iphigenia, *Poetics* 1461b), and mechanical resolutions (*Poetics* 1454a). Despite its tremendous influence on Western drama the *Poetics* should be read critically, with an awareness of how Aristotle's definitions fail to comprehend Euripides, rather than vice versa. Euripides won fewer first prizes in the dramatic competition (only five over his whole career) than did either Aeschylus or Sophocles. Yet his plays were clearly popular; there are accounts of Athenians captured in battle being released from slavery because they could recite Euripides's plays from memory. These plays' popularity may be the reason why more have survived to our day, and they are more different from one another in terms of genre, tone, and style than are the surviving seven plays of Aeschylus or the seven by Sophocles.

Lesser-known plays by Euripides, such as *Orestes, Phoenician Women, Herakles*, and *Cyclops*, are just as interesting as the better-known ones. Finally, Euripidean discontinuities seem less alien in the light of twentieth-century intellectual and cultural developments such as quantum mechanics, chaos theory, cultural relativism, and political cynicism. To American adolescents raised on *Pulp Fiction* and *South Park* they may seem downright familiar.

Ancient Performance Conditions

One way to use performance in the classroom is to discuss how ancient scripts were originally performed. Students often approach Greek drama with assumptions drawn from contemporary theater or film, thinking of professionals performing naturalistically in bright light to audiences in dark indoor spaces. Learning about the Greek theater's huge outdoor spaces, masks and elaborate costumes, music and dance expands their aesthetic horizons. Discussing the playwrights' contest, the state's role in presenting the festival, and its religious dimension helps them understand the social and material circumstances of artistic production. Performance conditions similar to those of football games and rock concerts show that Greek drama was not just "high culture" designed for an elite. Teaching about ancient performance conditions has been made easier by the appearance of many excellent guides to Athenian drama in performance. (See Csapo and Slater; Easterling, *Cambridge Companion*; Erp Taalman Kip; Green and Handley; Rehm, *Greek Tragic Theatre*; Taplin, *Greek Tragedy*; Walton, *Greek Sense*; and Wiles, *Masks, Tragedy*, and especially *Performance*. See also the discussion of Internet resources in part 1 of this volume.)

Trying to re-create the conditions and effects of ancient performance is usually deadly both in theatrical productions and in the classroom. Using selected characteristics of ancient performance in performance experiments, however, can be enlightening. When used in a performance context, information about ancient performance conditions changes from positivistic evidence, which must be learned, to performance choices, which can be discussed. For example, we know that only three actors performed all the individual roles in an Athenian play, although it is not always clear which roles were performed by a single actor in the original production (Damen). Experiments in which the same actor performs different roles in a particular script can bring up questions about the similarities and differences between characters, acting styles ancient and modern, and—since all roles were played by men—the performance of gender. In a University of California, Santa Cruz, production of *Alcestis*, for example, the same actor played Apollo, Admetos, and the Servant who serves the drunken Herakles. The performer changed his acting style in each role, yet the psychological and functional interconnections between these characters were fascinating.

Critiquing Performances of Euripides

Still another way to use performance in the classroom is to compare the written script with staging choices made in a production—ideally a live production or, failing that, a filmed version. A number of Euripides's plays have been filmed, and *Trojan Women* and *Iphigenia at Aulis* are available on videotape (Cacoyannis). Sometimes several different versions offer students the chance to compare different stagings. Of *Medea*, for example, there is a New York Greek Drama Company production on videotape that aims at historical authenticity and alterity (Steadman). The actors speak the Greek text with pitch accents, and the chorus's choreography is drawn from Greek vase paintings. There are two different productions of Robinson Jeffers's adaptation, one starring Judith Anderson (1945), the other Zoe Caldwell (1982). These can be used to show how Jeffers changed Euripides's script and how differently the two actresses perform the title role. Other film versions make more radical changes. Pier Paolo Pasolini's *Medea* begins by depicting Medea in Colchis, showing strong influences from anthropology, and in Jules Dassin's *A Dream of Passion* a contemporary Greek actress preparing to play Medea meets a woman who has killed her children.

Discussing staging choices can help demonstrate that performances of classical texts are always connected to their own historical context and affected by the artistic and ideological aims of their directors and producers. For example, at the beginning of Euripides's *Iphigenia at Aulis* Agamemnon describes the pressure he feels from the army's desire to launch the war against Troy. Cacoyannis begins his film *Iphigenia* with a forty-minute sequence in which this pressure is shown in detail. As a result Agamemnon's decision to sacrifice Iphigenia seems more inevitable and the king less responsible. Karelisa Hartigan surveys American productions of ancient drama over the last century (*Greek Tragedy*); Marianne McDonald's *Euripides in Cinema* and Kenneth MacKinnon's *Greek Tragedy into Film* contain good discussions of films based on Euripides's plays.

Creating Performances of Euripides

This approach is easy to use, requires no projection equipment, and is more valuable than critiquing, especially since many interesting Euripidean scripts are not available on film. It offers a more active way to use performance in the classroom, one that encourages students to interpret the plays, make their own staging decisions, and commit to them. Performance as a methodology does not resolve discontinuities; on the contrary, it requires that students confront discontinuities more immediately than they do in silent reading.

Using performance requires some shifts of focus and some new techniques, but the techniques are easy to learn, and there are many helpful materials available. The flexibility of performance makes it easy to integrate, since even a little complements and enriches the literature curriculum, and performance always feels like a reward. Performance teaching is very different from fully staging a production, and much easier. While theatrical producers and directors must consider the show as a product and focus their energies toward that end, teachers can concentrate on the process of making choices and realizing them. In a literature class, the point of acting out scenes is to explore the range of performance choices and their effects. Performances can be more or less lively, imaginative, or powerful, but there is no such thing as a definitively "right" or "wrong" performance. If performance is used in the classroom to present foregone conclusions or to hone or demonstrate performers' skills, the results can be deadly. If it is used as an experiment with open-ended results that cannot be known in advance, it can bring the literature classroom to life.

Translations

A good translation is important in teaching any ancient work, but in performance teaching a speakable, actable translation is essential. The actor Patrick Stewart once told a class of mine that he tries to avoid performing Greek tragedy because most translations are impossible to act well. Picking up the translation of *Antigone* we were using (Wyckoff), he proceeded to prove his point. But then he performed from memory several speeches from David Rudkin's version of *Hippolytus*, in which he had played Theseus:

> Hear me. Old neglected powers, hear me.
> All you, whose potency has been denied so long:
> from that dark deep to which we've banished you,
> hear us! Waken! Rise! We call you home.
> I have a son, unhusbands me. A son no son,
> unfathers me. Yourselves be father for me.
> Ascend before him into the day, to cover him
> from all his light, and your annihilation fall
> on him! Under that Sun do it: to leave him
> ruin on this earth. Else I'll know wrong in
> Nature's nothing; violation's nothing;
> and all our sense of boundary is vain.   (45)

Rudkin's version is far from literal. But the meter, the rhythm, the use of repetition, the alliteration all help an actor create the kind of huge vocal and emotional effect this scene requires.

Few translations capture the grandeur in Euripides, and even fewer realize the colloquialism and humor in his plays. For example, Orestes and Electra have a long scene (*Electra* 215–96) that ought to culminate in the recognition and reunion of brother and sister. Instead, both try to keep the recognition from taking place, Orestes because he does not want to fulfill his tragic role, Electra because she has an exaggerated idea about her absent brother. I translated an exchange from this scene thus:

> ELECTRA: I'm married, stranger. Might as well be dead.
> ORESTES: I'm sorry for your brother. Who's your husband?
> ELECTRA: Not the man my father would have chosen.
> ORESTES: Tell me, so I can let your brother know.
> ELECTRA: This is my husband's house, in the middle of nowhere.
> ORESTES: Looks like it belongs to a cowpoke, or a wetback.
> ELECTRA: He's poor, but decent, and has respect for me.
> ORESTES: Respect? What kind of respect can such a man have?
> ELECTRA: He's never been reckless enough to sleep with me.
> ORESTE : A vow of chastity? Or doesn't he find you attractive?
> (247–56)

In the original at line 252 Orestes says "ditchdigger or cowherd," but I wanted to make his social snobbery very clear to contemporary audiences. James Morwood's translation flattens the oddness here, including the last line's sarcasm; his note says solemnly that "sexual abstinence could promote purity and reverence" (Medea 195). Don Taylor, a professional director, keeps the liveliness of the original, as in the hilarious scene in *Helen* between the aristocratic Menelaus and the old female doorkeeper who shoves him around:

> MEN: Now look here old woman, you don't need to be rude.
>   I'll do what you say by all means, but abuse . . .
> CONCIERGE: You get out then! I'm just doing my job, I am,
>   Stranger, we don't want no Greeks round here!
>   (*Euripides* 154–55)

There are more translations of ancient drama available now than ever before, making it easy to consult various versions of a play. (Of course, the ideal result of such consultation is to encourage students—and teachers—to learn Greek!) In addition to the works of Robert Bagg, Mary-Kay Gamel, Derek Mahon, David Rudkin, and Don Taylor, actable translations include those by William Arrowsmith, Brendan Kennelly, David Lan, Kenneth McLeish, and Paul Roche. Even the most apparently literal translations involve choices and changes, such as explaining unfamiliar references and allusions. Describing Dionysos's journey to reach Greece, for example, Derek Mahon substitutes "hot Iranian plains, Saudi deserts and Indian ports" (11) for Persia, Baktria, and Arabia. Teachers should not be afraid to adapt translations to their own purposes by changing the language of a particular version (to eliminate obvious Briticisms, for example) or by combining several translations. Most translations have few if any notes; exceptions are the Focus Classical Library translations (Esposito; Halleran; Podlecki), a new series from Routledge that offers copious notes (see Blondell, Gamel, Rabinowitz, and Zweig), and John

Ferguson's volume with notes to Philip Vellacott's Penguin translations of *Medea* and *Electra*. When working on a particular script, students may find it interesting to compare later plays based on it, such as Wole Soyinka's The Bacchae *of Euripides: A Communion Rite*, Tony Harrison's *Medea: A Sex-War Opera*, and Charles Mee's *Orestes* and *Trojan Women: A Love Story*. Marianne McDonald discusses some of these plays in *Ancient Sun, Modern Light*.

Acting

A good place to start in the performance teaching of ancient drama is to have students perform monologues. In doing this exercise the performance teacher can draw on excellent resources in the theory and practice of acting. There are many different approaches to acting; most university acting programs teach Konstantin Stanislavski's techniques, which aim to help actors create naturalistic performances. Stanislavski's method assumes that dramatic characters can be treated as real people with a comprehensible psychological makeup that can be analyzed. This method is not entirely appropriate for ancient drama, but these techniques are a good first step in making ancient scripts less foreign by encouraging students to analyze from within, from a performer's point of view.

If the class is studying a particular play, the various monologues of a single character can be assigned to different students, or several students can be asked to perform a single monologue. Students can start by analyzing the "given circumstances"—all the details, external and internal, about the character and situation that can be gained from the play: age, status, personal history, attitudes, and so forth (Stanislavski, *Creating* 3–43). An added benefit of such analysis for Athenian drama is greater understanding of Greek myth. Then, following Stanislavski's argument that actors create powerful dramatic characters by identifying specific, concrete desires to make something happen, actors should identify the intentions of characters at various moments in the text: "On the stage do not run for the sake of running, or suffer for the sake of suffering. Don't act 'in general,' for the sake of action; always act with a purpose" (Stanislavski, *Actor* 37). Actors must study their scripts carefully to identify intentions and to use active verbs to name them. The intention may not be explicit in the words spoken but may be part of the character's psychological "subtext." For example, as Alcestis bids farewell to her husband, Admetus (*Alcestis* 280–325), an actor might decide that her intention is to glorify herself and to shame Admetus. Stanislavski encourages actors to keep their intentions strong to "raise the stakes" of the performance.

Since real people act from a variety of different impulses and motives, actors should be attentive to subtle changes in a character's intentions by dividing a speech or scene into units or "beats." A "beat change" occurs when a character's intention or the focus of the scene changes. Euripidean monologues are often organized in an explicitly rhetorical fashion, so that in studying them students can identify emotional beat changes by syntactic markers. In *Trojan*

Women, for example, Hecuba's speech accusing Helen (969–1032) and Helen's self-defense (914–65) contain clear transitional devices. Hecuba's logic wins the argument, and Menelaos seems to condemn his faithless wife, but since we know from other sources (such as Homer's *Odyssey*, bk. 4) that he took Helen back, his protestations (1036–59) have an ironic subtext.

To keep from getting lost in too many details, actors can identify larger units called "objectives" for individual scenes and a "super-objective" for the whole play. An actor playing Hippolytus, for example, might decide that his super-objective is to avoid pollution of any kind, not only sexual. Therefore, he does not reveal Phaedra's love for him to his father, although he has told the Nurse he will, and when Artemis reveals that Theseus too was the victim of Aphrodite, Hippolytus forgives his father. But performers must avoid "end-gaming"—flattening their performance in the light of what happens at the end of the monologue, the scene, or the play. Medea's plan to kill her children, for example, is formed only gradually, as she realizes the importance of children to males during her encounters with Kreon, Jason, and Aigeus. Performance takes place in real time, and good performers remain "in the moment," performing the changes in their intentions as they occur, watching and listening to everything that is happening onstage, and continuing on the basis of what they actually hear, see, and do.

Stanislavski's techniques for analyzing a play (called "table work" in a theatrical production) give students the same opportunities to discuss scene structure, rhetorical strategies, themes, and imagery as does literary analysis. But when this study is undertaken with a view to performance, the stakes are higher and more personal. "Always act in your own person. You can never get away from yourself" (Stanislavski, *Actor* 167). Performance requires performers to put themselves on the line, their voices into the words, their bodies into the gestures. Hence ethical questions can easily arise (should my character say or do this? would I?) and lead to discussions about values in different cultural contexts. Although "it is so much easier to lie when you are on the stage than to speak and act the truth," Stanislavski insists on honesty: "Avoid everything that runs counter to nature, logic, and common sense." Inexperienced performers tend to do too much business to cover nervousness, but Stanislavksi urges simplicity: "Cut 90 per cent!" (*Actor* 152–53). Since the unexamined role is not worth acting, at its most intense this process of textual analysis and self-examination can be downright Socratic.

Stanislavski's techniques were developed for acting the naturalistic plays of Chekhov, in which there is often a strong contrast between text and subtext. Influenced by Romanticism and Freudian psychology, contemporary students tend to consider character as an essential self that is expressed in behavior. Athenian drama, however, is more "presentational" than "representational." There is more rhetoric and less subtext, and conventions such as nonhuman characters, long monologues, and constructed dialogue consisting of alternating lines (stichomythia) are not naturalistic by twentieth-century standards.

But what constitutes naturalism differs in different performance circumstances, and in *Frogs* Aristophanes has Euripides boast that his characters speak in "natural conversational dialogue" (954). In any case, discussing whether Stanislavski's approach is appropriate for performing ancient drama can lead to good discussions about concepts of the self and the meaning of acting.

Although intellectual study is crucial to performance, actors must use their bodies effectively. Speech too is physical, not just mental. So physical exercises are essential to performance—warm-ups to focus attention and prepare the body for movement; games to set the mood and unite the group; and exercises specific to particular characters, scenes, or plays (for ideas see R. Cohen; Spolin). Guided improvisation exercises can expand students' understanding of characters and situations: students playing Medea and Jason can be asked, for example, to improvise the first meeting of these characters in Colchis. Physical work grounds learning in the body, making it memorable; students who think they will never be able to memorize lines, for example, quickly find that focusing on the physicality of the sounds of words they speak, on their location and movement while speaking, and on their relationships to other speakers makes this process much easier. A safe atmosphere in which critiques are delivered constructively is crucial, so performers can experiment without the risk of feeling foolish.

The nonverbal aspects of performance include gesture, proxemics (actors' spatial relationships), blocking (actors' movements), and the use of time. Membership in a shared culture gives students an intuitive understanding of these aspects and their social meaning, but performance makes their awareness and deployment of them more conscious and purposeful. One of the conventions of ancient theater is the use of what we would call stage directions in the dialogue, including references to entrances and exits, gestures and expressions. Although these are useful guides, contemporary performers should not take them as infallible. Performances in which the visual and verbal elements contradict each other can be electric, as are the best productions of ancient drama in modern dress. Besides, in some cases Euripides seems to be using the convention of spoken stage directions self-consciously. After Iphigenia and Klytemnestra have learned of Agamemnon's plan to sacrifice the girl, for example, Agamemnon asks Iphigenia why she is crying and holding her dress before her eyes and then accuses her and Klytemnestra of staging a scene for him (*Iphigenia at Aulis* 1127–28). Euripides's plays contain many such metatheatrical moments that call attention to the fact that the audience is watching a constructed artifact.

Directing

Since performers cannot see themselves (and should never be encouraged to use mirrors), even solo performers need directors. There are many models for directing, ranging from giving the actors complete freedom, to virtual dictatorship over all aspects of the production. In a literature classroom, where the focus is on experimentation rather than polish, the teacher can take the director's role in providing a framework, ideas, and feedback for the performers' work. There are many useful guides to directing; John Kirk and Ralph Bellas's *The Art of Directing* is a good place to start, while Alexander Dean and Lawrence Carra, in *Fundamentals of Play Directing*, go into more detail; for a full discussion of theatrical semiotics, see Erika Fischer-Lichte.

Since novice performers see monologues on the page as an unbroken column of print, they tend to perform these speeches at the same tone, pace, and rhythm throughout; the teacher-director can encourage students to vary these speeches according to their intentions and to take pauses where justified. Novices also tend to be "ungrounded" in their movements, shifting position or making random gestures. By demonstrating how powerful even the simplest movement becomes when it occurs against a background of stillness and concentration, the teacher-director can help performers decide which movements and gestures are effective.

Discussions of blocking and movement always involve questions about stage space and its meaning, another area in which the contrast between ancient and modern performance conditions can be fruitfully explored. In a proscenium theater, downstage (closer to the audience) is a powerful position, while upstage is weaker; entrances made from stage left (audience right) and exits to stage right are normal. In the Theater of Dionysos, spatial relations were quite different; see David Wiles, *Tragedy in Athens*, for interpretations of the meaning of performance in that space. But any area, indoors or outdoors, can be an effective performance space provided that its qualities are understood and exploited.

Most scenes in Athenian drama involve two characters, and usually only two speak even if a third is present. Addressing another character helps the speaker clarify intentions and beat changes in the relationship between the characters, and the listener needs to respond emotionally and physically and at times even try to interrupt (see *Medea* 550). The teacher-director can help the performers determine their blocking to make clear the meaning of the scene. In *Electra*, for example, Orestes begins to have doubts about killing his mother, and Electra must keep him in line (962–87). Blocking can express this dynamic in various ways: Orestes can rush around trying to find some means of escape while Electra remains stationary, firm in her intention; he can retreat as far as possible, and she can bring him back step-by-step as she rebuts each of his objections; she can circle him like a predator stalking its prey.

One of the most important elements of Athenian tragedy is the chorus, whose members react and respond to the protagonists, affecting the play's meaning not only by their spoken comments and songs but also by their constant presence onstage, listening and reacting. How many actors make a chorus? Euripides used fifteen; I have seen productions with as few as three, but I think that the minimum number in a fully staged production is six. Every increase in number changes the dynamic between chorus and protagonists. Whatever the number, the chorus's role is crucial, as ancient discussions of

Athenian tragedy indicate: a playwright whose script was accepted for the drama competition was said to have been "given a chorus." A director trying to get even five or six actors to work as a group understands why!

The choral songs (odes) are the most difficult aspect of ancient drama for modern performers. For the chorus to stand still and speak words in unison is not only theatrically deadly but historically inappropriate; the word *chorus* means "dancers," and the performers sang the odes as they danced. The words can be made intelligible by dividing the odes into understandable sections spoken by individual chorus members; students in the chorus can be asked to construct an individual character for themselves and choose phrases from the text that they think their character would say. But to individualize the chorus members works against the dynamic of the chorus-group versus protagonist-individual. Even the ancient audience may not have grasped the full verbal complexity of these songs in the swirl of music and dance, and in performance, theatrical effect is as important as philosophical import. If possible, music and movement should be integrated into the songs. A bit of percussion can accompany the words, a tape on a boom box can be played under them, the words can be set to a preexisting melody, or even (if there is a composer in the class) new music can be written. No matter what the results, the search for appropriate music helps students understand the meaning and tone of the choral songs: for example, the chorus's appeal to Aphrodite (*Medea* 627–62) can work as a gospel song, while the country setting of *Electra* might give its songs a country-and-western flavor. For inspiration, see *The Gospel at Colonus*, Lee Breuer and Bob Telson's musical version of Sophocles's *Oedipus at Colonus*, which respects (but does not revere) both the original script and its new context.

One of the advantages of the chorus is that it can serve some of the functions of a set, framing the action by its position and movement. The chorus can also enliven the long monologues typical of Athenian drama. The messenger speech, for example, a long report on offstage action often considered one of the stumbling blocks of this drama, can become a high point of the play. During a University of California, Santa Cruz, production of *Hippolytus*, as the messenger downstage described how Hippolytus's horses dragged him to death, Hippolytus stood on a chair upstage with chorus members as horses. The actor playing Aphrodite had been sitting onstage since her opening monologue, watching the action; now she walked forward and tipped Hippolytus out of his "chariot." As he rolled, screaming for mercy, she very slowly and carefully poured a bucket of stage blood over him. Such stagings need to be carefully choreographed so that they are more than mime or illustration of the words. In this case, the messenger speech was delivered at normal speed, while the upstage action was in slow motion, making the scene nightmarish.

This production, though fully staged, used very simple costumes and props. Theater is a material art, and the right prop or costume element can help performers perform and audiences understand. Simple choices, even if required by budgetary constraints, are often more dramatically effective than more complicated ones. Re-creating historically authentic items can be pedagogically useful, but seeking contemporary analogies to the items specified in the scripts sparks students' imagination, and familiar items can work better in performance—in addition to being much cheaper! For example, Medea might wear an exotic necklace or an animal-print scarf to hint at her otherness (though she probably should not look completely foreign, since she says she has worked hard to fit into Greek society; 11–12, 222–23). Travelers such as Orestes in *Electra* or Herakles in *Alcestis* can carry luggage: in our productions Orestes's expensive leather backpack suggested the privileged upbringing that allowed him to sneer at Electra's rustic home, and Herakles easily carried a large suitcase, complete with stickers from his Laborious travels, which Admetos's servant had to struggle to drag into the house. The title character in *Ion* has been raised as a slave in Apollo's temple at Delphi. If he wields a broom, mop, and bucket, his pride in his janitor's job can seem both touching and absurd. When his foster mother the Priestess appears, similar costuming for her can establish the link between her and Ion; we gave her a toilet brush and rubber gloves.

Any item repeatedly stressed in the script deserves special attention. The statue of Artemis in *Iphigenia among the Taurians* is frequently mentioned, and the actual statue is brought onstage (1158). In the original production this prop probably helped to focus the themes of cultural diversity central to the play. Taking a more psychological tack, we decided that to Iphigenia this statue symbolized her self, stolen by her traumatic experience at Aulis, so we commissioned a student artist to create a life bust of the actor. Connections with contemporary events can also be theatrically and politically effective. In our *Iphigenia at Aulis*, performed shortly after the Gulf War in 1991, Agamemnon wore an American general's uniform, and the chorus waved yellow ribbons. Such connections run the risk of flattening or distortion (see Taylor, *Directing* 33–39). Bold choices and combinations are appropriate, however, to Euripidean discontinuity, provided their aim is to make it new, not to make fun of it.

Athenian drama was performed in mask, and in performance experiments masks are powerful tools. They are easy to acquire; instead of using prefabricated ones, students can make their own—for example, from aluminum foil covered by masking tape. But the use of the mask in Athenian tragedy is no simple matter. Was it a religious element? Was it considered necessary because of the large scale of the theater or because actors played more than one character? Did it help the actors embody their characters? Scholars of ancient drama do not agree. David Wiles provides a thoughtful discussion, although he focuses on comedy rather than tragedy (*Masks*). In twentieth-century theater, masks are often used to create a Brechtian alienation effect (see Smith). Various uses of the mask can be tested in the classroom, but they need careful preparation and discussion.

Parallel performances of a single scene offer a satisfying culmination to performance teaching. Several groups of actors, each with a student director, can be asked to think about the given circumstances, decide performance style, break the scene into beats, identify intentions and objectives, and work out blocking. If desired, the instructor can create clear contrasts between the groups by assigning different objectives for the scene to each one or by having one group perform in mask, the other unmasked. After the performances, the class can discuss and compare the results. The performance teacher needs to guide such discussions carefully, so that the comments focus on what observers saw and how they interpreted it, instead of criticizing the performers' effectiveness. Under these circumstances performers quickly understand the importance of being bold and making clear choices, and they should be rewarded for their courage.

Another useful experiment involves juxtaposing scenes from different plays that have some formal and/or thematic similarity. For example, Medea's deception of Jason (869–975) can be compared with Admetos's deception of Herakles (*Alcestis* 509–50) or Agamemnon's deception of Iphigenia (*Iphigenia at Aulis* 640–85). Performing similar scenes in plays by different playwrights, such as the debates between father and son in Sophocles's *Antigone* (635–780) and in Euripides's *Hippolytus* (902–1101), quickly illuminates the differences between them in structure, characterization, tone, and effect. This technique can also be used to compare ancient and modern plays, testing how scenes of intergenerational conflicts in, say, Eugene O'Neill's *Desire under the Elms*, Arthur Miller's *A View from the Bridge*, or David Mamet's *Oleanna* compare with such scenes in Euripides.

A staged reading, with scripts in hand, can vividly illuminate characters, relationships, and issues. A fully staged production requires many hours of preparation, but the range of decisions and the coordination of different aspects give insights far beyond those that result from scene work. Since even full productions are experiments, focusing on the process as well as the product can help keep participants sane under pressure. Productions give opportunities to involve colleagues and students in different areas—literature, theater, politics, history, art. They offer to a wider audience the chance to experience ancient drama, and preshow talks and postshow discussions can amplify the audience's understanding.

The original performances of Euripides's plays gave Athenian performers and audience members a chance to engage with crucial issues. In today's United States, where community seems illusory and most people regard art as a commodity that they consume rather than as a process in which they can participate, performance can give contemporary Americans roles to play in the communal, enlightening, and joyful process of creating art.[1]

NOTE

[1]My understanding of Euripidean drama has been shaped by working on productions of *Medea*, *Hippolytus*, *Alcestis*, *Electra*, *Iphigenia at Aulis*, *Iphigenia among the Taurians*, and *Ion*. Many of these productions were supported by various agencies at the University of California, Santa Cruz, and during the course of them I learned invaluable

lessons from Christopher Grabowski, Tim Earle, Dale Robinson, George Chastain, Andrew Doe, Paul Graf, Sommer Ulrickson, Robby MacLean, John Maloney, and Greg Fritsch. Many thanks to Thomas A. Vogler and Hank Vogler for their advice on this essay.

Euripidean Stagecraft

Michael R. Halleran

Drama literally means "thing done." The original audience for an ancient Greek production sat in the *theatron*, literally "viewing place." I rehearse these two well-known facts to emphasize that Greek drama was something acted, performed to be seen (as well as heard) by its audiences. In fifth-century Athens, tragedies were typically performed only once and at a glorious religious festival attended by as many as fifteen thousand viewers. At this point, the Greek book trade was not very extensive, and very few Athenians would have had the opportunity to read the plays that were performed at the annual festival. The fundamental, if not the exclusive, mode of experiencing these plays for their original audience was in performance. When we approach these plays in the classroom, we therefore need to consider and explore their theatrical potentialities. This assertion should not be taken as a polemic against other forms of "reading" Greek tragedy. The original production, while holding a special place in the history of the play, does not uniquely impart meaning. Meaning is constructed by readers and audiences. At the same time, only folly would lead us to ignore one of the most salient features of dramatic literature—that is to say, its theatricality.

With a few notable exceptions (Aeschylus, *Eumenides* 117–29 being the most familiar), the original texts of Greek drama, whether the early ones on papyrus or the later medieval manuscripts, do not contain stage directions. What we know about ancient productions and stage actions is inferred primarily from the words in the texts themselves. We also are informed about the ancient stage and some of its conventions by the material record, including representations on vase paintings, as well as by archaeological excavations of the actual theaters. Knowledge of the physical stage, costumes, and gestures derived from these various sources helps to shape our understanding of ancient stagecraft. Our understanding is imperfect, of course, and one should always remember that all the stage directions indicated in translations are the translator's (or an editor's) judgment. Many are uncontroversial, but some are rightly contested. One should always be willing to challenge these stage suggestions and invite one's students to develop their own ideas on this subject.

What, exactly, do we know about the ancient theater? This question poses a vexed set of issues, which I can address only cursorily here. The original Theater of Dionysus in Athens does not survive, and its reconstruction is not without controversy, but we know something of its shape and function. We know that central to the performance was a large dancing area (*orchestra*), perhaps originally rectangular but later circular, measuring some seventy feet in diameter. This area was primarily for the chorus, whose members would dance there while singing their parts. Located at one edge of the orchestra was the *skene* (pronounced "skaynay"), a building (originally temporary and of wood, later permanent and of stone). This stage building, perhaps thirty-five to forty feet long and twelve feet high, was, along with the *orchestra*, the chief focal point for the audience. It represented whatever the world of the play described it to be—palace (typically), tents, cave—and served also as a changing room for the actors. The *skene* had one central double door, which allowed for the actors' comings and goings, and by the later fifth century in all likelihood two side doors in addition. Remarkably, it is unknown whether in the fifth-century theater there existed what we call a stage, that is, an elevated platform on which the actors performed. Most likely, the actors performed on a slightly raised platform that extended out from the *skene*. What is essential to bear in mind is that the actors were not cut off from the chorus either physically or in the theater's psychic space. Actors and chorus are in regular dialogue and debate and may have come into physical contact as well. Threats are made across the two areas, and on rare occasions the chorus could even enter the *skene*. The impressive edifice that was the Hellenistic stage, lofty and theatrically distant, had not yet developed.

Perhaps the most challenging aspect of Greek tragedy to communicate to a contemporary audience is the chorus. (On the chorus, see Gould, "Tragedy"; Goldhill, "Collectivity"; Henrichs, "Why.") A group of fifteen (originally maybe twelve), its members sang and danced its parts, moving choreographically across the large open space of the *orchestra*. The great musicals of the 1940s and 1950s offer some parallel for the faux spontaneity involved, but nothing in them corresponds to the chorus's constant presence during the play. The chorus arrived onstage early in (or even at the start of) the drama and, with rare exception, remained until its conclusion. The chorus's space was the *orchestra*, and while chorus members engaged with the actors and threatened to enter the *skene* (something that occurs only once in extant Euripides), their distinction from the actors was marked by their physical location in the theater. This constant presence produces some "awkward" moments, as plots are devised and secrets revealed in their hearing, and characters must therefore often swear them to secrecy. They uphold their vow of secrecy in *Hippolytus*, to the young man's destruction, but violate it in *Ion*, throwing that play's events into a new (and needed) direction. The Corinthian women's complicit silence in *Medea* makes possible the murder of their king and his daughter (as well as Medea's own children) and offers a powerful commentary on these actions.

The dramatic function of the chorus is a perennially debated question, and detailed discussion lies beyond the scope of this essay. But I want to emphasize that chorus members are not a static participant in the play's action. Nor are they the "voice of the poet," the "idealized spectator," or any other monolithic construct. It is true that the chorus members in tragedy tend to be more conservative and more cautious than the other characters, but they do have a role *in* the play and are not mere outside observers. They are characters in the play, integrated into the drama to varying degrees. The Corinthian or Trozenian women in *Medea* and *Hippolytus*, respectively, fit easily into the action, and the suppliant band of *Suppliant Women* and the choral bacchants of *Bacchae* are integral players in their respective dramas. In *Phoenician Women*, however, the chorus members that give the play its name are awkwardly situated in this Theban saga. One member of the chorus, the *coryphaeus* (chorus leader), also stands apart and interacts more directly with the actors, in spoken rhythms as well as in song. In visualizing ancient productions, one should keep in mind the chorus's presence and the backdrop it offers to the surrounding actions.

The action of the plays occurs outdoors, in front of the location represented by the *skene*. This was a dramatic convention, but it also reflected the fact that much of the everyday and political activity in classical Athens took place in the open air. The openness of this theatrical space is noteworthy. Built into the southeast slope of the Acropolis, the theater was large, public, and visually and acoustically connected to its environment. The conceit of the modern stage is the "missing" fourth wall—allowing the audience to see into others' living rooms, kitchens, offices, and bedrooms. In the ancient theater there was no missing wall, nor was there a curtain. The play began not with the unveiling of a tableau but with the drama's opening words—or even before then (see below). There were also very few stage properties. Sophocles is said to have introduced scene painting, but it was probably minimal, and a play such as the *Ion* atypically makes elaborate use of real (or imagined) painting on Apollo's temple at Delphi (185–218).

The theater also had two long entrance ramps on either side of the *skene*, called *eisodoi*, from which the actors and chorus could make entrances and exits. The first choral song is commonly called the *parodos* because it would often be sung as the chorus arrived down one of these ramps (sometimes called, less accurately, *parodoi*). These long ramps provided a powerful tool for the playwright to manipulate stately exits, surprise entrances, sorrowful and slowly moving funeral processions, and so on. In the later Greek theater, the two entrance ramps came to represent two distinct offstage areas—the ramp to the audience's left was imagined to lead to the country, the ramp to the right to the city. But this convention had not yet formed during Euripides's career. In his time, the play indicated (roughly) where the two ramps led. Along with the door(s) leading into the *skene* these ramps formed a triangle of theatrical focus. At times the pattern of comings and goings helps to build the play's meanings. For example, the polarity between city and country at the heart of *Bacchae* is underscored visually. The manic and miraculous activities all come from one side of the stage, while King Pentheus controls his palace. His doom is multiply signaled when he departs in maenadic dress and down the ramp leading to the wilds of Cithaeron. (See Wiles, *Tragedy* 133–60, on the theatrical and symbolic use of the *eisodoi*.)

The unseen is also part of Euripides's plays. The fifth-century stage's conventions presented the audience with a constant physical setting and placed all the play's visible action before it. But the "unseen" places are also part of how the playwright constructs his drama. In *Medea*, for example, Medea controls the interior, as well as the outside, of the palace represented by the *skene*: she is heard (wildly) from within before she even appears onstage; she debates and then later dupes Jason before the palace. When, at the play's end, Jason attempts to enter the palace, he is thwarted by Medea on high in her dragon chariot. Of course, she murders her children inside the palace, too. The palace's interior remains throughout the play unknown to the eye but present to the imagination. It is the site of mania, murder, and magic, all kept beyond our eyes and Jason's reach. Similarly, other offstage areas, sometimes not even visible in their exterior, can play a key role in the texture of the play. The battlefields in *Children of Heracles* and *Phoenician Women*, for example, are essential to the movement of those plays.

Just as the unseen can be important to a play's dynamics, so too can the unheard. Silences, often unnoticed on the page, can be powerful onstage. A character's not speaking tends to be lost in *reading* a text, but combined with a physical presence silence can have a larger effect on a scene's meaning. Perhaps the most potent example comes from Sophocles's *Oedipus the King*, where the king and the Corinthian messenger engage in a tight, stichomythic exchange for more than sixty lines while Jocasta, discovering the truth of her husband's/child's identity during the course of this dialogue, stands silently and passively as her world begins to collapse. In *Hippolytus*, the most likely staging of the central scene (Halleran, Aris ed., 200–01) shows the Nurse continuing with her failed supplication of Hippolytus and the young man savagely attacking both the Nurse and Phaedra while Phaedra herself stands out of the way— in earshot but not part of this scene. Phaedra and Hippolytus never address each other anywhere in the play, and their profound miscommunication is underscored by her mute presence in this, the only scene in which they are onstage together. Some caution is in order, however, when interpreting such silent presences. Dialogue in Greek tragedy tends to be between only two characters. True three-way dialogue is actually rare in tragedy, even in Euripides. We must accept the convention of fifth-century theater that tended to present characters in dyadic combination, even when more than two characters were onstage, and be careful not to interpret too aggressively the periodic absence from conversation of a given character onstage.

In recent years, scholars have come to talk about the "grammar of dramatic technique." Such a grammar is descriptive more than prescriptive (i.e., it outlines patterns more than "rules"), and it lays out some of the important features of ancient stagecraft. In teaching Euripides and the other Greek tragedians, teachers should bear in mind several general patterns concerning performance.

Some Fundamental "Rules"

The fundamental dynamic of Greek drama flows from the dual registers of actors and chorus. The actors typically spoke their lines, while the chorus, fifteen in number and acting as a group, sang and danced. The interplay of spoken and sung verse (with choreographed accompaniment), of individuals and a group provides the plays with much of their rich texture and complexity. Just as these two constituent parts of tragedy are distinguished formally, the perspectives they offer often bring views into crisp counterpoint.

All participants (actors and chorus) wore full-faced masks covering the whole head. This practice may well reflect drama's ritual origins, and it has many important consequences for interpretation. Psychological drama in the modern sense, as created by, for example, Ibsen and O'Neill, was absent from the fifth-century stage. The mask, with its unchanging visage, was a powerful way to deflect attention from the psychology of the individual toward a more limited range of social and ethical types. Aristotle boldly claims that tragedy is not about human beings but about actions and life (*Poetics* 1450a16–17). Although this statement is polemical in intent, it correctly focuses on the action as the heart of these dramas.

Unlike, for example, a Shakespearean play, where it is not uncommon to have six, seven, or more actors onstage at a given time, Greek tragedy worked with smaller groups, favoring one or two actors onstage at any given time. In fact, the practice followed by the tragedians was to use only three actors in total. This number refers to actors with speaking parts, not the number of roles in a dramatic production. A single actor could play more than one role, his changes of mask and costume making the transitions. For many plays we can determine the probable assignment of parts among the actors. Attempts to find patterns of significance in the distribution of parts (an individual actor playing the parts of, say, sworn enemies or husband and wife in the same play) have not found wide acceptance.

As a consequence of a relatively unbusy stage and few actors, individual arrivals and departures have greater significance. In fact, Oliver Taplin, amplifying Aristotle, has demonstrated that the basic structure of Greek tragedy involved the alternation of speech and song (*epeisodion* and *stasimon*) framed by exits before the songs and entrances after them (see *Stagecraft*). This demonstration has two immediate and related corollaries: entrances and exits are structurally fundamental to Greek drama, and the links between these stage actions and the songs they frame should repay careful attention.

Visual Echoes

Nuances of Euripides's dramatic technique can be explored under several rubrics. The synaesthetic heading "visual echoes" is meant to emphasize that significant repetition in theater need not be verbal but can be visual as well, sometimes reinforcing verbal cues, sometimes not. Examples of such "echoes," of varying specificity and intensity, are plentiful in Euripides. An example from *Alcestis* shows how powerfully verbal and visual markers can join forces. At the moment of her death, Alcestis collapses, having just bid farewell to her husband,

Admetus, in a line with two changes of speakers, an extremely rare structure in tragic verse. Later in the play, when Heracles returns with the veiled Alcestis, whom he has rescued from the dead, he insists on Admetus's receiving her into his house and taking hold of her to indicate his agreement. Admetus has fought against receiving this "stranger" into his house because it is clear that this would break his vow to his dying wife not to remarry. At the moment of his acceptance of the veiled woman (receiving her as a husband would a wife), Admetus shares with Heracles a line involving that same very rare phenomenon of two changes of speakers, just as he did with Alcestis at the moment of her death. Alcestis's death and "rebirth" are thus marked by verbal and visual echoes, underscoring the multiple ironies in the tale of the wife who dies for her husband only to be betrayed by him when he "remarries" her.

Bacchae contains several effective mirror scenes, including the large frame of the play created by the two appearances of Dionysus: first in mufti and then (presumably) in his full divine dress. The shift from Pentheus as hunter to hunted is also conveyed through a mirror scene (Taplin, *Greek Tragedy* 138–39). When the "stranger" (Dionysus in disguise) first arrives before Pentheus, it is as an object of prey, the captured prisoner chained and led in by Pentheus's men. But after Pentheus agrees to wear maenadic garb to investigate the women in the mountains, it is now Dionysus (still in disguise) who is in command, leading a psychically captured Pentheus to the hills and his ruin. This complete turnabout is seen in Pentheus' dress—the outfit he mocked as effeminate in the first scene, he now wears—and in the "echo" of that earlier scene's situation.

Entrances and exits in *Heracles* present what might be the most sustained set of visual echoes in all of Euripides. Heracles arrives in the nick of time to rescue (or so it seems) his family from threatened murder at the hands of Lycus. When he leads his family into the apparent safety of the palace, the gesture echoes verbally and visually the family's entrance *from* the palace at the start of the scene, which had seemed to mark their certain death. Tears accompany both prominent stage actions, the repeated verb "pull" (*helko*) appears in each instance, and Heracles explicitly contrasts the one with the other: "So your entrances into it are fairer / Than your exits from it, right?" (Halleran 623–24). He says he will lead into the house these "little boats in tow" (631). This safety of the house and Heracles's rescue are illusory. Ruin, replaced by rescue, reverts to ruin with the maddening of the hero into the murder of his family. But at the play's end, Heracles, himself now rescued by Theseus, departs not from the house but from the city of Thebes, escorted by Theseus like a "little boat in tow" (1424). The rare verbal image and the repeated stage action (a led departure) join these two events and complete the triadic progression, underscoring the play's larger shifts from rescue to ruin and back again.

Plays may also echo each other. *Orestes*, an unpredictable play from late in Euripides's career, offers a visual echo of an earlier play, *Medea*. *Medea* concludes with a scene of Jason trying to force entry into the palace only to be thwarted by a triumphant Medea on high. Twenty-three years later, *Orestes* presents the same situation. Menelaos arrives to stop what he presumes is Orestes's murder of his kin, and his demands that the palace doors be opened are met with Orestes on the rooftop threatening Hermione. Then the playwright, having echoed his earlier drama, offers a third tier to the scene. Whereas Medea seemed to act with divine authority, here Apollo appears on high and undercuts Orestes's apparent power and sets the following events on a new course.

Only Connect

For all its stylization and formality, Greek tragedy frequently made use of physical contact to express meaning. A single touch can alter the course of the play and our responses to it. Two examples give some idea of the dramatic potential of physical contact. In *Hippolytus*, Phaedra has determined that she will die by starvation rather than betray her husband by yielding to her passion for her stepson. She will not even talk about it lest her will and her good name be endangered. Her nurse, however, is eager to save Phaedra's life, whatever the cost. The Nurse's insistent attempts to get Phaedra to explain her plight seem futile—until she grasps Phaedra by the knees in supplication (325–35). This simple act changes the play's direction. Phaedra yields before the socioreligious compulsion implicit in supplication and reveals her passion for Hippolytus. This touch allows the play to move forward (it threatens to stop short if Phaedra dies in silence), as Phaedra tells her secret but does so "involuntarily." It also problematizes our response to Phaedra—inviting the audience to consider her virtuous for revealing her secret only under "compulsion" and at the same time to wonder about the conventionality that causes her to yield to this touch.

Similarly, the crucial moment in *Medea* when Creon forgoes his better judgment and grants Medea one more day in Corinth is achieved by the touch of supplication (324–54). The power of this touch breaks Creon's prudent resolve to exile Medea and leads to a rare instance of a character expressly doing something against his better judgment. He loses his daughter's and his own life because of it. Shortly hereafter, we see Medea express her contempt for Creon and acknowledge her manipulation of this ritual touch to achieve her ends.

Objects

The spare stage must have lent great weight to the few stage properties that were used in the original productions of these plays. In Sophocles's *Electra*, the urn with the "dead" Orestes's "ashes" provides the focus for a gripping scene and successful deception, while the bow in *Philoctetes* has visual, mythological, and symbolic meanings. Euripides does not seem to have used objects as such prominent vehicles for visual meaning, but he did take advantage of them. Heracles's bow in *Heracles* provides a strong example. Early in the play Lycus debates with Heracles's mortal father, Amphitryon, about his son's alleged cowardice in fighting with a bow at safe distance. The length of this debate has puzzled many scholars, but its full importance is not realized until later in the play. Heracles comes to the family's rescue, carrying his bow, only to use this very weapon when he is maddened into killing his children. Later he challenges his heroic status when he wonders whether he should leave the bow behind. His decision to continue carrying it, despite the ruin it has brought to his family, marks the moment of willingness to accept life's painful vicissitudes and his life as Heracles the hero.

In *Ion*, a play of fortune and recognition, the crucial moment when mother and son turn from intended mutual bloodshed to happy reunion is achieved through a wicker basket. This basket once held the infant Ion and tokens of his birthright. Now the Delphic priestess, the Pythia, appears to give it to Ion as he threatens Creusa, his mother (unknown to him), taking refuge at the altar. As Ion examines the basket and wonders about his mother's identity (while she is right before him), Creusa recognizes the basket she abandoned her child in years before, leaves the altar, and risks her life to claim her son. She is able to accurately identify the tokens left in the basket and establish herself as Ion's mother. The tokens themselves—the infant's blanket woven with a Gorgon's head, snake-shaped jewelry, and a miraculously preserved olive wreath—all resonate with the play's themes of Athenian history, autochthony, and power.

Several plays involve supplication at an altar—for example, *Children of Heracles*, *Suppliants*, *Heracles*, and *Helen*. In each of these the stage property representing the altar serves as an impressive visual marker of the crisis being enacted onstage, as each play opens with a group or individual taking refuge at the altar. Even before the play's first word, physical contact with the altar (essential for its potential protection) indicates the imminent danger that will drive the action of the drama.

The *skene* building itself can evoke a powerful response over the course of a tragedy. Most famously, in Aeschylus's *Oresteia* the house, represented by the *skene*, provides a concrete symbol of the multigenerational internecine violence in the family of Atreus. Attention is focused on it at once by the unusual opening scene in which a watchman lies on its roof. In the first two plays of the trilogy, the audience goes on to witness the control exerted over the house and household by Clytemnestra, the Furies who dwell on it (as imagined by Cassandra), and the battle to control it.

In *Alcestis* the house, which Admetus addresses in his opening words, reflects the wedded life he shared with Alcestis, as well as his hospitality (to Apollo and Heracles). Later it comes to represent Admetus's failure to die instead of his wife, then his betrayal of her, and finally their reunion. The tents of the Trojan women in the play of that name are a visual reminder of their fall from royalty to slavery. Dionysus's power is seen in the "palace miracle" in *Bacchae* in which Pentheus's palace is imagined to be leveled. The staging of this scene is controversial (I tend to think it was effected more by illusion than by pyrotechnics), but however it was staged, the destruction of the palace, represented by the *skene*, is fundamental to the shift in the balance of power between Pentheus and the "stranger."

Corpses can also serve as powerful visual effects. In Sophocles's *Ajax*, the hero's corpse dominates the entire second half of the play. Funeral processions in *Suppliants* and *Trojan Women*, for example, also highlight dead bodies. Such processions, along with other slow, stately, or solemn entrances are typically underscored by the use of a different meter (anapests) to announce their arrival, even when an arrival at that moment in the play would not normally be announced (Halleran, *Stagecraft* 11–18). In *Alcestis*, a funeral procession for the dead Alcestis provides a bizarre backdrop for the argument conducted by her husband, Admetus, and his father, Pheres, over their mutual unwillingness to die. The corpse's presence helps to create a dissonant note for this scene in the elusive overall tone of the play.

Hippolytus makes significant thematic use of bodies. First, the audience sees a moribund Phaedra lying on a couch while being carried onstage by attendants. Later, after she has taken her life, her corpse, holding the lying tablets, is presented to Theseus and the audience. Her mute corpse bears powerful testimony against Hippolytus and persuades Theseus that her false charges of rape against his son are true. Throughout the debate between father and son over his innocence, Phaedra's corpse remains a constant presence, an irrefutable (false) witness and the visual backdrop to the debate. In the scene following Hippolytus's departure (and the removal of Phaedra's corpse), a messenger reports Hippolytus's encounter with a bull sent by Poseidon from the sea and his near-fatal condition. When Hippolytus returns near death, his arrival echoes Phaedra's earlier entrance. Then at the play's conclusion Hippolytus, now vindicated by Artemis, has a second encounter with his father. The pitiful reconciliation between father and son closes with Theseus veiling the corpse of the son whose death he caused.

In *Heracles*, the maddened hero, having killed his wife and children and been subdued by Athena, awakens tied to a pillar and surrounded by the carnage he has wrought, the corpses of his family. Initially confused by his surroundings, he gradually discovers where he is and what he has done and decides to take his own life for shame. Theseus's arrival, however, intervenes, and the long final scene in which Theseus persuades Heracles to continue living is played out amid the corpses of his own flesh and blood, murdered by his own hand. His soul-searching debate with Theseus and his decision to not commit suicide but accept the limitations of his mortality, and therefore to continue living despite the blood on his hands, gain in power from the physical presence of the corpses throughout this scene.

Special Devices

Two mechanical devices added to the possibilities of stage production in Euripides's dramas—the *ekkyklema* and the *mechane*. The precise nature and even the fifth-century use of these devices are questioned, but the plays themselves argue strongly for their employment in Euripidean drama.

Since the interior of the *skene* was not visible through a "missing" fourth wall, the Greek theater developed a way to bring interior scenes to the audience's view: the *ekkyklema*, which was a wheeled platform coming out from the central doors of the *skene*. It did not have to be used all the time since the conventions placed the actions outside, before the *skene*, and narrative and imagination played a role in conjuring up interiors to the audience's mind's eye. But the potential dramatic effects of making the interior visible were too powerful not to exploit. In an earlier period of the Greek theater interior objects might have been carried onstage by extras, but the development of the *ekkyklema* allowed for a simple, if artificial, way to display interior scenes to the audience. The *ekkyklema* could hold tableaux of various types—corpses being the most frequent. Its use in *Hippolytus* and *Heracles* to make visible what has hitherto been only reported shows the powerful effect of "ocular proof."

Whereas the *ekkyklema* increased the playwright's potential expanse at ground level, the *mechane* expanded his vertical scope. This was a cranelike device that allowed characters to appear on high, either held aloft or carried to the rooftop. Euripides clearly favored using the gods as characters in his dramas: of the seventeen extant tragedies, thirteen present at least one divinity (and another a ghost). Sophocles, by contrast, used this device only once in his extant seven plays—at the end of *Philoctetes*—and this instance is generally described as an example of Euripidean influence. The gods that appeared while other characters or the chorus were onstage certainly appeared on the roof or in the *mechane*. Impressive and unreachable, they appeared literally above the mortals. Members of the audience had to adjust their vision to include this new location of dramatic action. The appearances of gods at the start of plays, before the arrival of other characters, are more problematic. It is possible that they, too, appeared on high, but they might also have appeared at stage level, with their distance from mortals being suggested in other ways (Mastronarde, esp. 272–80; Halleran, *Stagecraft* 8–10).

Medea's use of the *mechane* to effect her escape at the end of *Medea* adds to the impression that she is in fact godlike in the savage revenge she exacts from her faithless husband, who, in turn, seems impotent against this great fury. For all her concern for Hippolytus, Aphrodite remains aloft, without tears for her mortal beloved, at the end of *Hippolytus*. The sudden appearances on high of divinities grip the imagination and move the plays into another register. At a fundamental level, Greek tragedy constantly explores the relationship of mortals and immortals; here the gods, made manifest, assert themselves physically in the action, even while remaining aloof. Interpretations of these scenes vary widely (see most recently Dunn), but whatever views we adopt we should take into account the particular and particularly Euripidean ways these gods are presented onstage.

Outlining Your Own Greek Drama: A Creative Project

Adele J. Haft

In 1982 a gifted student and playwright asked me if he could compose a drama for Greek and Roman Tragedy in Translation, a second-year course open to those who have passed English composition at Hunter College, City University of New York. By the end of the semester, Timothy Flannery had submitted the detailed outline for a play about Marsyas, the satyr whose mastery of the flute embroiled him in a fatal contest with the god of the lyre, Apollo. Flannery later finished his tragedy, and in 1985 he directed *Marsyas: An Attic Resurrection* at Theater for the New City, an off-Broadway venue in Manhattan's East Village.

Watching that play take form, I realized that an entire tragedy class could benefit from such a project. Over the past decade, I have required students to create their own "classical Greek tragedy." More specifically, they outline the play's contents and compose a finished section of two or three pages. All plots and characters are based on a classical myth not portrayed in a surviving full-length Greek or Roman drama. (See the appendix for the project description handed out on the first day of class.)

Although the prospect is terrifying at first, most students eventually take pleasure in competing to produce one of the three works that will be read during the drama contest on the final day. Outlining a Greek drama challenges their creativity as they grapple with issues of theme and characterization, the playwrights' different styles, and the peculiarities of Athenian production and performance during the fifth century BCE. The process helps students visualize and understand the unfamiliar aspects of classical Greek drama: an omnipresent chorus, infrequent changes of scene, the absence of a curtain and stage lights, the necessity of portraying action out of doors and in daylight, the restriction of dramatic time to twenty-four hours, the taboo against depicting violence onstage, and the assignment of speaking parts to no more than three male actors—all of whom wear masks.

The dramas my students create are intensely personal, but certain myths reappear time and again. Arachne's weaving contest with Athena, Orpheus's descent for Eurydice, Phaethon's insistence on mounting his father's solar chariot, Procris's death at the hands of her husband, Niobe's loss of her children, and Pygmalion's attempt to create an ideal woman—all are favorite subjects. The project has been so successful that I use it instead of the essay or research paper that normally supplements the exams in classical tragedy courses. And, as you will see, it has a special relevance for those of us teaching Euripides.

Introducing the Project

On the first day of class, I inform my students that thirty percent of their grade will derive from outlining a tragedy of their own. To counter their inevitable fears, I reassure them that the entire semester will be spent preparing for the project.

My first steps are to read the project description aloud and relate the plots of the tragedies that are essentially intact. I also make available J. Michael Walton's *Living Theatre*, which provides detailed appendixes listing the names, titles, settings, characters, and type of chorus in extant plays; the titles of lost plays; and glossaries of terms.

Over the next several weeks, the students sift through collections of myths to find two or three that particularly fascinate them. Since our classical mythology courses inspire many students to study ancient tragedy, their only difficulty is deciding which myths they enjoy most. I urge those who have little or no acquaintance with the myths to consult works on reserve—particularly Ovid's *Metamorphoses*, Robert Graves's *Greek Myths*, and Simon Hornblower and Anthony Spawforth's *The Oxford Classical Dictionary*. Students then discuss their choice of myths with me. In individual fifteen-minute conferences, we agree on a myth that meets the spirit of the project.

The Oxford Guide to Classical Mythology in the Arts, 1300–1990s (Reid and Rohmann) is particularly helpful for familiarizing students with the original sources for their myths. This two-volume reference provides alphabetical synopses of the mythic characters, describes the art they inspired, and cites sources of their myths in Greek and Latin literature. If students cannot decide on a myth, I often use the guide to find one compatible with their interests. Every student leaves my office with a copy of the page(s) relevant to their myth. So that all have access to the most important sources, I place on reserve translations of Homer, Hesiod, Pindar, Diodorus Siculus, Vergil, Ovid, Apollodorus, Pausanias, and Hyginus. One month before the project is due, I ask students to submit a brief description of the myth, setting, characters, and type of chorus they intend to flesh out in their tragedy. This ungraded assignment stimulates uncommitted students to schedule a conference with me and others to discuss a change of topic if their research has proved uninspiring.

Preparing for the Project in Class

So that students understand the foundation on which to mold their plot and characterizations, I spend part of every class demonstrating how the ancient Greek tragedies were constructed. The first two classes conjure up a day at the theater in fifth-century Athens. Using slides, I encourage students to comment on the differences between ancient Greek performances and their modern-day counterparts. For those interested in pursuing the subject, I recommend several works available at Hunter: H. C. Baldry's *The Greek Tragic Theatre*, Margarete Bieber's *The History of the Greek and Roman Theater*, Arthur Pickard-Cambridge's *The Dramatic Festivals of Athens*, Rush Rehm's *Greek Tragic Theatre*, Oliver Taplin's *Greek Tragedy in Action*, and T. B. L. Webster's *Greek Theatre Production*.

During the semester, my class reads thirteen plays—at least half of them by Euripides. As we begin each, I outline the play's formal structure on the board. In this way students quickly become familiar with the various parts of the ancient drama—their terms, meaning, and traditional sequence. They learn that a prologue is followed by the *parodos* (choral entrance song), then by several *epeisodia* (acts or spoken scenes) separated one from another by *stasima* (choral odes), and finally by the *exodos* (conclusion and "exit" song). On the outline I include a brief description of the action, line numbers, and characters in each part of the drama. I also highlight a character's first appearance to demonstrate how often the playwright introduces a new character into a new act. For example, here is the beginning of one outline of Euripides's *Iphigenia* (or *Iphigeneia*) *at Tauris*:

1–122   Prologue: **Iphigenia** relates her dream of Orestes's death. Unseen by Iphigenia, **Orestes** and **Pylades** discuss Apollo's oracle and Orestes's fear of this strange place.

123–235   *Parodos*: The Chorus of Temple Maidens and Iphigenia grieve over Orestes's supposed death.

236–391   Act 1: Without bringing Pylades and Orestes onstage, the **Herdsman** tells of their capture. Ignorant of their names, Iphigenia inures herself to the fate of these fellow Greeks but attributes to Artemis the Taurians' barbarity to foreigners (see England xxvi–xxix).

The outline emphasizes that, in the prologue at least, three different actors are employed. A complete outline enables students to see how no more than three actors can play all the characters, except the nonspeaking parts. It also suggests the possible distributions of roles among the actors. In the *Iphigenia at Tauris*, the protagonist naturally assumes the part of Iphigenia, the leading character present in every act before the *exodos*; in the finale, he might switch to another female role—that of Athena, the play's deus ex machina (the god who appears on high from a mechanical crane). The second actor could portray Orestes in the *parodos* and acts 2 through 3, the Herdsman in act 1, and the Soldier-Messenger in the *exodos*. The third actor might play the role of Pylades in the *parodos* and acts 2 through 3 and the role of Thoas in act 4 and the *exodos*.

A complete outline has another benefit: it shows how the choral odes provided actors with time to change their masks and robes in the *skene* (tent or stage building) before assuming another role in the next act. Since our translations cannot convey the subtle rhythms of the Greek original, it is sometimes difficult to surmise from them where one part of the drama ends and another begins. For this purpose, indispensable guides are found in the commentaries on individual plays published by Oxford (e.g., Owen's *Ion*; Dodds's *Bacchae*; Barrett's *Hippolytos*) and by Aris and Phillips (e.g., Conacher's *Alcestis*; Cropp's *Electra*). In their notes these editors identify the line numbers of the various parts, and in their introductions they often suggest which roles might have been assumed by each of the three actors.

Early in the second month, I request—as five percent of their final grade— that students outline the structure of a required Euripidean play and diagram the roles they would assign to each actor. After this material is presented in class, those who have not performed satisfactorily are asked to repeat the exercise for the next tragedy. Anyone who continues to have difficulties must seek help after class, since it is vital that all students understand the structure of Greek drama before they undertake their projects in earnest.

Other assignments emphasize the content of the tragedies. Early in the semester, I divide the class into groups of four to six students. In the class preceding our first discussion of a play, I assign each group a different question to consider: How is a specific character depicted? What is the role of the chorus? Where is the play set and why? How ought a particular passage be analyzed? Since we devote two classes to each play, at the end of the first class I give the groups twenty minutes to discuss their assignments and elect a leader to present their ideas during the second class. In the next class, each of the six leaders offers a four-minute synopsis to the class and submits to me a two-page essay for criticism before the final project.

Both oral and written presentations receive grades, and every student is required to act as leader once during the course. These exercises invite students to actively engage the plays. Analysis of specific issues also helps them perform better on the essay and passage analysis sections of their exams, and it has the further benefit of focusing on the distinctions between the actors and the members of the chorus, allowing students to generalize about the content of the actors' speeches in contrast to that of the choral songs.

No modern rendition of the Greek tragedies can restore the music or choreography of the originals. Yet there is no more exciting way to come to grips with these plays than by a visit to the theater. Given the expense of tickets and the complexity of students' schedules, however, I find that videos offer an equitable way of introducing the ancient plays and a director's vision. I show two or three in class. Among them are Michael Cacoyannis's *Trojan Women* (1971) and *Iphigenia* (1977); Jules Dassin's *A Dream of Passion* (1978), an interpretation of the *Medea*; and Peter Weir's *Picnic at Hanging Rock* (1975), which, like the *Bacchae*, explores the fatal attraction of the irrational. Viewing these films gives students ideas and confidence when creating their own projects.

The Drama Contest

The climax of my course is the drama contest, which takes place on the last day of class. As far as possible, we attempt to simulate the procedures used at the Great Dionysia in Athens during the fifth century BCE. A week and a half before the last class, students submit their drama projects, and I, in the role of eponymous archon, select the three best. The final day of class compresses events once spread over six or seven days. In the spirit of the *proagon*, held a few days before the Great Dionysia began, I summarize the plots of the three selected plays. For the ancient audience, hearing the synopses offered by the three playwrights—spectacularly accompanied by costumed actors, choral members, and musicians—was both playbill and further enticement. In fairness to my audience of playwrights, I summarize the plot of every one of their plays and announce honorable mentions. The class then selects ten students as judges and the contestants read their tragedies aloud, thus collapsing into forty-five minutes the three days traditionally reserved for the ancient performances. After the judges list the three contestants in order of preference, they slip their votes into an "urn." (I use a Saco de Toro "Bullie," a vessel made from a bull's scrotum, to remind the class that a bull sacrifice preceded the ancient contests dedicated to the god of drama, Dionysos Eleuthereus.) At least five of the ballots are picked at random to determine which contestants receive first, second, and third prize. The winner is crowned with a wreath of ivy—symbolizing the god's promise of immortality—and each contestant selects from an assortment of desk copies provided by the instructor. Invited guests attend the festivities and share the food and wine following the contest.

Euripides and Outlining Your Own Greek Drama

This project works especially well in translation courses where Euripides is taught alongside the other ancient tragedians and where techniques of production and performance are considered as meaningful as issues of theme and characterization. Students do not have to produce Euripidean-style plays. Yet, not surprisingly, they gravitate toward those techniques and themes most associated with his unusually large corpus of surviving works. Students may admire Aeschylus's epic dimensions, complex word imagery, and lengthy choral odes or Sophocles's dialogues involving all three actors. But they usually do not possess the sophistication or time to replicate these strengths. Euripides also seems more accessible. Students frequently imitate the messenger speeches that appear in almost every Euripidean drama; or his familiar prologue speaker, who provides the audience with vital information; or his habit of shifting our sympathies midway through the play; or his trademark deus ex machina to predict the future of the characters. Euripides's domestic settings and intrigues, his relentless demythologizing of heroic figures of myth, the conflict between his characters' masks and actions, his fascination with abnormal psychology, highly charged emotions, and sensational effects—all make him very "contemporary." The growing diversity of our student population seems certain to ensure that Euripidean drama will become even more popular. Our students relate well to his nonaristocratic characters, his treatment of women and children, his ambivalence toward war and its advocates, his contempt of hypocrisy. Perhaps most appealing of all is the humanity Euripides manages to convey through his characters' blend of weakness and good intentions.

APPENDIX
OUTLINING YOUR OWN GREEK DRAMA: PROJECT HANDOUT

Choose a Greek or Roman myth that has not survived in dramatic form from antiquity and develop this myth into a "typical" Greek tragedy. You will not be writing an entire Greek tragedy. Instead, you will outline the plan for one, peopling it with at least six suitable characters and providing a short example of "finished" dialogue, monologue, or choral ode. Keep quotations from your sources to a minimum; if you include a quotation, be sure to cite your source and page(s) in parentheses.

The entire project should be no longer than twelve single-spaced, typed pages; double-space between paragraphs, speakers, and the parts of your drama. Please follow the format below, and see me as soon as possible about your choice of myth and approach to it.

Cover Page (p. 1)
Include your name and the title of your play. Remember that the titles of most classical plays derive from the name of the chorus (e.g., *The Trojan Women*) or leading character (e.g., *Hippolytos*).

Part 1 (pp. 2–3): Cast of Characters and the Chorus
Use as a model the list of characters preceding each play we have read, but add the following information:

1. A description of the chorus and every character and the reason(s) why each appears in your play. (No more than 3–4 sentences per character or chorus, please.)

2. An indication of which actor you would assign to each character. (After the name of each character, put in parentheses "Actor 1," "Actor 2," or "Actor 3.") Remember that the Greeks used no more than three actors in each tragedy. Make sure that you do not have one actor playing two parts simultaneously. And do give the actors sufficient time to change between roles.

3. A short description of the setting and why you've chosen it.

Part 2 (pp. 4–8): Outline of Play
Outline the entire contents of your play, describing briefly what happens and what is said in each monologue, dialogue, and choral ode. For guidance, refer to the play outlines I have put on the board. You will want to adhere to the following sequence for the parts of your play: a prologue (whether a monologue, dialogue, or both); a *parodos* (choral entrance and song); act 1, introducing at least one new character; a choral ode; act 2, introducing another new character or characters; a choral ode; and so on, through to the *exodos*. In the left-hand margin, supply line numbers for each part to give an indication of the relative "length" you would assign to your episodes. (Note that most ancient Greek tragedies range from 1000 to 1700 lines.)

Part 3 (pp. 9–11): Finished Episode
Isolate one extended monologue, dialogue, or choral song that epitomizes the message of your play. It should contain many of the important themes

and images recurring throughout your play. Compose this episode in its entirety.

Part 3 is the most creative part of your project. Though you have drawn on a wealth of sources for the rest of your exercise, in this section your own voice should be heard: use your own words and particular slant on the myth you have selected. While sticking to the skeleton of the myth as it has been handed down, provide your own motivations for your characters' actions. Give your gods their normal traits, but not necessarily those presented in the myth you have chosen. Let your chorus or invented characters shed light on unfamiliar aspects of the myth's meaning or a mythic character's psychology. In other words, do not quote or even paraphrase your sources here but create something uniquely your own.

Part 4 (p. 12): Bibliography

List in alphabetical order all the sources that you used to research your project. Follow the guide for citations in the most recent *MLA Handbook for Writers of Research Papers*.

The Importance of Debate in Euripides— and of Debating Euripides

Gary S. Meltzer

One of the most successful classes I have ever taught was a debate on Euripides's *Medea*, which I set up with the following assignment:

> Prepare for a debate in which everyone in the class will participate and argue pro or con the following statement: Although she commits a horrible crime, Medea wins our sympathy as a victim of a misogynistic society and a cruel husband. She shares the heroic traits of other tragic protagonists; she is intense, brave, and clever. Like Ajax, she is obsessed with avoiding mockery; like Achilles, she is intent on obtaining vengeance. Please write out your arguments for or against the statement above (a couple of paragraphs will do). Also, anticipating at least one argument on the other side, write out a paragraph of rebuttal. This assignment is to be turned in.

On the day of the debate, I divided the class into two teams and asked each team to present its case. Then each side had the chance to rebut the other side's arguments. Finally, a general discussion ensued that was freewheeling and lively, engaging students' intellect and emotions.

Why was this debate so successful, I wondered? Part of the answer stemmed from the debate format itself. Everyone was expected to prepare the question in advance and to share his or her response with the rest of the class. Being part of a team seemed to make even shy students feel more at ease. But not all debates work equally well, as I knew from previous experience. The particular question I devised was provocative and controversial, admitting no easy answers: can a character who kills her own children gain our sympathy? A character as complex as Medea cannot fail to elicit strong, and perhaps contradictory, emotional responses in the audience. Medea's crime shocks us because it violates our most basic assumptions about the "maternal instinct," human nature, and civilized life; and yet, as monstrous as Medea's crime is, the human dimensions of her plight are drawn so vividly as to be capable of winning our sympathy: her bitter hatred of the husband who has abandoned her, her anguish as an isolated foreigner in Corinth, her vacillations about her intended crime, and her desperate attempts to rationalize it. Adding to the complexity of Medea's characterization is the fact that she does seem to be "cast in the heroic mold" of tragic protagonists who are male (Foley, "Medea's Divided Self" 74, 76). Euripides's ability to create such characters—and situations— helps to explain why Aristotle called him "the most truly tragic of the tragic poets" (*Poetics* 1453a26–30).

So, the success of the debate also derived, at least in part, from the complexity of the protagonist. Medea's characterization resists ideological pigeon-holing: it reinforces traditional gender stereotypes in some ways, but at the same time, it offers us an extraordinarily empathetic look at women's lives in fifth-century BC Athens (one has to look no further than Medea's opening speech [214-66] for a masterful illustration of this). My students volunteered a number of their own strong reactions to Medea's character during the debate. One student saw her as victimized by her "jerk of a husband"; another, referring to the stories of Medea's involvement in the killing of both her own brother and Jason's uncle (Graves 153a, 155e–h), described her as a "serial killer." Other Euripidean characters, both female and male, are equally controversial: one thinks of Phaedra and Hippolytus in *Hippolytus*, Pentheus in *The Bacchae*, and *Hecuba* in the play named after her.

The success of the debate says something about the provocative nature of Euripidean drama in general, I realized, as I reflected further: it not only invites debate but also demands it. The art of questioning is a vital part of Euripides's own "teaching" (the Greeks used the same term [*didaskolos*] for both "teacher" and "dramatic poet"). This art of questioning—characterized as it is by a sustained, self-conscious examination of myth, rhetoric, and even of drama itself—distinguishes Euripides from his predecessors. Indeed, the greatest Euripidean tragedies are powerful, open-ended texts that offer much evidence for conflicting interpretations. We have reason to believe that Euripides's drama was as controversial in his own day as it is in ours. The comic playwright Aristophanes, a contemporary of Euripides, crystallized this aspect of his tragedies by making him a character in the *Frogs* who boasts that he taught the Athenians to question and criticize everything (971–79). Indeed, Euripidean drama, with its iconoclastic portrayal of cowardly heroes and noble peasants and its questioning of the existence of the gods, subverts the whole mythic tradition of the Greeks.

Students of Euripides need to understand, however, that the questions posed in his drama reflect wider controversies in late-fifth-century Athens—a time of rapid social, political, and intellectual change that resembles our own turbulent age. In his capacity to question, Euripides exemplifies the radical skepticism of a period that is known both as the "Greek enlightenment" and as the "intellectual revolution." Understanding developments in this period, therefore, is essential if one wishes to understand Euripidean drama.

Let us begin, then, by identifying three key trends of the era: a new, self-conscious interest in rhetoric and debate; a questioning of old aristocratic norms and mythic truths; and concomitantly, a growing emphasis on man's powers of reason and logic. The rise of democracy provides an important context in which to place all these trends. Democratic reforms in Athens in the early and middle fifth century BC permitted greater participation by ordinary citizens in the political process. A group of itinerant teachers known as Sophists arose to meet the greater need for instruction in how to debate in the assembly and to plead one's case in the law courts. Their claim to be able to teach the skills of rhetoric and debate to any interested citizen willing to pay their fee certainly had a democratic aspect. Formerly, eloquence had been considered a gift the gods bestowed on kings and poets, "masters of truth," in Marcel Detienne's phrase. Now, in Euripides's age, anyone who was properly trained in rhetoric could, in principle, learn to argue well (a sophistic belief that is perhaps reflected in the well-crafted speeches of both women and lower-class characters in Euripidean drama).

The Sophists developed types of argumentation that still survive in our courts, political forums, academic discourse, and everyday life. They taught, for example, the use of "double arguments" (*dissoi logoi*), the art of arguing both sides of a question that is still used today in law school (Guthrie 316). Other procedures of argument used in law courts and political debates in both ancient Athens and modern America include appeals to nature versus nurture (custom, law), advantage or expedience, likelihood or probability, and lastly, justice (Guthrie 48, 169, 178–79). And yet, as popular as sophistic teachings were among the Athenian elite, the boast of some Sophists that they could make the "weaker argument appear the stronger" (Guthrie 188) struck some critics, especially Plato, as corrupt; in the *Republic, Gorgias,* and other Platonic dialogues, Socrates attacks the Sophists for arguing without any regard for the morality or justice of the case they were making. Emblematic of this alleged disregard is the definition of justice offered by the Sophist Thrasymachus as the "advantage of the stronger " (*Republic* 338c, in *Dialogues*).

The Sophist Protagoras's claim that "[o]f all things the measure is man" (Robinson 245) perhaps epitomizes the bold new faith put by the Greek enlightenment in man's powers of reason and analysis. Indeed, during this period, Athenians put growing confidence in the power of rational discourse and debate to attain a form of truth superior to the old, mythic truths— whether through cross-examination in the courts, debate in the assembly, or philosophical inquiry. Adding to the turbulence of Euripides's age were several other factors: the challenge of early philosophers to mythic explanations of the cosmos (the pre-Socratic philosopher Anaxagoras, for example, argued that the sun was not a god but a "red-hot stone" [Robinson 187]); the political upheaval of the Peloponnesian War between Athens and Sparta (431–04 BC); and the rise of prose, which marked a shift from a "song culture" to a "book culture" (Herington 3–4).

The influence of this intellectual revolution on the text of Euripides is enormous, varied, and many-faceted. An intense concern with rhetoric—its morality, its powers, its limitations—pervades the dramas. Although Euripides has been attacked by critics from Aristophanes to Nietzsche as sophistic, his dramas contain blame as well as praise of the new art of rhetoric. For example, Hecuba praises persuasion as "the only art whose power / is absolute" (Arrowsmith, *Hecuba* 817–18), but Phaedra attacks it as a "deadly thing which devastates well-ordered cities" (Grene, *Hippolytus* 486–87). Euripidean drama subjects traditional and innovative values alike to critical inquiry—a point neglected by those who condemn the playwright as a radical iconoclast.

In fact, anxiety about the power of sophistry pervades Euripidean drama, but two examples should suffice. Suspecting that his son, Hippolytus, has raped his wife, Phaedra, Theseus utters the following lament:

> If there were
> some token now, some mark to make the division
> clear between friend and friend, the true and the false!
> All men should have two voices, one the just voice,
> and one as chance would have it. In this way
> the treacherous scheming voice would be confuted
> by the just, and we should never be deceived.
> (*Hippolytus* 925–31)

After she has been betrayed by Jason, Medea voices a similar complaint about the lack of a touchstone to distinguish truth from lies:

> O God, you have given to mortals a sure method
> of telling the gold that is pure from the counterfeit;
> Why is there no mark engraved upon men's bodies,
> By which we could know the true ones from the false ones?
> (Warner, *The Medea* 516–19)

Both Theseus and Medea speak of deceptiveness and sophistry as universal human problems for which they can only offer utopian solutions. Some feminist critics argue that it is the female protagonists of the two plays under discussion who epitomize the destructive power of persuasion: Phaedra's false accusation of rape against Hippolytus results in his death, and Medea uses her cunning to gain revenge on Jason by killing their sons (Rabinowitz, *Anxiety* 143, 163–65). However, the role of these admittedly deceptive female characters is paradoxical, insofar as they also expose or highlight the hypocrisy of their male antagonists. Medea paints a convincing portrait of Jason as a conniving opportunist, and it is a male character, after all—Hippolytus—who gives us the most famous bit of sophistry in all Greek tragedy: "My tongue swore, but my mind was still unpledged" (*Hippolytus* 612).

Hecuba furnishes yet another example of the paradoxical portrait of female characters in Euripides. On the one hand, she uses feminine wiles to avenge the loss of her son at the hands of Polymestor (Rabinowitz, *Anxiety* 121–22). On the other hand, she attacks the sophistry of politicians like Agamemnon who "cringe for favors from a screaming mob" and of Polymestor himself, whom she attacks as one of the "sophists who make a science of persuasion, / glozing evil with the slick of loveliness" (*Hecuba* 1193; 256–57).

The distrust of sophistry expressed by many Euripidean characters—both female and male—reflects anxiety about the new importance of rhetoric in an age that questioned old beliefs. As vexing and duplicitous as the traditional gods could be, one could be reasonably sure about how to win their favor, avoid their wrath, and appease them when necessary; moreover, prophets and sooth-sayers knew how to interpret their signs and omens accurately. People could, after all, count on gods such as Zeus and Apollo to protect certain principles of justice and truth; any oath sworn by Zeus or oracle delivered by Apollo was deemed reliable, and Zeus himself enforced the law of hospitality. But now, in the new age, when either impersonal cosmic principles or human self-interest reigned in place of the old gods, to whom could one appeal in the face of injustice? Characters in desperate situations sometimes invoke cosmic principles instead of the anthropomorphic Olympian deities, as Hecuba does here:

> O power, who mount the world, wheel where the world rides,
> O mystery of man's knowledge, whosoever you be,
> Zeus named, nature's necessity or mortal mind,
> I call upon you [. . .].   (Lattimore, *The Trojan Women* 884–87)

We have already seen how Theseus and Medea, when confronted with crises of their own, expressed a longing for a transcendent, infallible sign of truth.

Indeed, a whole series of Euripidean characters ask versions of the question, Where can a clear, sure sign or voice of truth and justice be found, if truth and justice are no longer defined by the gods but have become the subject of partisan debate? The young democracy came to regard the ability to test arguments through the skillful use of debate and cross-examination as a fairly reliable means of reaching the truth. But this new confidence in rhetoric and logic may have been misplaced: What happens if a defendant is in the right but does not present his case as well as his opponent does? Or what happens if a judge or jury is unfairly prejudiced against a defendant? Euripides's *Hippolytus* dramatizes both of these dangers. After Phaedra commits suicide and leaves behind a letter incriminating Hippolytus, Theseus too quickly rejects his son's pleas of innocence and condemns him to death. In doing so he is swayed both by a low estimate of Hippolytus's character and by the misleading "evidence" of Phaedra's suicide and letter (Meltzer 175–76). He finds out too late that Hippolytus was telling the truth and that Phaedra succeeded in making the "weaker argument appear to be the stronger" (Guthrie 188). Dilemmas like the one faced by Theseus prompt a variety of Euripidean characters to reflect not only about the existence of the gods, the meaning of truth, and the accessibility of justice but also about the nature of language and the workings of rhetoric.

Indeed, formal debates in Euripides often mirror debates between the old and new modes of thought in the wider culture. For example, in *The Phoenician Women* (Wyckoff), a quarrel between two brothers about which one should be king of Thebes becomes in effect a debate about debate itself:

POLYNEICES: The word of truth is single in its nature;
              and a just cause needs no interpreting.
              It carries its own case. But the unjust argument
              since it is sick, needs clever medicine. [. . .]
ETEOCLES: If all men saw the fair and wise the same
              men would not have debaters' double strife.
              But nothing is like or even among men
              except the name they give—which is not the fact.
                                              (469–72, 499–502)

For these mythic characters of the heroic age (predating the fifth century BC by many centuries) to be using sophistic terms and logic creates a jarring, anachronistic effect. The Athenian audience would just as surely have picked up on these contemporary allusions as we ourselves would, if we heard Hamlet say, "To be or not to be—let me deconstruct the question!"

Formal debates often represent crucial, even climactic scenes in the dramas. These debates may take the form of trials, replete with legal vocabulary. Indeed, Euripides's trial scenes incorporate the "courtroom drama" that must have been as popular with Athenian audiences as it is with us today (Collard, "Formal Debates" 63). In *Hippolytus*, Theseus wrongly finds Hippolytus guilty of rape; in *Hecuba*, Agamemnon serves as judge in hearing the cases presented by Hecuba and Polymestor. These and other debates, like the one in *The Phoenician Women* just discussed or the one between Hecuba and Helen in *The Trojan Women*, are so improbable as to break the mythic frame of the play. The failure of these debates and "trials" to reach the truth or produce a just outcome certainly makes a comment on the young Athenian democracy (Meltzer 175).

Debates, whether formal or informal, also serve as important structuring principles of Euripidean drama. For example, the debate between Artemis and Aphrodite frames the action of *Hippolytus,* and the debate between Dionysus and Cadmus caps the action of *The Bacchae*. At the same time, both these debates dramatize the clash between traditional and contemporary views of the gods—and of divine justice—that was taking place in the surrounding culture. The most profound Euripidean dramas, such as *Hippolytus* and *The Bacchae*, eschew any easy morals by calling into question the very notion of a single truth or simple justice.

An understanding of sophistic modes of argumentation is vital for appreciating the subtext and subtlety of the verbal contest in Euripides. Perhaps the best way to demonstrate the importance of these types of arguments is to examine a scene from one of Euripides's plays that deploys them all: the debate between Death and Apollo in *Alcestis* (Lattimore 28–76). First, a little background on the play: Admetus is fated to die, but in return for his hospitality the god Apollo has decided to save his life, if someone else will agree to die in his place. But no one, not even his aged parents, is willing to do so, until his wife,

Alcestis, volunteers. In the opening scene of the play, Apollo attempts to dis-
suade Death from snatching Alcestis off—or at least to delay her death. The
ensuing debate between Apollo and Death takes the form of a stichomythia
("line-speech"), a fast-paced argument in which two characters exchange
pointed one-liners. Let us briefly examine part of this confrontation, in which
the characters' use of sophistic arguments turns to comic effect:

DEATH: Ah!
You at this house, Phoebus? Why do you haunt
the place. It is unfair to take for your own
and spoil the death-spirits' privileges. [. . .]

APOLLO: Never fear. I have nothing but justice and fair words for you.

DEATH: If you mean fairly, what are you doing with a bow?

APOLLO: It is my custom to carry it with me all the time.

DEATH: It is your custom to help this house more than you ought. [. . .]

APOLLO: Is there any way, then, for Alcestis to grow old?

DEATH: There is not. I insist on enjoying my rights too.

APOLLO: You would not take more than one life, in any case.

DEATH: My privilege means more to me when they die young.

APOLLO: If she dies old, she will have a lavish burial.

DEATH: What you propose, Phoebus, is to favor the rich.

APOLLO: What is this? Have you unrecognized talents for debate?

DEATH: Those who could afford to buy a late death would buy it then.

APOLLO: I see. Are you determined not to do this for me?

DEATH: I will not do it. And you know my character.

(28–31, 38–41, 52–61)

At the beginning of this scene both Apollo and Death allude to the principle
of justice. Death claims it is "unfair" for Apollo to transgress on his territory by
first rescuing Admetus from death and then trying to forestall Alcestis's death
as well (30–31). Apollo counters by insisting that he harbors no ill intentions
toward Death: "I have nothing but justice and fair words for you" (38). Death
challenges this assertion by asking Apollo, "If you mean fairly, what are you
doing with a bow?" (39). The art of arguing well, of constructing "fair words,"
will apparently not suffice for Death, who, in questioning Apollo's need for a
bow, employs the sophistic distinction between words and deeds. Apollo counters by insisting that he carries the bow out of habit and not out of any violent
intent: "It is my custom to carry it with me all the time" (40). In explaining his
actions Apollo relies on the sophistic principle of "custom," only to have Death
throw the same term back at him: "It is your custom to help this house more
than you ought" (41).

Later on in the exchange, with Death still insisting on his rights, Apollo
resorts to trying to buy him off with the promise of a "lavish burial" if Alcestis

is allowed to die old (56). Here, Apollo tries to appeal to Death's sense of self-interest; it would be to his *advantage* to wait, since he would benefit from a more expensive funeral. With the witty riposte, "What you propose, Phoebus, is to favor the rich" (57), Death accuses Phoebus of not being sufficiently egalitarian, a clear allusion to Athens's democratic ethos. In another reference to democratic practices, Apollo responds by expressing surprise at Death's "unrecognized talents for debate" (58). Unmoved by this piece of flattery, Death insists that he cannot make an exception for Alcestis, because if he did, other wealthy individuals would inevitably try to postpone their deaths as well—a witty appeal to the principle of likelihood or probability. Finally, Death caps off the exchange by showing his determination to carry Alcestis off, no matter how cleverly Apollo argues; Death's reference to his inflexible "character" (61) harks back to the sophistic principle of "nature," counterbalancing Apollo's earlier reference to "custom."

Euripides's original audience would doubtless have delighted in hearing these great gods conduct this debate in terms that resonated so clearly for their own times. The rapid-fire nature of the exchange, combined with the clever spin each character puts on the sophistic terms he tosses into the fray, would certainly have contributed to this delight. Part of Euripides's genius is his ability to update mythological scenes by injecting them with references to contemporary thought. After reading this scene, however, one can better understand the criticism that Euripides's drama degrades the high art of earlier tragedy and trivializes the traditional gods, who may remind us of lawyers trading sophisms. But one could well select other scenes in which Euripides's use of sophistic devices adds to the psychological complexity of his characters and enhances the tragic effect of his dramas.

An understanding of Euripides's use—and examination—of debate and rhetoric is, therefore, essential to coming to grips with the issues raised by the plays. But, to return again to the question I posed at the outset, why does debating these issues in class work so well, and, more broadly, why does Euripides appeal so much to us? One important answer is that many of his questions are, in fact, our own: we, too, live in a highly rhetorical and litigious age; we, too, are experiencing an "intellectual revolution" as we shift from the age of the book to the information age; we, too, are undergoing a crisis in values, voice, and meaning. Like the Athenians of Euripides's age, we pride ourselves on our rationality and inventiveness even as we fear relying on these powers too much. In postmodern America as in ancient Athens, a great chasm divides an elite corps of scientists and intellectuals from the masses of people who reject science and logic in favor of mystic practices and traditional religion.

A central question of our times—just as it was of Euripides's—is whether our confidence in democratic practices is justified. We also maintain a certain faith in rhetoric as the foundation of our system of government, even as we share a distrust of its potential for abuse. Can debate, cross-examination, and oratory lead to truth and justice in the political and legal arenas? The controversy about the O. J. Simpson trial only heightened the suspicion that lawyers are paid exorbitant fees precisely to make the worse cause triumph over the better. The fact that we suspect the motives of our politicians as well was clear from the debate over the impeachment of President Clinton (whose sobriquet "slick Willie" branded him as the archetypal Sophist).

After conducting the *Medea* debate in class, I suggest taking a vote and discussing who won and why. Was the winning side "right" in some way—or did it simply manipulate the arguments better? Can the truth of the matter finally be attained? How may this discussion help us understand the strengths and limitations of our own political and legal system? These are quintessentially Euripidean questions, and the answers can shed light not only on Euripides's drama and his age but also on our own postmodern condition.

Teaching Euripides, Teaching Mythology: Ideology and the Hero

Paul Allen Miller

This essay examines the ways in which Euripides's *Iphigenia in Aulis* and *Electra* can be used in a large Introduction to Mythology course to illustrate the changing role of mythology in Greek society. Beginning with a brief discussion of the role of mythology in the largely oral societies of Homeric Greece, in which poetry and narrative were the primary means of cultural instruction, I discuss the ways in which such a course allows students to see how myth functions primarily, in Roland Barthes's terms, to make the cultural appear natural (129, 142). In the tragedy of fifth-century Athens, however, the role of myth became more complex as it increasingly functioned as a tool for the self-representation of the polis. I illustrate this process in class by contrasting the function of the hero in Homeric epic with that exemplified by the figures of Agamemnon and the house of Atreus in Aeschylus's *Oresteia* and Euripides's *Iphigenia in Aulis* and *Electra*. In the *Oresteia* (458 BCE), myth is self-consciously rewritten as an allegory of the evolution of the polis, so that the fate of the hero and his clan are directly associated with rise of the rule of law and the transition from a clan-based revenge theory of justice to the triumph of the Athenian law courts under the patronage of Athena.

The *Iphigenia in Aulis* and the *Electra* of Euripides, however, while continuing to meditate on the fate of the house of Atreus, represent a fundamental break with the Aeschylean use of mythology as an allegorical representation, and thus naturalization (in Barthes's sense of making the cultural appear natural), of the rise of the polis. They instead use mythology as a means of ideological criticism and for the demystification of ruling assumptions. This shift not only represents the different uses to which mythology can be put within a society but also demonstrates its sensitivity to changes in social context: the *Iphigenia in Aulis* (405 BCE) and the *Electra* (c. 413 BCE) contain clear allusions to the Peloponnesian War that was then exhausting Athens. The *Iphigenia in Aulis* thus portrays Agamemnon as vacillating and cowardly, concerned more about his political fortunes than about the fate of the Greeks, his wife, or his daughter. The *Electra*, however, shows both the play's namesake and Orestes possessed by an obsessive desire for revenge founded more on ressentiment for their fallen station in the wake of their father's murder than on a desire for justice. The greed and cynicism that motivate them, in turn, are played out against the explicit backdrop of the failed Athenian expedition to Sicily (415 BCE). This rewriting of the story Aeschylus used in the *Libation Bearers* is far more skeptical and corrosive of traditional values than Sophocles's *Electra* is.

Mythology thus in the established polis of the late fifth century ceased to be primarily a means of legitimating existing institutions, as it was in Aeschylus, and became instead a tool for social criticism in the face of the looming crisis precipitated by a disastrous war. Euripides's plays offer an excellent vehicle for demonstrating the changing function of mythological narrative in a complex and evolving traditional society. In turn, they invite students to examine how such narratives are used in other times and places both to legitimate and to question dominant ideologies and institutions.

Mythology in Homeric Society

Since the pioneering work of Milman Parry, it has been widely recognized that the Homeric poems and the mythology they represent are the products of a vast and deeply rooted tradition of oral composition. Basic story types and patterns of heroic behavior were passed down from generation to generation as part of a complex and evolving set of narratives whose roots can be traced back to a common Indo-European mythology and poetry, at least 1,200 years before the accepted date for the composition of our version of the Homeric poems, circa 800 BCE (Kirk, "Homer" 7; Nagy, *Comparative Studies* and *Pindar's Homer* 23, 54–55, 435–36). This tradition was profoundly conservative, preserving memories of material practices, such as chariot warfare, that had long since passed out of existence. The investment of such considerable amounts of emotional and intellectual energy in the poetic preservation of the past would have served normative as well as aesthetic functions. The oral tradition was the primary means of cultural and ideological transmission in a society that lacked any other reliable means of record keeping (Havelock 29, 46, 94–124, 159; Nagy, *Pindar's Homer* 55n19, 368, 404, 430; Thomas 51; Rose 57; Thalmann 32). The narratives of the Homeric poems constituted one of the chief structures through which the societies of ancient Greece defined what it meant to be a subject and what social positions were available to subjects. They naturalized cultural constructions and preserved them from one generation to the next (Rose 55). Thus in the *Iliad*, while Agamemnon and Achilles quarrel over whether it was right for Agamemnon to take the war prize of Achilles, the code by which such determinations should be made is itself never questioned. The basic nature of honor, glory, and justice is not open to negotiation in the Homeric poems, only their application is. Consequently, Odysseus never questions whether the suitors should die at the end of the *Odyssey*, and when Thersites, the lone commoner to speak in the *Iliad*, questions Agamemnon's fitness to rule, he is publicly humiliated by the aristocratic Odysseus with the assent of all present. The hegemony of the ruling elite and of their code is never seriously called into question.

Mythology in the Oresteia

On one level, Aeschylus's *Oresteia* represents a narrative sequel to Homer's Trojan epics. In it, we follow the story of Agamemnon's homecoming after the sack of Troy, his betrayal and murder at the hands of Clytemnestra, and the subsequent tale of Orestes's revenge and the final purgation of his blood guilt. On another level, we are dealing with something far more complex. Where the Homeric stories served as paradigms of proper behavior, attaining a quasi-legal status in Greek society (Frow 179), the retelling of those stories in the more self-consciously literary medium of tragedy allowed the addition of an allegorical dimension absent from the Homeric tales. Where the original epics were Panhellenic, the common heritage of all Greeks, extant tragedy adapted those myths to the public and political requirements of the Athenian polis (Romilly, *La modernité* 183; Goldhill, *Aeschylus* 1–21), thereby creating more complex and overdetermined sets of meanings. The mythology now functioned on at least two levels simultaneously. Thus, on the one hand, Aeschylus's trilogy presents the traditional story of Agamemnon's murder and Orestes's vengeance as a paradigm of filial piety, in much the same way as it is evoked in the *Odyssey*. On the other, the story now tells of the rise of the rule of law in the Athenian polis so that the fate of Orestes is directly associated with the transition from a revenge theory of justice to the establishment of the Athenian law courts under the patronage of Athena. The goddess now functions not only as a cult figure but also as a mediator between the rigid legal and patriarchal drive toward abstraction represented by Apollo, who sponsors Orestes, and the primal forces of blood, soil, and the feminine embodied by the Furies, who are Clytemnestra's advocates. The heroic figures of myth have retained their status as paradigms of behavior whose function is to make the cultural appear natural, but the increasing complexity and overdetermination of their relation to the extraliterary context has left them open to new forms of allegorical appropriation.

Euripides's Iphigenia in Aulis

The world of Euripides was very different not only from that of Homer, from which it was separated by almost four hundred years, but also from that of Aeschylus, a generation earlier. Aeschylus lived in a confident and triumphant Athens that had just emerged from the Persian Wars with its independence and democracy intact and a newly acquired empire in tow. The Athens of Euripides, and particularly the late Euripides of the plays we are examining, was one in which demagoguery and imperial arrogance had plunged the city into a disastrous thirty-year war with Sparta and where the forces of a new intellectual skepticism embodied by the Sophists—itinerant teachers of the rhetorical and political arts—had eroded belief in the traditional values represented by the heroes of the oral tradition (Foley, *Ritual Irony* 18, 45; Romilly, *La modernité* 6-9, 22–28, 119–24). The same myths that in Homer served as paradigms whereby the cultural was made to appear natural, and in Aeschylus served as the raw materials for the allegorical representation of the rise of the polis, in Euripides become the means of criticizing the very ideology they once helped to legitimate (Hartigan, *Ambiguity* 13).

The *Iphigenia in Aulis*, one of Euripides's last plays, performed posthumously in 405 BCE, retells a portion of the Agamemnon narrative from the period immediately preceding the Trojan War. The event it portrays is the ritual murder of Agamemnon's daughter to placate the goddess Artemis and thus allow the becalmed Greek expedition to continue sailing to Troy. This is a crucial point in the traditional story since her death not only makes the Trojan War possible but also causes Clytemnestra's murderous rage against Agamemnon as depicted in the *Oresteia*. The characters in the play invite comparison with those found in the stories of Homer and Aeschylus, but in each case Euripides's heroes are found wanting (Rabinowitz, *Anxiety* 38). The only character who is able to rise above narrow self-interest is Iphigenia (Rabinowitz, *Anxiety* 52), whose heroic resolution to accept her sacrifice is thrown into even higher relief by both the unworthiness of the cause, recovering a runaway wife, and the vicious nature of the people for whom she gives her life (Foley, *Ritual Irony* 66, 97; Hartigan, *Ambiguity* 180). The tragic grandeur of her gesture persists despite the ends it will be used to achieve, not because of them.

The play opens with a portrait of Agamemnon as a study in vacillation (Rabinowitz, *Anxiety* 40–41; Foley, *Ritual Irony* 95). He has neither the courage to reject the murder of his daughter and return home a failure nor the resolve to accept the horror of victory's price. Instead, we see him composing and destroying letters that alternately warn Clytemnestra of the fate awaiting their daughter and summon her and Iphigenia for a sham marriage to Achilles. In his opening conversation with the Old Man, his servant, he rejects the heroic pursuit of glory that underwrites the values of the Homeric warrior (Rabinowitz, *Anxiety* 40; Romilly, *La modernité* 146–47): "I am jealous of men who without peril / Pass through their lives, obscure / Unknown" (C. Walker 16–18). The servant is shocked and must recall his master to his station, "I don't like words like this from a king" (28). Such an inversion of normative social roles, wherein master and man change positions, is unprecedented in Homer and Aeschylus, and the sign of a world out of joint.

Agamemnon's own, internal ambivalences are, in turn, writ large in his confrontation with Menelaus, who has intercepted the Old Man as he tried to deliver to Clytemnestra a final warning from Agamemnon (Rabinowitz, *Anxiety* 40–41). It is Menelaus who originally pushed Agamemnon to agree to a deed from which he had shrunk in horror, and Menelaus does not hesitate to try to subvert the old servant's loyalty to his master, a blow against the very nature of the social order in a slave-holding society (304–05). Instead of being a paradigm of heroic behavior, Menelaus is portrayed as exclusively concerned with his own interests. He is more than willing to slaughter Iphigenia if it will help him regain possession of Helen. His charge that Agamemnon is nothing more than a politician who put on a deceptive public face to receive the coveted command of the army implies that Iphigenia is to be sacrificed at the altar of her father's political vanity (337–44). In the last years of the disastrous Peloponnesian War, the irony of this charge must have had particular resonance with an Athenian audience that had itself been convinced by ambitious politicians to follow an ultimately ruinous course (Hartigan, *Ambiguity* 165; Romilly, *La modernité* 62). Menelaus then charges that many men fail to achieve their political ambitions because they become weak like Agamemnon (366–72). Agamemnon responds, arguing that Menelaus is both a slave to passion and an inadequate husband: in short, he charges him with effeminacy (381–87). The heroes of Homer and Aeschylus are reduced here to schoolboys trading taunts. The absurdity of their respective positions is only heightened by Menelaus's subsequent and sudden change of heart and Agamemnon's refusal to relent from their original purpose (477–533). The rapid and all but unmotivated shift of each brother to the other's position produces a radical ambiguity that is initially resolved through the depiction of both as cowards, fearful of Odysseus's wrath if the Trojan campaign were called off, and is then finally sublimated into Iphigenia's willing self-sacrifice (Rabinowitz, *Anxiety* 41; Romilly, *La modernité* 58–59).

The other great hero of the Trojan narrative, Achilles, fares little better in the play. He is portrayed as a self-centered rhetorician whose anger at Agamemnon is motivated not by the outrage about to be done to Iphigenia but by Agamemnon's failure to seek Achilles's permission to use his name:

> What would have been fitting, if he had wanted
> This snare and pretext, then he should
> Have requested from me the use of my name.
> As it was, I knew nothing, and so
> To your husband, chiefly through faith in me,
> You surrendered your daughter.
> *Perhaps*—I might have granted him use
> Of my name—for the sake of Greece. [. . .]   (961–66)

This is not the volatile hero of the *Iliad* whose adherence to the heroic code ultimately leads to his own destruction but a calculator of self-interest enraged at Agamemnon's failure to consult him before using his name to commit a crime. The anger of the Iliadic Achilles is excessive but noble; that of his Euripidean counterpart is base and easily curbed (Hartigan, *Ambiguity* 167–69). His promise to defend Iphigenia against the whole Greek army recalls the heroism of Homer but is never put to the test (Rabinowitz, *Anxiety* 44).

In the end, the sole hero of the play is Iphigenia. It is her sacrifice that suspends the radical ambiguities that threaten to undermine the progress of the traditional Trojan War narrative (Rabinowitz, *Anxiety* 42). Yet this act does not raise her to the level of the paradigmatic Homeric hero, but rather it falls into the bathos of the multiple ironies that enfold it. As Helene Foley summarizes, "Iphigenia dies for an army seized by an uncontrollable lust for violence," and her desire to save Achilles from dying for a woman is "undercut by his later death for Helen" (*Ritual Irony* 92). It is a glorious but, from a coldly rational point view, useless gesture.

Euripides's Electra

The *Electra*, while performed eight years before the *Iphigenia in Aulis*, picks up the story at the same point as Aeschylus's *Libation Bearers*, the middle play of the *Oresteia* trilogy. The Trojan War is over, Agamemnon is dead, and Clytemnestra sits on the throne of Argos. Where in Aeschylus Electra is the dutiful daughter, bearing sacrifice to the grave of her father and withdrawing into the house while Orestes performs the actual acts of vengeance, in Euripides she is characterized not only by her rage and resentment but also by her active participation in her mother's murder. The poet in this case is building on the precedent established by Sophocles's *Electra*, a play whose performance date is unknown but that is generally believed to antedate Euripides's *Electra* (Denniston xxxiv–xxxix; Romilly, *La modernité* 95; Hartigan, *Ambiguity* 107n2; Michelini, *Euripides* 185–87). In the Sophoclean version, Electra is portrayed as a sterile virgin, alienated from both her household and her community and consumed with a thirst for vengeance (Foley, *Ritual Irony* 43). She is prepared to undertake the murders herself when she hears the false report of Orestes's death, and she later begs him to commit the ultimate outrage of leaving Aegisthus's corpse unburied. The play ends with neither the triumphant sublimation of blood vengeance into legal justice, as in the *Oresteia*, nor a sense of guilt and horror, as in Euripides (Goldhill, *Aeschylus* 93–95 and *Reading* 269–70). Thus, in the introduction to her Chicago translation of Euripides, Emily Vermeule sums up the relation between the Euripidean Electra and her Sophoclean antecedent as follows: "Euripides adds new insights, mainly Electra's failure to distinguish right from wrong; her daydreams limited to clothes, marriage, money [. . .]. While [. . .] pushing Sophocles' character to its logical extreme, he has lost sight of the spiritual strength with which Sophocles endowed her" (3).

The most notable difference between the Euripidean, on the one hand, and the Sophoclean and Aeschylean retellings of the Electra myth, on the other, is the marriage of the title character to a poor farmer. On the level of the narrative itself, this alteration introduces an immediate ambiguity. Electra sees her marriage as a deliberate humiliation by her mother. Yet in the farmer's opening speech we find out that Aegisthus had planned to have Electra killed to prevent her from having children who could challenge the legitimacy of his and Clytemnestra's reign. The marriage to the poor but noble farmer was a compromise suggested by Clytemnestra: a way of sparing her daughter's life while ensuring that she and her consort would be secure from any pretenders to the throne (22–34). Thus, the act that Electra sees as a deliberate affront is actually one that saves her life. If Clytemnestra were really the mercenary monster that Electra claims she is, she would have allowed her daughter to be put to death. The bid to save Electra's life is testimony to Clytemnestra's continuing maternal love.

On another level, the marriage to the poor farmer is a mere device to introduce the theme of class difference, which is central to the basic ideological, and ultimately epistemological, thrust of the play (Romilly, *La modernité* 193–96). Electra's hatred of her mother is in fact motivated more by ressentiment than by grief for her father. She characterizes Clytemnestra as a monster, yet when Clytemnestra believes that her daughter is about to give birth she rushes to her humble home to perform the necessary rituals. Her actions do not conform to Electra's portrait, and we begin to question the daughter's motivation (Goldhill, *Reading* 253). A careful reading of Electra's opening speech to Orestes reveals that her hatred of her mother is fueled far more by jealousy of Clytemnestra's wealth than by an unquenchable desire for justice (304–19; Hartigan, *Ambiguity* 115, 123).

Things are not what they appear, and class difference is one of the strongest wedges Euripides drives between the worlds of being and seeming. Thus the poverty of the noble farmer and the pettiness of the aristocracy lead to a radical questioning—unthinkable in Homer and Aeschylus—of the traditional Greek equation of moral value and social position. Yet, the play itself offers no alternative epistemological paradigm that would restore a stable relation between the phenomenal world and the values it is supposed to represent, that would again make it possible to judge from appearances. Euripides leaves us in a state of epistemological uncertainty (Goldhill, *Reading* 258). This combination of a deep questioning of traditional class-based ideology and a thoroughgoing intellectual skepticism is most completely embodied in Orestes's tirade on the impossibility of making valid personal and social judgments when confronted by anomalies such as the poor but noble farmer:

> How then can man distinguish man, what test can he use?
> the test of wealth? that measure means poverty of mind;
> of poverty? the pauper owns one thing, the sickness
> of his condition, a compelling teacher of evil;
> by nerve in war? yet who, when a spear is cast across
> his face, will stand to witness his companion's courage?
> We can only toss our judgements random on the wind.
> (Vermeule 373–79)

This moment of demystification, in which Orestes is made to recognize the limits of traditional ideology, produces no real clarity, no new understanding by the characters of either their own or others' actions. Indeed as Karelisa Hartigan notes, Orestes himself fails each of the tests he proposes: he "is solid proof that noble families often have cowardly sons" (*Ambiguity* 110–11). Appearances are deceiving, and even those who announce that appearances are deceiving are not to be trusted. Euripides here produces an ethical *mise en abyme* in which the ground for all positive judgment falls away beneath his spectators' feet (Goldhill, *Reading* 252).

Another example of this same double logic can be seen in the deliberate recollection of the scene in Aeschylus's *Libation Bearers* where Electra recognizes the presence of Orestes through three tokens: the matching of his footprint to hers; the matching of a lock of his hair to hers; and the recognition of a swatch of fabric she had woven for him when they were children. When the Old Man, who was Orestes's tutor, presents the same three tokens to Euripides's Electra, she demonstrates their logical absurdity. First, brother and sister almost never have the same size foot, and besides the soil is too rocky to leave a recognizable imprint. Second, the hair of a brother and a sister is often quite different, while it is not uncommon for completely unrelated people to have similar hair. Third, since Electra was a small child when Orestes left, how could she have possibly woven him a garment, and even if she had, how could a grown man possibly wear a garment woven for a boy (520–45)? This scene, however, does more than reveal the absurdity of the Aeschylean original. It implicitly indicts Aeschylus's belief in an intelligible universe guided by the will of Zeus (Romilly, *La modernité* 23). Aeschylus's world is one in which the will of the gods penetrates the very nature of things. The arbitrary, the contingent, the meaningless have no place in the *Oresteia*, but the Euripidean universe is one whose very substance constantly threatens to dissolve. Still, to leave matters there would be merely to substitute a negative certainty for a positive. Euripides's project in this play is more radical. He is not simply substituting the skepticism of the Sophists in place of the traditional verities of Aeschylus: although Electra's logic in refuting the Old Man's signs is impeccable, they are nonetheless revealed to be true. Orestes is there (Goldhill, *Reading* 247). Appearances *are* deceiving, but so is the belief they are not to be trusted.

In the same way, at the play's end when Orestes and Electra have murdered Aegisthus and Clytemnestra, they are flooded with feelings of guilt, even though their actions were authorized by both the oracle of Apollo and the necessity of blood vengeance, so powerfully evoked by Aeschylus. Yet both murders pervert a ritual context. Aegisthus is killed when his back is turned. He is making a sacrifice and treating Orestes and Pylades as guest friends (Hartigan, *Ambiguity* 116). He is shown not as a tyrant but "as a respectably generous host, properly sacrificing to the Nymphs" (Goldhill, *Reading* 253). His murder in this context is an outrage unthinkable in Homer. Likewise, Clytemnestra is lured to her death only by the summons to perform a ritual for the birth of Iphigenia's fictional child. Only by exhibiting maternal piety is Electra able to pervert a rite for the celebration of birth into the occasion of her mother's murder (Foley, *Ritual Irony* 43–44). It is not that Clytemnestra and Aegisthus do not deserve retribution for the death of Agamemnon, but should it have been this retribution, by these people, and for these reasons? As the Dioscuri sum up at the end of the play, "Justice has claimed [your mother] but you have not worked in justice" (1244). There are times, in short, when justice is not just, when the difference between being and seeming yawns immeasurably wide.

The *Electra* of Euripides begins with the basic situation found in Aeschylus's *Libation Bearers*. In that play, myth still serves a paradigmatic function. Electra is a model of daughterly duty, and the final result of her and Orestes's actions is not the perversion of ritual norms but the establishment by the polis of new forms of justice through the inauguration of the court on the Areopagus. In Sophocles's *Electra*, the title character's exemplary actions are neither celebrated nor condemned. Electra no longer is the retiring, dutiful daughter. She is consumed with anger and revenge. But her motives and their fundamental epistemological grounding are never directly called into question. In Euripides's version, however, the possibility of making such final judgments is put into doubt, as is the possibility of myth itself serving as a model of behavior (Goldhill, *Reading* 250). It is not that Aeschylus's trilogy has an express public and didactic purpose, whereas Euripides's *Electra* does not, but that Euripides's message is fundamentally different. He seeks not to persuade his audience to conform to a single moral code but to warn them of the dangers, the inherent immorality, the epistemological impossibility of such a code and of its foundation in illusions, deception, and cynical self-interest (Goldhill, *Reading* 256).

I start from the premise that the goal of a mythology class is not to teach students to memorize arcane details whose primary purpose is to prove one's membership in the cultural elite but to come to an understanding of how myth functions in society. The literary works of ancient Greece are especially valuable in this regard because through them we can see with particular clarity how the same basic narratives— in my example, the story of the house of Atreus— come to serve radically different functions. The works of Euripides are especially useful from this perspective because they demonstrate how stories that have been used to reinforce a hegemonic ideology can, in certain contexts, be used to call that very ideology into question. This example in turn encourages students to become both more aware of the myths that structure their lives and more effective critics of them.

The *Poetics* in Euripides's Green Room?

Dale Grote

I wanted to read a little something about the tragic hero.
Now I'm having to learn Aristotle's philosophy. Who has
time for this?

—Comment left on a *Poetics* Internet site

No one could be faulted for minimizing the *Poetics* in a course on Greek tragedy. The work is fragmentary; its prose is compressed; its ideas are complicated when they're not hopelessly obscure. Its most energetic defenders acknowledge that the work we now have is at best a script for Aristotle's lectures. At worst, it may be notes taken by students who attended them. It is also clear from internal and external evidence that what we call the *Poetics* is only the first chapter in a more comprehensive study of poetry. We know that we are missing part 2 of the *Poetics*, which took up comedy, and that Aristotle published a complete work, *On the Poets*, now lost. The state of the document we do have and the loss of what we do not make it hard to reconstruct his important conclusions in much detail. What we can see is mostly disliked. Does anyone really try to define the genres anymore? Even the concepts that at first seem promising—*katharsis* and *hamartia*—are mysterious and have no obvious application to any of the extant tragedies. The most famous obituary for the work as a useful interpretive instrument for Greek tragedy was written by Cedric Whitman (*Sophocles* 29–41), himself a classicist and distinguished scholar of Greek theater. Finally, with a small change, the cry of despair of the student quoted above could be that of the professor or teacher: "I just wanted to teach a little something about Aristotle's tragic hero. Now I'm having to learn Aristotle's philosophy. Who has time for this?" So the question is, Is there a way to make responsible, yet limited, use of the *Poetics* in a general course on Euripides or tragedy?

Like the Bible, the *Poetics* is more often read from than read and with similar results. The context is forgotten, and what is left is either misunderstood or put to uses for which it was never intended. Although there is no direct evidence for it, nearly everyone believes that the *Poetics* is, at least in part, Aristotle's defense of poetry against the attacks made by Plato, most notably in book 10 of the *Republic*, written in the 370s. His famous instruction to banish the poets had two justifications: the poet's art is twice removed from reality since it imitates an imitation, and it appeals directly to the emotions, most notably pity and fear, and hence to the irrational, which is not healthy or useful.

There are an undeniable logical rigor and purpose to Aristotle's treatise, both of which perhaps can best be seen at some distance. So, with due apologies for simplifying what is complex, here is an essential summary.

> Chapters 1–5: Human beings have an indwelling impulse for *mimêsis* (imitation, representation, enactment, or portrayal). The poetic art (*poiêtikê technê*) is an expression of this instinct. There are many forms of the *poiêtikê technê*, which are distinguishable by what they imitate, how they do it, and with what materials. The one we discuss in this essay is tragedy. Tragedy evolved from earlier forms of poetry, eventually nearing its final form, and our objective is to define it.

> Chapter 6: Tragedy can be succinctly defined as an enactment in words with certain formal elements of a serious action that arouses pity and fear in the audience for the purpose of a *katharsis* of such emotions. (It's maddening that Aristotle does not define or give any examples of *katharsis* in the *Poetics*, although in another work [*Politics* 1341b36] he refers us to a "clearer" definition of the term in the *Poetics*. He is perhaps referring to book 2 of the *Poetics*, which is not extant.) There are six identifiable qualitative elements of tragic *mimêsis*: plot, character, thought, language, song, and spectacle. The last five elements certainly contribute to *katharsis*, but plot is the soul of the tragedy. Accordingly, most of what I discuss here has to do with the different kinds of plots and with the one kind of plot that is the best at producing this tragic reaction.

> Chapters 7–14: Plots must have a manageable size and a logical unity of events. The simple plot moves from good to bad fortune without reversals or recognitions. The complex plot has them. By the way, tragedies also have a number of quantitative parts: prologue, episode, exode, and choral songs (the *parodos* and the *stasimon*). Some tragedies also have a song sung from the stage and lamentations. Returning to the plot, the best kind of tragedy is one that shows us a good but not perfect man, whose status is diminished in the end because of some *hamartia* he

makes. (Aristotle does not define *hamartia* or even provide an example of it. The normal meaning of the word is a mistaken judgment or error. No one believes any longer that it means "tragic flaw" or any other moral or personal defect that leads to tragic action.) He should be about to kill, or about to be killed himself by, someone close to him, but at the last moment, through a simultaneous recognition on the part of the would-be killer and victim, there is a reversal of events and the destruction is prevented.

Chapters 15–22: Turning to the other materials out of which a tragedy is composed, we receive advice about character, the kinds of recognition that are possible and which is best, diction, thought, and other technical matters so as to strengthen the tragic experience of *katharsis*. So much for tragedy.

Chapters 23–26: There are some interesting implications and applications of what we have covered. Among other things, we can distinguish tragedy and epic from each other using the principles of definition employed above. It also follows that tragedy is superior to epic because tragedy's effects are more powerful, varied, and compact.

Setting aside temporarily the more attractive mysteries of the *Poetics*, we already have sufficient grounds for bringing in Aristotle. After my students have read their first couple of plays, I give them this assignment: Collect your thoughts and write a few notes on the question, What is tragedy? This creates panic, as it seems that the question is not just unanswerable but also impertinent. After gathering, comparing, and compiling various efforts, we reach a hopeless muddle and are ready for Aristotle's help. Even if in the end we cannot accept or find a useful application of his definition, Aristotle's method, rigor, and ambition never fail to impress.

Next, for Aristotle the soul of tragedy is the ordering of events called plot; accordingly he has plenty to say about it. The basic ingredients in a proper tragic plot are what he calls reversal (*peripeteia*), discovery or recognition (*anagnôrisis*), and calamity or suffering (*pathos*), all of which, in his judgment, should be linked together in a tight causal mechanism. The discovery should bring the reversal that leads to the calamity:

> Chapter 11: A *reversal* is a change of the situation into the opposite, and this change is, moreover, probable or inevitable—like the man in the *Oedipus* who came to cheer Oedipus and rid him of his anxiety about his mother by revealing his parentage and changed the whole situation. A *discovery*, as the term itself implies, is a change from ignorance to knowledge, producing either friendship or hatred in those who are destined for good fortune or ill. A discovery is most effective when it coincides with

reversals, such as that involved by the discovery in the *Oedipus*. A *calamity* is a destructive or painful occurrence, such as a death on the stage, acute suffering and wounding, and so on.

Now we have a program for a closer look at the substance of the plays. Students can be instructed to watch for and describe the moments of reversal and discovery that lead to the calamity in each of Euripides's tragedies that are covered in the course, an inquiry into which often proves abundantly fruitful. Euripides is fond of twisting his plots through surprises, disappointments, and other mechanisms of misdirection.

An extended, and perhaps more complex, application of this analysis would be to follow Aristotle's closer prescriptions for the reversal, calamity, and discovery (chapter 13 through to the end of chapter 16). Here, as much as anywhere else in his writings, we can see how Aristotle's mind works, as he undertakes an empirical investigation within a strongly teleological framework. Again, I summarize:

> There are only a finite number of possibilities for tragic plot: a supremely virtuous, supremely vicious, or somewhat virtuous agent performs, or just avoids performing, some act of violence, either knowingly or unknowingly, against someone related or not related to him or her, and the result is good for all, bad for all, or good for some and bad for others. The tragic theater is not meant to be mere melodrama, where the wicked get their deserts and the good prosper in the end. The purpose of tragedy is to create deep feelings of pity and fear, and the best way to do that is as follows: A somewhat virtuous agent nearly performs some act of violence against a family member out of ignorance that is corrected by a recognition. There are many ways to effect the recognition, but the most skillful way is to have it come about, not as a result of some prop or complicated inference, but as a result of something the agent is already doing that is in accord with the plot itself. An example is the way Iphigenia recognizes Orestes in *Iphigenia at Tauris*. It can be expected that she would want to send a letter back home given her situation. Hence in the play the recognition is not forced. We can also see that by the recognition, the act of violence against a family member that would have been committed in ignorance is avoided.

There is a problem in these chapters that cannot be easily explained. On the one hand, Aristotle says that tragedies should end unhappily. In fact, he says that Euripides is thought to be "the most tragic" of the tragedians because, whatever his other faults, his plays end as tragedies should. On the other hand, Aristotle says that the best plot is one where the calamity is avoided, as in *Iphigenia at Tauris*. No one kills or harms anyone. So we have Aristotle in chapter 13 saying that the most tragic plays end unhappily but then saying in chapter

14 that the best tragedies avoid the calamity and, one would suppose, end happily. One defensible way out of this difficulty that has been offered is to say that nearly performing a dreadful act can be as terrible and pitiful as actually performing it. But this is just a guess, and not everyone is persuaded by it.

The best thing to do is to bracket the problem off and move on to issues that are more feasibly and quickly addressed. We must always remind ourselves and our students that the first order of business is to study the plays, not Aristotle. Other, less distracting questions might be the following: Which of the plays end happily either in part or in whole? Which of the principal agents observe or violate Aristotle's prescription that they be good yet not supremely good? Chapter 16 provides a very manageable typology of recognitions: from signs, through artificial contrivance (where the poet inexpertly inserts words or dialogue that do not fall naturally out of the plot), memory, and reasoning. Try to pick out which of these methods Euripides uses in the plays.

In marshaling the evidence for the definition of tragedy, Aristotle both praises and criticizes Euripides. We have seen that Aristotle defends Euripides against those who fault him for writing plays that end in misfortune (*dystychia*): "This is right [way for plays to end]. The greatest indication of this is that such plays seem to be the most tragic in staged competition. Even if he doesn't organize other things well, Euripides is thought to be the most tragic of the poets" (ch. 13). But what are his faults?

1. His choruses are not as tightly involved in the action as they should be: "The chorus too must be regarded as one of the actors. It must be part of the whole and share in the action, not as in Euripides but as in Sophocles" (ch. 18).

2. His Menelaus and Iphigenia are examples of inept characterization: "As an example of motiveless degradation of character, we have Menelaus in the *Orestes*; of character indecorous and inappropriate; [. . .] of inconsistency, the *Iphigenia at Aulis*—for Iphigenia the suppliant in no way resembles her later self" (ch. 15).

3. The resort to the deus ex machina in *Medea* violates the principle that plots should have a sort of logical orderliness to them, that events should flow one to the next in a way that is probable or understandable: "Clearly therefore the denouement of each play should also be the result of the plot itself and not produced mechanically as in the *Medea*. The deus ex machina should only be used to explain what lies outside the play, either what happened earlier and is therefore beyond human knowledge, or what happens later and needs to be foretold in a proclamation. For we ascribe to the gods the power of seeing everything. There must, however, be nothing inexplicable in the incidents, or, if there is, it must lie outside the tragedy" (ch. 15).

4. The second half of the double recognition scene in the *Iphigeneia at Tauris* is badly handled: "In the second place come those which are manufactured by the poet and are therefore inartistic. For instance, in the *Iphigeneia* [*at Tauris*] Orestes revealed himself. She was revealed to him through the letter,

but Orestes says himself what the poet wants and not what the plot requires. So this comes near to the fault already mentioned, for he might just as well have actually brought some tokens" [Aristotle doesn't like tokens] (ch. 16).

The obvious application of these remarks is to ask the students to review for themselves the scenes or characters that Aristotle has targeted. A larger project would be draw up a list of other examples from Euripides's tragedies that further illustrate these criticisms: needlessly debased or inconsistent characters, inartistic recognition scenes, and use of the deus ex machina that radically interrupts the flow of events.

Clearly none of these projects will produce enduring contributions to scholarship on the *Poetics*. But they will create a sense of cooperation with Aristotle: to understand tragedy and think about the experience it creates.

APPENDIX

Chapter 6, where Aristotle presents his definition of tragedy, is the key to understanding the intent and structure of the *Poetics*. Unfortunately, it is also the most compressed chapter. In order to warm my students to the *Poetics*, I distribute this imaginary reconstruction of the whole of the original lecture with all the explanatory asides and answers to questions coming from the audience. I also include an explication of the notion of *katharsis*, which presents only one of many competing analyses. Aristotle is speaking:

Yesterday we spent some time establishing several key points. First, and most important, unlike the assertions of some that poetry is not a discipline at all and hence cannot be an object of knowledge, I hold that it is something that can be described with scientific accuracy. Poetry is a part of the larger genus of activity that is embedded in human nature called imitation, and as such poetry must have a positive role to play in the human experience. Next, there are different kinds of poetry, each of which can be differentiated from the others in terms of what it does, how it does it, and the materials out of which it is built. Poets do more than just absorb what poets before them have done. Without being fully aware of what they are doing, they are nevertheless adhering to certain fixed principles that reside in the different forms of poetry. This is why, when asked, they can't say precisely what it is they are doing at any given time, as Plato has written, but . . .

Yes, down here. A question. Now, just a moment. I didn't say that poets are stupid. Consider a farmer. He may not be able to explain in any scientific way why he uses fresh water on his crops and not salt water or why one side of a hill is better for grapes than the other. Frankly, as a farmer, he probably doesn't need to know the precise biology of every plant or animal on his farm. He can be a reasonably successful farmer by following rules and procedures that he doesn't fully understand, though I would maintain that the best farmer would also be a scientist of farming, thus basing his decisions on a sure knowledge of his art rather than simply following the customary ways of other farmers. But because most farmers don't possess this kind of knowledge themselves, it doesn't mean that they aren't acting within a body of principles that are fixed and certain. Please remember that in this school our duty is to study phenomena and extract what is knowable. What I do reject categorically, however, is that poets are simply opening themselves to the divine and scribbling out whatever their daimon dictates. It takes study and practice, and that means the poet is learning something. It's that "something" that is the object of our study.

So, then, the different species of poetry can be shown to have a natural history, growing through stages, very much like a living organism, until they each approach their mature form. We can't really know a thing unless we see it growing through its stages, so that's why I talked about the early history of tragedy. Tragedy has a form, a "whatness" that defines it. And all that which we call tragedy takes part in it to one degree or another. This does not mean that any one tragedy expresses the form perfectly. In fact, none that I know of does, though some come closer than others. The reason we're taking up tragedy first is that it is most respected among thoughtful Athenians for embodying something noble and uplifting. There will be time in future lectures to perform the same kind of analysis to the other genres of poetry, like comedy, epic, and what have you. Let me wind up today's lecture with a summary of what we've covered so far and an indication of what we'll take up in the next lectures. I'll be defining tragedy as follows: "Tragedy is a *mimêsis* (representation, portrayal) of an action that is serious, complete, and of a certain magnitude, using embellished language [. . .] in the form of action, not of narrative; through pity and fear effecting the cleansing (*katharsis*) of these emotions."

Do you understand what we're doing? We are threading our way through the various forms of *mimêsis* to the one we want to study by identifying the differentia. What is new here is the last clause: "through pity and fear effecting the cleansing (*katharsis*) of these emotions." This is the goal of tragedy, nothing more, nothing less, and all the parts of tragedy have a role in effecting this purpose. In future lectures, we will study the various parts of tragedy—plot, character, thought, song, diction, and spectacle—and show how a perfect tragedy should handle these elements to enhance this tragic experience. For now, let me give you something to think about.

We know that Plato doesn't care for poetry because, among other things, its appeal is emotional, and emotions complicate the mental apprehension of truth. Indeed, we can think of many people who would not just support this idea but also argue that we are more alive as human beings in our emotions than in our intellect. This perversion, Plato argues, needs no encouragement. Therefore, tragic poetry can serve no good end.

I can't agree that emotions are inherently dangerous or that they can't be trained. First, we should not try to deny the role of properly tuned emotions in a man of good character. Or, to put it another way, the formation of proper character needs the training of the emotions, too. To feel love, hate, wrath, mercy, and so forth when we should is the mark of a good upbringing. Consider pity and fear. Pity is the emotion we feel when we see someone suffering in a way that is undeservedly harsh for the mistake that has been made. I'm going to argue later that the perfect tragedy should depict a fine but not perfect man who makes some mistake that we can well understand and might have made ourselves under the same circumstances, but who is then subject to suffering that goes far beyond what is deserved. To continue, fear is the emotion we feel when we realize that we are also subject to suffering. Not only are these emotions needed for proper moral action, they are also socially necessary. Can you think of a stable society built from people who lack these two feelings? Social arrangements are hardly more than extrapolations of an innate feeling of affection (*philia*), of which pity is a part. And some amount of fear is needed for self-preservation. But an excess of pity and fear would be equally destabilizing in a society. No wrongdoers would ever be punished; no courage in the defense of the city would be possible. Then where would we be?

In tragedy, we see that the emotions of pity and fear are paramount. This is a fact. We start from there. It must follow that piling on pity and fear somehow effects a refinement or retuning of pity and fear in the audience. It loads them up precisely in order to purge the excess. Not to eliminate them, mind you, but to purge the excess. This is all I mean by *katharsis*. See you next time.

At Home and Not at Home:
Euripides as a Comic Character

Laura McClure

Although in recent years critics have freed themselves from traditional notions about Euripides, many modern assessments still owe their views to Aristophanic comedy. This trend began in antiquity with the scholia to Euripides, where critical remarks about the poet's technique may be traced directly to Aristophanes, an author with whom early commentators were reasonably familiar (Lord). By the nineteenth century, Friedrich Nietzsche in *The Birth of Tragedy* took Aristophanes's portrayal of the poet at face value: Euripides had triumphed over Aeschylus and debased the tragic art by affiliating it with rhetoric and the specious philosophizing of Socrates. Because of the pervasive influence of the comic poet on later interpretations of Euripides, Attic Old Comedy provides an excellent pedagogical tool for introducing undergraduates to Euripides's plays. The highly political aspect of comedy further affords a wealth of insights into the social and political context of Athenian drama. And because it continually comments on the tragic genre, even portraying it as a poetic rival, Aristophanic comedy is our best fifth-century source of information about the ancient theater and literary criticism.

Literary and Cultural Background of Athenian Drama

That Euripides's plays make up a significant part of the reading for three quite distinct courses that I teach—Classical Mythology, Gender and Sexuality in the Classical World, and Civilization of Ancient Greece—underscores his pedagogical versatility. In the civilization course, students read the plays of Euripides and Aristophanes as part of a lengthy unit on the Athenian empire in the classical period. The plays of Aristophanes serve a key role in this particular course: not only do they illuminate, in a very engaging way, the often contradictory and elusive drama of Euripides; they also help students grasp the sociopolitical climate of late-fifth-century Athens and the role played by the dramatic poets within it. The large size of this course (about 120 students, with no teaching assistants) necessitates a lecture format and precludes extensive writing assignments or in-class discussion, although students are frequently asked to write a few sentences in response to questions designed to generate discussion. Students first read two or three plays by Euripides (I like to include either the *Hippolytus* or the *Helen* because of their relevance to the comic plays), followed by two plays of Aristophanes, either *Acharnians*, *The Poet and the Women*, or *Frogs*.

Although the two poets differed in age by almost a generation—Euripides was born around 480 BCE and Aristophanes around 450 BCE—they overlapped in the dramatic competitions for almost two decades. The comic poet first presented Euripides as a character in the *Acharnians*, his earliest extant play, which was produced around 425 BCE. This pattern of parody and comic mockery continued over the next twenty years, with Euripides appearing as a character in both *The Poet and the Women*, staged in 411 BCE, and *Frogs*, produced in 405 BCE. Comic travesty of Euripides was apparently quite popular with the audience, since two of the plays featuring the tragic poet as a character received first prize, and the *Women of the Thesmophoria* may have. Aside from introducing Euripides as a character into these three plays, Aristophanes also repeatedly quotes tragic verses and parodies scenes, especially from plays such as the *Telephus, Alcestis, Aeolus, Bellerophon, Sthenoboea, Hippolytus, Helen*, and *Andromeda*, many of which are now lost. The large number of references to Euripides's work in the rest of the comic corpus attests to the remarkable popularity of the tragedian in his own lifetime (Ehrenberg 281; Harriott provides a useful table of Euripidean quotations in Aristophanes [6]). Even allusions to plays written several years earlier and produced a single time on the Athenian stage appear to have been familiar to the spectators. (How they knew these lines remains a mystery: written copies may have circulated, tragic actors may have recited passages from past performances, or spectators may have simply had an aptitude for recalling the poetic and linguistic details of the tragedies they had seen.)

By the time the students in my course encounter Euripides, they have learned about some of the rapid social and political changes experienced by the Athenians in the second half of the fifth century. The sophistic movement, heralded by the arrival of the Sophists Protagoras and Anaxagoras at Athens around 450 BCE, is essential to understanding the poetic milieu of both poets. Encouraged by the patronage of the popular Athenian statesman, Pericles, the intellectual innovations of the Sophists promoted a kind of ethical relativism and privileging of rhetoric that pervaded Athenian artistic and political discourse for the rest of the century. During this time, Athens experienced an unprecedented explosion of literary and artistic creation: Euripides staged his first play, the *Daughters of Pelias*, in 455 BCE, shortly after the death of Aeschylus, and continued to compete with Sophocles for dramatic victories over the next three decades. In the world of the visual arts, Pericles inaugurated an ambitious building program, financed by the heavy taxes levied on Athenian subject-allies, beginning with the construction of the Parthenon in 447 BCE and the Propylaea, its gateway, in 437 BCE.

Also important to understanding Athenian drama is the close connection between the city-state and the five-day festival in honor of Dionysus, where tragedy, satyr drama, and Attic Old Comedy were performed. The character of Aeschylus in the *Frogs* ascribes to the dramatic poet, whom he refers to as the *didaskalos* ("teacher") of the polis ("city-state"), the responsibility of creating good citizens by inculcating civic ideology and traditional values. The dramatic festival itself also had a political dimension: held at the end of March and open to the entire Hellenic world, the festival became an occasion for displaying the

power and wealth of Athens (Goldhill, "Great Dionysia"). The opening ceremonies of the festival further strengthened the link between the dramatic plays
and the state: Athenian generals poured the opening libations; a panel of
judges, one from each of the city's ten tribes, evaluated the plays; the city's
benefactors received awards; the male children of the war dead marched
across the stage in full armor; and, after the founding of the Delian league, the
tributes paid to Athens by subject-allies were displayed to all.

The citizens who attended the theater experienced the spectacle placed
before them as another facet of the discursive life that defined the polis. In all
aspects of their political lives, the Athenians engaged in the contest of words
either as actors or as spectators not only in their deliberative assemblies and
law courts but also in the theater. They were "spectators of speeches," says one
speaker in Thucydides as he chides the Athenians for sitting at the feet of
Sophists and for putting pleasure in listening above all else (3.38.4–7). A passage from Aristophanes's Wasps further suggests how much the Athenians
identified the performative realms of the theater with those of the law courts:
after describing the various types of entertainment offered jurors by desperate
defendants, Philocleon, addicted to jury duty, wishes someone would take legal
action against the tragic actor Oeagrus so that he might perform one of his
Niobe speeches for the jury (562–880).

Persuasion and the Art of Rhetoric
in the Democratic Polis

Because of the importance of persuasion to the democratic institutions of the
polis, the dangers of speech and the vagaries of language are a substantive issue
in many Athenian plays, beginning with Aeschylus and intensifying in the work
of Euripides and Aristophanes during the last third of the fifth century.
Although the Athenians strongly valued verbal expertise and poetic skill, they
nonetheless exhibited a deep-seated ambivalence toward the art of rhetoric,
particularly when it became the means for nonaristocratic members of the
polis to gain access to political power. Aristophanic comedy repeatedly reinforces this idea; in the Clouds, the Just Argument maintains that the best form
of education for the city's youth should consist of learning traditional songs, not
the art of rhetoric (964–68). In the view of the conservative elite, rhetoric
eroded the power of the upper classes by teaching wealthy, but often not well-
born, boys how to speak persuasively, thereby allowing them unprecedented
access to political life. Under the tutelage of the Sophists, a new class of politicians, the demagogues, gained a foothold in the public sphere by appealing
directly to the dêmos ("citizen body"). Their presence appears responsible for
the growth of the popular courts in the 420s and for the focus on rhetoric evident in the plays of both Euripides and Aristophanes.

The Athenian love of words manifested itself in another way in the theater.
The spectators conjured by Aristophanes, and Attic Old Comedy in general, as

well as the keen interest in poetic genres exhibited by these works, suggest the widespread attention of the Athenian public to literature and literary issues. According to the comic poet Strattis (fragment 1, Kassel and Austin), the dramatic audience could distinguish between "play" and "performance" and frequently criticized tragic actors for their poor performances. The actor Hegelochus's famous mistake while delivering a line from Euripides's *Orestes* earned him incessant ridicule from the comic poets, all because his breathless delivery of *galên* instead of *galên'* changed the intended meaning of the sentence from "I see the *calm* after the storm" to "I see the *weasel* after the storm" (Euripides's *Orestes* 279, my trans.; cf. Aristophanes, *Frogs* 303–04). Another comic fragment shows the important role played by Euripides in these contemporary literary debates: he appealed to the sophisticated, "over-subtle spectator" who "hunts after sententious phrases" and "euripid-aristophanizes" (qtd. in Heath, *Political Comedy* 285). Similarly, Aristophanes in his *Frogs* portrays Euripides's own literary sensibility as an adventure in poetic phrasing (96–102). The clever expressions quoted by Aristophanes, like "Air, domicile of Zeus" or "the foot of Time," and catchy one-liners, like "It was not my mind that swore" (*Frogs* 100–02), encapsulate in miniature his dramatic technique and sophistic outlook and may have been allusions particularly familiar to all the spectators (Michelini, *Euripides* 89). Aristophanes also attributes to Euripides an extensive library (*Frogs* 943, 1409), a novel feature of daily life by the end of the fifth century and one probably connected with the Sophists, because they were known for their use of the relatively new technology of writing.

Euripides and Comic Criticism: Rhetoric and the New Education

For those teaching Euripides primarily from a literary, rather than a cultural, perspective, Aristophanes provides significant insight into the workings of the theater and ancient views of literary criticism, particularly through his use of the tragic poet as a dramatic character. Thus in the *Acharnians*, the first of Aristophanes's plays to feature Euripides, the protagonist, Dicaeopolis, visits the house of Euripides to acquire a beggar's costume and persuasive rhetoric to win the audience's sympathy (393–480). Enlisting the help of student performers (costumes or masks may be provided), a teacher might use this scene as a starting point for elucidating several of the stock themes relating to Euripides repeated in this and later plays. The initial exchange between Euripides's savvy slave and the slow-witted petitioner sets the tone for the whole scene: "Is Euripides at home?" asks Dicaeopolis. "He's at home and he's not at home, if you know what I mean" (396–97). The circuitous answer given by the slave paints the poet as a vacuous, long-winded philosopher who intellectualizes drama, a character type also identified with Socrates in Aristophanic comedy. In *Clouds* the comic poet makes Euripides the favorite poet of Socrates's new pupil, the spendthrift son of Strepsiades (1378). In another passage, Aristophanes credits both Socrates and

Euripides with promoting the dangerous new education and its central art, rhetoric, rather than the traditional music taught in the past:

> It is not elegant to sit by Socrates and chatter (*lalein*),
> throwing away traditional music and poetry,
> and omitting the most important part of the tragic art.
> (*Frogs* 1491–95; my trans.)

The verb *lalein*, a word that Aristophanes uses here about Socrates and elsewhere associates with Euripides, signifies the kind of idle chatter practiced by lower-class men in the marketplace and by gossiping women. In this view, philosophical discourse and Euripidean drama represent idle and superficial pursuits attractive only to the nonelite members of Athenian society.

Euripides's Democratic Art

By portraying a poetic contest between Aeschylus and Euripides in the underworld, the *Frogs* also provides an excellent starting point for conveying fifth-century views of Euripides (and Aeschylus), as well as contemporary interest in literary criticism. Like the scene in the *Acharnians*, the *Frogs* portrays Euripides as a chatterbox with a "well-hinged tongue" who fills the stage with babbling characters (*Frogs* 891). According to Aeacus, such prattle has attracted a formidable following in the underworld consisting mostly of criminals, highwaymen, thieves, burglars, and parricides, susceptible targets of Euripidean rhetoric (*Frogs* 771–73). This democratic speech figures prominently in Euripides's own drama, where everyone gets a chance to speak—the wife, the slave, the master, the maiden, and the old woman (*Frogs* 949–50). Aristophanes repeatedly criticizes Euripides for portraying such commoners in his drama, especially beggars and those with infirmities. According to Aeschylus in the *Frogs*, this type of artistic innovation denigrates the tragic art, which should portray men not as they are but as they should be (1445). Elsewhere Aristophanes plays up the equation between clever speech and low birth with his favorite Euripidean insult, that the tragic poet is the son of a greengrocer mother (*Acharnians* 457, 478; *Frogs* 840, 947; *Knights* 19; *Poet* 6, 387).

Euripides and Metatheater

The scene between Dicaeopolis and Euripides in the *Acharnians* introduces another important theme, the association of the tragic poet with the art of disguise and tragic mimesis: "By your knees I entreat you, Euripides, give me a rag from any old play of yours. I have to make a long speech to the chorus and it means my death if I don't speak well" (414–17). By the end of the fifth century, *mimesis* was apparently a term of literary theory (see Taplin, *Comic Angels* 68n4), and it appears as a major preoccupation in Attic Old Comedy. In

The Poet and the Women, the tragic poet Agathon tenders a theory of poetic mimesis, one that comically confuses physical reality with dramatic illusion: "If a (male) poet creates a play about women, / he must make his body adopt their mannerisms" (151–52; cf. 154–56). That is, the playwright must dress and act the part of a woman when composing female roles. This theory of mimesis has a moral dimension in the *Frogs*, where Aeschylus blames Euripides's plays of sexual passion for inducing Athenian wives to commit suicide out of shame; such tales, he asserts, should be kept off the Athenian stage (1050–54).

In addition to its preoccupation with literary mimesis, the *Frogs* repeatedly ascribes theatrical innovations to Euripides, including his penchant for changing traditional scene types, such as recognition scenes or the deus ex machina ("god from the machine"), and his use of comic elements and genre mixing (Heath, *Political Comedy* 217–18). In addition, the play also contains an abundance of technical criticism aimed at Euripides: the poet is taken to task for daring phrases, as discussed above, his linguistic style, and his preference for the consonants *s* and *l*. The bulk of the criticism, however, is reserved for his tendency to end each verse with the same monotonous metrical pattern, embodied by the phrase *lêkythion apôlesen* (*Frogs* 1208–50). The tragic poet is also denigrated for his innovations in choral meters and for his incoherent and inappropriate monodies (*Frogs* 1309–64).

Given his associations with dramatic and stylistic innovations, Euripides becomes a symbol of metatheater or "playing with the play" in several comic scenes. Although Attic Old Comedy frequently breaks the dramatic illusion by calling attention to itself as theater, this technique rarely occurs in a serious genre like Attic tragedy. When the case has been made for metatheatrical discourse in tragedy, it has most often been in connection with Euripides, in plays like *Electra*, where the recognition parodies that of Aeschylus's *Libation Bearers*, or the *Bacchae*, where Pentheus's cross-dressing of Dionysus strongly echoes a similar scene in Aristophanes's own *The Poet and the Women*. For Aristophanes, and probably for the audience, Euripides embodied notions of theatricality, mimesis, literary parody, and dramatic metadiscourse. Thus in *Acharnians*, his character allows us a glimpse into the workings of the theater when he provides Dicaeopolis with the rags and rhetoric, the major components of tragic drama, with which to persuade his interlocutors. In *The Poet and the Women*, he serves as the Relative's dresser, costuming and depilating him until he resembles, although not very convincingly, an Athenian housewife. In true comic fashion, Aristophanes reverses his role at the end of the play by having Euripides disguise himself as a woman, the pandering Artemisia, in an attempt to rescue his kinsman and elude the Archer.

Euripides's Notorious Women

The parody of individual Euripidean plays constitutes another aspect of Aristophanic metatheater. In *The Poet and the Women*, when the Relative's disguise is about to be revealed, he plays in turn the parts of Telephus threatened with death by the Greeks, Palamedes unjustly condemned to death by the Greeks, Helen in the clutches of Theoclymenus, and Andromeda about to die at the hands of the sea monster. Indeed, *The Poet and the Women* may be viewed as a deliberate response to Euripides's *Helen*, a play performed at the city Dionysia during the previous year, and its interplay of comic and metatheatrical elements, its flaunting of tragic conventions, and "its complex intertextual relationships with a famous predecessor which it parodies" (Heath, *Political Comedy* 219). In this sense, Aristophanes shares some of his dramatic techniques with his tragic predecessor, blending genres in similar ways, but with a distinctly different purpose, to critique the tragic genre and declare comedy the dramatic victor. By continually pitting tragedy, in the form of parody, against comedy, the poet demonstrates the superiority of the comic art form.

For those interested in exploring the issue of gender in Euripides, Aristophanes's *The Poet and the Women* provides excellent commentary on the tragic poet's representation of women and the "gendering" of dramatic genre (for a detailed treatment of this idea, see Zeitlin, "Travesties"). In this play, a glib Euripides persuades his kinsman to infiltrate the women's celebration of the Thesmophoria, a civic fertility festival in honor of Demeter, where the tragic poet is to be prosecuted for slandering women in the theater. The speech (384–432) catalogs some of the slander Euripidean drama has perpetuated about women, that they are whores, man chasers, tipplers, betrayers, chatterboxes, good-for-nothings, and a curse to men (392–94). This scene reinforces Aristophanes's frequent allusions to the scandalous women of Euripidean drama: of the twelve plays quoted most often by the comic poet, six are named after a notorious female, like Medea or Sthenoboea. Other plays feature lustful or promiscuous women: the *Aeolus* relates the incestuous affair of Macareus and Canace; the *Meleager* portrays a violent Atalanta, and the first *Hippolytus* (the play probably cited most) features a lovesick wife on the verge of adultery with her stepson (Harriott 5).

But *The Poet and the Women* does more than portray Euripides as a recalcitrant misogynist: the play fashions the tragic poet Agathon into a symbol of the emasculated art of new tragedy, invented by Euripides and perpetuated by his successors, while juxtaposing comedy as the virile, remedial discourse that "makes men" in the city. The association of the tragic poet with an enervating feminizing drama is again underscored in the *Frogs*, when Aristophanes pits the manly, heroic drama of Aeschylus, embodied by his *Persians*, against the democratic, womanish art of Euripides. From a pedagogical standpoint, *The Poet and the Women* compels students to confront the idea of gender as a social category by raising the questions, How can literary discourse be gendered? What purpose does the association of comedy with masculinity, incarnated by the hairy, oafish, and ithyphallic Relative, and tragedy with effeminacy serve? What does the play say about the function of the dramatic poet in the democratic polis? Teaching this play in my gender course truly became a turning point for the students, because it helped them recognize that gender categories are not absolute but can be deployed in service of social and political ideology.

The scene at the Thesmophoria also introduces another important Aristophanic theme relating to Euripides, his atheism (*Poet* 451), a charge also brought against Socrates. The comic poet accuses him not only of worshiping abstractions, like Aether ("Air"), instead of traditional deities (*Poet* 272; *Frogs* 100, 311, 892), but of actually inventing them (*Frogs* 889). Thus the widow who sells religious garlands in *The Poet and the Women* complains that her business has fallen off because of Euripides.

While Attic Old Comedy may serve as a very rich source of observations about the ancient theater, its audience, its techniques, and the playwrights who competed in it, one must not take its representation of Euripides at face value, as Nietzsche did. Instead, the fictional construction of Euripides should be understood as part of the ongoing polemic Aristophanes established between the tragic genre and his own poetic task as a comic poet, between the new Athens and the old one. Performed during a time of crises, at the end of a thirty-year war with Sparta, soon after the deaths of the tragedians Sophocles and Euripides, the *Frogs* sets forth the issue more cogently and urgently than any of the other comedies. Although the debate between the tragic poets in the *Frogs* may suggest the popularity of literary criticism among Athenian theatergoers, as well as their fondness for Euripides, it is predominantly a debate about politics, about whether rhetorically gifted but corrupt men should rule instead of those who uphold tradition. For, according to Aristophanes, dramatic poets have a didactic task: "to make the men in the cities better" (*Frogs* 1009–10).

As the poet of the radical democracy who brought beggarly and verbose heroes to life on the stage, Euripides contributed to the demise of the polis in Aristophanes's view. The tragic art of Euripides made the Athenians lazy and garrulous, liable to insubordination and gullible to deception. Even the god of tragedy learned Euripides's lessons: at the end of the *Frogs*, Dionysus extricates himself from his original pledge—to restore the tragic poet to the city—by a bit of verbal equivocation borrowed from the *Hippolytus*; when asked to explain his change of heart, the god quips, "It was my tongue that swore—my choice is Aeschylus"(*Frogs* 1471). At the same time, it cannot be denied that the tragic poet exerted a strong artistic influence on Aristophanes's own art; the neologism coined by Cratinus around 423 BCE, "to euripid-aristophanize," suggests how closely linked the two poets were in literary sensibility and in the minds of the spectators. Aristophanes, like Socrates and Euripides, may be viewed as just another of those tiresome intellectuals wandering around Athens at the end of the century (Heath, *Political Comedy* 10).

Myth and Allusion in Sophocles's *Women of Trachis* and Euripides's *Herakles*

Mark W. Padilla

This essay addresses the topic of how Sophocles and Euripides selected and adapted mythical material for the purposes of shaping a tragic narrative. Students of Athenian tragedy can sometimes fall into a trap whereby it is assumed that the featured narratives and protagonists belong to a universally known and shared tradition and that it was the mainstay of a dramatist to translate this stock of tales in relatively simple ways into the medium of the tragic theater. In fact, playwrights combined a passive and active engagement with the selected myths for a featured play, weaving together in the strands of their tragic projects elements from older and newer presentations of a particular story, as well as incorporating freely invented material created for the occasion of the play's production at the festival of the Greater Dionysia. The occasion to consider the processes by which tragedians shaped a tragic story out of inherited mythic material is useful, for the exercise encourages teachers and students to reflect more openly on why a dramatist chose to emphasize certain motifs and events and to place them in their featured narrative order.

The task of forging a tragedy from epic and other genre sources is one common to all early playwrights: even Aeschylus, a playwright commonly identified with Archaic sensibilities, radically refitted his inherited tradition to render it available to the new possibilities of theatrical spectacle (Easterling and Knox 291). Sophoclean and Euripidean drama, produced in the middle and late fifth century BCE, provides striking opportunities for us to consider this process of mythical adaptation and, more important, to see how the resulting tragic text could yield its audience a complex and multilayered theatrical production. Euripides's *Herakles* and Sophocles's *Women of Trachis* each feature the figure of Herakles—a well-attested hero in the late sixth and fifth centuries, a hero-god whose central importance in the explosion of vase-painting production in the late sixth century may have influenced the very origins of Greek drama (see Padilla, "Herakles"), and a figure whose attestations and attributes in myth, literature, cult, political expression, and iconography have been the subject of intense study in recent years (see also Padilla, *Myths*). Armed with this knowledge about the hero, we can lay bare some of the creative decisions made by Sophocles and Euripides in their respective productions of the *Women of Trachis* and *Herakles*.

Sophocles's Women of Trachis

The tales of Herakles, which Sophocles interjoins in the *Women of Trachis*, are notoriously difficult to separate out into individual strands, in part because of the speculative endeavor of assuming what is traditional and what is innovative.

Nevertheless, the play is clearly a compilation of old mythical motifs, of motifs coined around the time of the play's composition, and Sophoclean inventions. (Earlier treatments of this issue include the discussions in the commentaries on the play by Jebb; Kamerbeek; Easterling, Trachiniae; and Davies, "Lychas' Lying Tale." Further discussions may be found in Shapiro, *Myth* 155–60; Kraus; and Gantz 431–34, 457–63.) Of the older myths, the play integrates at least five that are stock myths involving Herakles. The first is the hero's servitude to the Lydian queen Omphale, a punishment that more typically follows Herakles's attempt to steal the Delphic tripod and, possibly, his murder of Iphitus. A second myth centers on the palace of Oechalia and involves a folktale pattern involving the stock themes of arrogance and punishment, the spear-won bride, and the woman who brings down a heroic man. Here, Herakles falls in love with Iole, the daughter of his host, King Eurytus, during a symposium. Though Herakles later wins an archery contest whose prize is the girl, Eurytus refuses to give Iole to Herakles, perhaps because the hero is already married to Deianira, because he is not sufficiently refined to be her husband, or for some other reason. Herakles later returns to Oechalia and takes Iole by force and kills the sons of Eurytus. This story was the subject of a seventh-century epic, the *Sack of Oechalia*, attributed to Creophylus of Samos, and was included in the *Herakleia* of Panyassis, an uncle of Herodotus. The story of the "Eurytidae" was featured in a half-dozen vases manufactured from 500 to 480 BCE, and the tragedian Ion composed a play on the subject in the early second half of the century (see D. Williams 138–39). A third myth involves Herakles's sacrilegious murder of Iphitus, a tale recounted by Homer (*Odyssey* 21.22–30). The fact that Iphitus is a son of Eurytus would help explain the violence, except that Iphitus supports the hero in his bid for Iole. (See Apollodorus 2.6.1; adding to the complication, the scholiast of the *Women of Trachis* on verse 354—*scholia* is ancient commentary information originally written in the margins or between lines of manuscripts—states that Pherecydes, a writer roughly contemporary with Sophocles, related that Herakles sought Iole as the wife of Hyllus, his son.) An earlier tradition perhaps differentiates between the two Iphituses (or whatever their names were), and the surviving accounts involve a conflation.

The fourth myth that Sophocles uses is Herakles's marriage to Deianira, an event that Sophocles brings forward in time so that it takes place before the murder of Iphitus and the Lydian servitude. Hesiod (Merkelbach and West, fragment 25.20–25) knows of the marital union, and its origins thus reach back at least to the early sixth century—as discussed in an important treatment of this issue by Jennifer March (49–77). Apollodorus (2.7.6–7) and Diodorus Siculus (*Bibliotheca Historica* 4.35.36–38), whose postclassical versions differ on a number of points from Sophocles's version, recount the story. Herakles wins Deianira as a bride by defeating her suitor in battle, the shape-shifting river god, Achelous. Herakles learns about Deianira from her brother Meleager during his journey to Hades, as memorably depicted by the fifth-century Athenian poet

Bacchylides (Campbell, vol. 4, poem 16), an account that shares verbal parallels and thematic overlap with the *Women of Trachis*. (Evidence is unfortunately lacking for scholars to determine which text is the earlier. In addition to the commentaries, see March 62–66; Segal, "Sophocles' *Trachiniae*" 106n30; and Platter.) Though Deianira's home was originally in Calydon, Sophocles's shift of her origins to Aetolian Pleuron seems to speak to the tragedian's project of removing the heroine from her "heroic" past, to characterize her as a domesticated wife (Williams and Dickerson 6). Whether Herakles took his new wife to Thebes or the Argolid, Thebes is currently the home of his mother and the residence of their children other than Hyllus, while the Argolid is the location of his murder of Iphitus. It is because of this murder that Herakles and Deianira move to Thessalian Trachis, a city near the Malian Gulf west of Thermopylae, under the protection of Ceyx. Ceyx is the city's king and a guest-friend of Herakles, and Sophocles sets the play's action before his palace.

A fifth myth featured in the play takes place after the marriage, though exactly when it occurs in their exilic movements is not clear. When Herakles and Deianira need to cross the Euenus River, the centaur Nessus, who worked the ferry service, tries to rape Deianira, and Herakles acts to rescue her. The theme of Herakles saving a woman from a lusty centaur was probably a generic one—given the evidence of vase painting from the early Archaic period—and the version of the rescue of Deianira seems originally to have involved use of the club or sword rather than the bow. Moreover, the Archaic poet Archilochus knew of this event (West, fragments 286–88), and he treats the theme of the contest for Deianira, positing that Achelous appeared in the form of a bull, in contrast to Homer's depiction of him as a river (West, fragment 287). Moreover, Maryline Parca has suggested that Deianira's reference to herself as a faded flower looks back to Archilochus's (recently unearthed) "Cologne Epode" (182). If Sophocles thus relied on Archilochus for some details, his hero, by contrast, is able to deliver an arrow into Nessus before the centaur can succeed with his sexual violence. To what extent the mythical tradition before the fifth century connected this (attempted or completed) rape with the actions leading to Herakles's death is unknown: some of the motifs that Sophocles uses to interconnect them—most strikingly the motif of the poisoned blood but also the arrow shot, the love charm, and the theme of the dead killing the living (see March 64)—may be his own or may be found in Bacchylides or another relatively recent poet. Hesiod did know of the poisoned cloak, but whether or not he connected it with the actions of Nessus remains speculation. However, the detail of Diodorus Siculus (4.36.5) and Apollodorus (2.7.6)—that Nessus gives to Deianira some of his sperm mixed with blood—suggests the existence of an earlier legend that Sophocles chose to modify, either in the interest of decorum or to render the story compatible with the failed rape; in the play, Deianira refers only to the centaur's blood.

The play also posits that Nessus gives Deianira some of his blood to keep in an amulet as a magic philter, a present contaminated by the poison coating Herakles's arrows. Deianira later places this mixture on a cloak that Herakles wears, thinking that it will end his infatuation with the captured Iole, but she is ignorant of the fact that the mixture is a deadly poison. Sophocles's Deianira, therefore, does not know beforehand the results of her actions, but it remains a question whether previous artists made her more complicit in the murder, along the lines of a jealous and scheming Medea figure. Sophocles, as already noted, renders Deianira innocent and essentially domestic. However, Apollodorus (1.8.1) relates a second mythic tradition in his portrayal of her as "Amazonian": she has a penchant for warfare, and she drives a chariot. Similarly, a scholiast (in Apollonius, *Argonautica* 1.12.12) states that she even fights alongside Herakles! In the light of this competing material, scholars have debated about the degree to which her characterization in the play includes elements of the aggressive Deianira. This assessment ranges from the view of her role as passive and weak, akin to Tecmessa in the *Ajax*, with the ironic effect that the "dominating" Herakles is brought down by a "subservient" Deianira (see McCall), to a reading stressing a more ambivalent heroine (see Hester; cf. March 51–52), to the notion that her character in the play incorporates the etymology of her name and represents a pattern of "murderer of man" (see Errondonea).

As part of the telling of the tale, Sophocles inherits and develops further the ethical problem posed elsewhere in poetry—namely, the reconciling of Herakles's own excessive possession of violence (*bia*) with modern notions of law (*nomos*) (cf. Merkelbach and West, Pindar fragment 169; Campbell, vol. 3, Stesichorus, fragments of *Geryoneis*).

Still another contemporary reference in the narrative is the manner of Herakles's death. Herakles directs his son to take him to Mount Oeta and to end his life there by immolation. This version of his death connects with his apotheosis, a motif, however, whose first attestations are vase paintings from around 460 BCE. Since Herakles was probably raised to the status of godhood only a century before (and with early Athenian support), perhaps the immolation apotheosis was also invented in Athens through an attempt to fill in the particulars about how Herakles was translated from man to god (see Boardman, "Herakles in Extremis"; Shapiro, "*Hêrôs Theos*"). Though the play does not make an explicit allusion to the apotheosis, the detail in the last scene that Hyllus need not light his father's pyre on Mount Oeta—the location of a cultic site for the hero-turned-god (see Stinton, "Apotheosis")—anticipates the emergence of Philoctetes for this role, a "favor" that Herakles rewards by giving him his bow. (Scholars who discuss the question of whether and how the play refers to Herakles's apotheosis include Hoey, "Date" 69n1 and "Ambiguity"; Stinton, "Scope"; C. Segal, *Tragedy* 100; Holt; Linforth; and Calame.) The question of whether the play thus refers in any substantive way to Herakles's apotheosis is yet another debated topic but one that, I believe, is largely moot: in the mid–fifth century, Athens had actively pursued the immortal cult over the heroic one and was likely instrumental in developing the idea during the sixth century BCE. Polis graphic artists, moreover, routinely featured Herakles as a god rather than as a hero in the second half of the fifth century, an interesting but sharp contrast with the extant poetic material. Assuming that Sophocles expected a largely Athenian audience in attendance at the Greater Dionysia for the play (a notion reinforced by the early springtime scheduling of the festival, when sailing in the Aegean was treacherous), the idea of Herakles as anything but a god works against the cultic evidence (Fuqua 59–60n155).

Having inherited some or all of this older and newer mythical material, Sophocles strategically connected and embellished it. Herakles has finished his labors, is married to Deianira, and is living with her in Trachis. In other accounts of this stage of Herakles's life, he and his new wife are forced to leave her home after Herakles kills a servant of Deianira's father in fit of rage (Apollodorus 2.7.6). In Sophocles's version, as already noted, Herakles's murder of Iphitus has necessitated their departure. In some other accounts, moreover, Herakles's servitude to Omphale takes place earlier in his life and is set for a period of three years. But as the play opens, Herakles has had to serve the Lydian queen for only one year, the year that has just passed. (Apollodorus 2.6.3, attempts to reconcile the two traditions.) Deianira is unaware of this servitude, as she is of his whereabouts for the last fifteen months. Like Euripides (as we shall see), Sophocles thus constructed a distinct and individualized Herakles myth for the purposes of his drama.

The cluster of characterization embodied by Herakles in Euripides's probably earlier work, *Alcestis*, combines Herakles's established comic-satyric identity with his superhuman and Olympian associations. It is possible that Euripides in this play first developed the hero in the "round" fashion required by the tragic stage (see Padilla, "Gifts"). Though Sophocles takes this process further by locating Herakles's tragic identity in the context of a *nostos* (return) theme, Sophocles maintains the hero's connections with the divine and super-heroic but also tilts the hero back toward the bestial and darker pole of mythical representation and in a way that is largely stripped of overtly positive satyric, folkloric, and enlightened elements. The composite mix of his dramatic identity is, however, just as rich and multisided, but the savagery in the characterization may well be the object of Sophocles's artistry—a portrayal that contains the darkest elements of his other protagonists. The portrayal of Herakles continues to challenge readers to find the kind of redeeming qualities featured in the roles of his other tragic protagonists. Perhaps this inquiry has been misdirected, since the statement that Sophocles is making demonstrates that a greatly popular figure of Athenian civic and religious culture and expression, and one largely reserved hitherto for more lighthearted drama, is nevertheless available for such grim characterization (one can recall his dark portrayal of Athena in the *Ajax*). In this fashion, the playwright inverts the manner in which he can "recover" the tragic nobility of such pariahs as Oedipus, and it is an interesting exercise to wonder if the *Women of Trachis* was produced in the same program with *Oedipus the King*. The two plays serve as ideal complements on several thematic levels.

Euripides's Herakles Mainomenos

Sophocles introduced many elements into the myths of Herakles's final mortal period of life. He also altered and conflated several existing mythic themes. Euripides was less ambitious about the rewriting of the hero's biography, but he made several striking changes. Most important, Herakles's murder of his Theban family follows rather than precedes the completion of his Eurysthean labors (Bond discusses the evidence of other sources for the story [xxviii–xxx]). This inversion thus allows Herakles to enter the play without the guilt and pollution of the murders and thus as a hero much celebrated throughout Greece for the completion of amazing deeds for the sake of noble aspirations. Amphitryon states vaguely that Herakles has been "cleansing the land," motivated either by Hera or through "necessity" (20–21).[1] Just before this statement, however, he offers another, and likely novel, motivation. Amphitryon has been forced into exile from Argos because of his accidental murder of his father-in-law, and Herakles has agreed to labor for Eurystheus to compensate for this death.

Another set of variables is found in the related issues of how many sons he has with Megara, what their ages are at death, and how they meet their deaths. In Euripides's play, a *mainômenos* ("mad") Herakles possesses and kills three sons with his weapons. But other sources of the tale provide different numbers of sons, ranging from two to eight. Pherecydes, a writer roughly contemporary with Euripides, states that the hero throws his five sons into the fire (Jacoby, fragment 3, F14), a motif that Ulrich von Wilamowitz-Möllendorff considers to be the earlier tradition (2: 85). Pindar, the early classical poet from Thebes, indicates that the sons are old enough to be slain in battle (he describes them as "fitted out with bronze" [*Isthmian* 4.81]), and states that their number is eight.

Thebes, the setting of the play, is the polis where Herakles is born and raised. On reaching manhood Herakles marries Megara, the king's daughter, a reward that Herakles earns, as later attested accounts relate, because of his aid in defeating the oppressive Teleboans (Diodorus Siculus 4.10.6; Apollodorus 2.4.11). Herakles has now been absent from the city to complete his labors, and as is typical in Theban politics, the throne has become subject to usurpation. The usurper is Lycus, descendant of a former *tyrannos* of the same name. Lycus has killed Creon, the Theban king and Megara's father, and now wishes to bolster his position by executing Megara and her children, who have been left in the protection of the aged Amphitryon. Since there is no evidence for this usurpation prior to the play, it is probably Euripidean. The theme not only provides a basis for the plot to unfold—Herakles must arrive to save his family—but also allows for political themes to emerge.

In one such scene (157–205), Lycus squares off with Amphitryon on the issue of which type of warrior is the most noble—hoplite or archer—in the context of whether Herakles is deserving of honor. This theme resonates with a debate in contemporary Athens over the social status of the archer and hoplite. Depictions of Herakles show him deploying differing weapons, but his association with the bow is particularly old. His connection with the bow, however, experienced a hiatus after the Persian Wars, a phenomenon attested to by the metopes at Olympia, which feature a club-wielding Herakles (see B. Cohen). The sculptors of the temple seem to have wanted to distance Herakles from his Scythian and Persian dress styles that had developed in connection with his archery prowess, styles that became less appropriate in the wake of Persia's attacks on Greece. Euripides revives the depiction of Herakles as archer, but with an interest separate from the Greek-barbarian tensions more relevant earlier in the century. The depiction of Herakles as bowman, as noted, resonates with social class tensions, a theme extending out of Herakles's predicament as the supposed son of Zeus who must labor for an inferior mortal cousin (Eurystheus); indeed, Lycus himself questions Herakles's paternity (148–50). The bow traditionally devalued its user because of its cheaper cost; well-to-do citizens could afford the gear of the hoplite and thus join this more respected branch of the polis's armed forces. Scythian slaves, employed as "Athenian policeman," may also have been outfitted with this weapon traditional to their national heritage, an association that further debased the use of the bow. But as we know from the account of Thucydides (4.31–39), the archer corps played an important role in Athens's successes in the conflict at Sphacteria. This achievement in turn bolstered the social standing of archers. Euripides's depiction of Herakles as a bowman is something of a paradox in this context: his status as an archer provides him with godlike immunity in battle (cf. Apollo and Artemis), an advantage that Amphitryon advertises in his retort to Lycus (195–201); however, Herakles's use of the bow compromises the communal regard (*timê*) that naturally emerges from participation in hoplite formation (I address this issue more fully in "Gorgonic Archer").

Another area of mythic adaptation is found in the emergence of the hero's Panhellenic status and completion of a "catalog" of labors (see Brommer; Philips; Gantz 381–416), an idea that seems to have emerged from the Olympia metopes just referred to, but one that also received a boost from the two plays under consideration. In the *Women of Trachis*, the chorus of maidens praises a Herakles who toils on behalf of all Greece, and Herakles later reviews some of his exploits. The *Herakles* then condenses these two topoi; its chorus, in a long ode, recounts the exemplary labors of the Panhellenic Herakles (348–450). The most recent labor of the hero is a journey to the underworld (to bring up Cerberus), an undertaking that seems to chorus members to be inherently more difficult to complete and a journey from which they worry that he may never return. The *Herakles* makes no mention of the hero's apotheosis—a fact that has led to some debate about whether this aspect is reflected in the play. But the question is largely irrelevant. Theseus's offer to give Herakles some of his hero cults (1323–33) does not necessarily imply a ratification of a chthonic aspect: the play's Attic spectators likely worshiped Herakles as a god in these same cults (see Verbanck-Piérard). A more pertinent issue lies in the query that Amphitryon poses to his foster son about how he managed to return from Hades (610). Herakles's response that he availed himself of the (Eleusinian) Mysteries (613) perhaps possesses an anachronistic ring, given the attention this motif received over a century before on vase paintings (Boardman, "Herakles, Peisistratos"). The scene borders on the comic, and Euripides is poking fun at the Heraklean tradition as he does elsewhere in the play.

The theme of the *mainômenos* Herakles presents another issue for us to consider. Euripides's treatment of it in the play represents our first well-known example of it. In the *Cypria*, part of the Trojan cycle perhaps produced in the sixth century, the figure of Nestor makes reference to the *mania* of Herakles, but there are no details (Davies, *Epicorum, Procli Cypr. Enarr.*, line 38). Pausanias concurs that Herakles kills the children while *mainômenos* and seems to indicate that Stesichorus (Campbell, vol. 3, fragment 230) and Panyassis (Davies, *Epicorum*, fragment 1) know about this deed. Herakles is a warrior of exceptional *menos*, a capacity for violence that can cause warriors to adopt unstable behavior. Herakles can possess a bestial demeanor and savage aspect (cf. Homer, *Odyssey* 11.608; Apollonius, *Argonautica*, 4.1436–40; Nauck, Euripides, *Syleus* fragment 689), and this paradigm perhaps provides a context for his madness. The treatment of the madness theme outside the play, moreover, does not always square with Euripides's account of it; as noted above, Pherecydes makes Herakles throw his sons into a fire. Perhaps, therefore, Euripides has not invented the theme of Herakles's murder of his family but has embellished it. In particular, the speeches of Lyssa and Iris in the middle of the play and the subsequent "messenger speech" are highly theatrical, and their roles in the story are probably first incorporated here. Amphitryon's presence in the house during the attack and Athena's protection of him by pelting Herakles with a stone are also likely the innovations of Euripides.

Athena is the ally of Herakles, and thus is not remarkable in this role, but the play may also feature her as a preparation for the entry of the Athenian Theseus. After the madness scene, Theseus enters the stage from Athens on hearing word of the trouble in Thebes. He discovers an unconscious Herakles surrounded by the corpses of his family and the wreckage of the house. When Herakles awakens, Theseus persuades Herakles not to kill himself and to come to Athens. Theseus provides this generosity to his friend because Herakles himself had just rescued him from Hades, where he had traveled with Perithous in a rash attempt to abduct Persephone. This last event is also the subject of a tragedy named *Perithous*, produced by either Euripides or Critias, and it, too, featured the theme of heroic *philia* (friendship). The *Herakles* probably draws on this play for its presentation of their discussion. The two plays, for example, feature the topic of the appropriateness of Herakles for Athenian civic sensibilities. Herakles constitutes a dynamic, powerful, and prestigious hero, but he is also a loner whose relationships with others, as the debacle with his family demonstrates, can end unhappily—as we have also seen in Sophocles's *Women of Trachis*. Perhaps, like the tragic Ajax, Herakles is a figure best appropriated after death, as in the hero cults that Theseus promises to give Herakles. If so, then Euripides's *Children of Herakles* may attempt to incorporate this other Herakles into Athenian life (see Pozzi). Indeed, one may question whether Herakles's presence is appropriate in Athens, given the earlier entry into the city of another famous child killer, Medea. In Euripides's *Medea*, Aegeus honors Medea's supplication plea by offering her asylum in Athens, an invitation that she takes up to escape persecution after murdering her children. Though Medea subsequently bears more children with Aegeus, her presence in the court is nearly disastrous for the king when she plots to murder the newly arrived Theseus in an attempt to secure her own children's access to the throne (see Sfyroeras). Theseus is also rather quick to adopt Herakles for his polis and appears more interested in how this illustrious hero can bolster his prestige than he is in the problem of Herakles's pollution. Theseus's expressed impiety is also marked by sophistry (see Strauss 116). It is interesting, moreover, that while the *Medea* concludes with a reference to a cult that will honor the murdered children, the *Herakles* does not offer this ritual viewpoint, even though Thebes possessed a cult for them (Pindar, *Isthmian* 4.79–84).

The notion that Herakles and Theseus would be featured together is not a novel one. It had been a fixture of Athenian mythic expression for over a century, in the media of poetry, vase painting, and temple art. Thus if Theseus's aid to Herakles in this specific narrative context is an innovation, it is not their linkage that is significant. What may be significant, however, is the likely original idea of featuring in one tragedy two figures typically represented as a *sôtêr*. Theseus plays a similar role in Euripides's *Suppliants* and Sophocles's *Oedipus at Colonus*, and his son, Demophon, plays a *sôtêr* in the *Heraclidae*. One message, therefore, that emerges here is that while Herakles can save others, he and his generational line required the help of Theseus and his generational line. Herakles may be mighty, but he is dependent, as it were, on the more urbane sensibilities that Theseus typically embodies.

Euripides's image of Herakles as an "involved parent" would also seem to be an innovation. This persona, for example, is largely foreign to his portrait in the *Women of Trachis*. Herakles, however, is a prodigious progenitor in myth (see the list compiled by Gruppe, cols. 1091–94; cf. Athenaeus 13.556), even if many of the stories of his procreative exploits are likely the product of aristocratic families eager to include the illustrious hero among their ancestors. (His most prodigious procreative feat is his impregnation of fifty or forty-nine daughters of Thespius.) Herakles, moreover, does possess roles outside the *Herakles* that also feature a positive association with children, marriage, and the household. Herakles appears with his family or bride on pots probably made in the early sixth century, and this iconographic theme continues into the fourth century. On an early Melian amphora, for example, Herakles seems to be paired with Deianira while they are taking leave of her parents (see "Herakles" 1690 in *Lexicon*; Schefold, pl. 57c). A more common motif depicts Herakles with Deianira as he reaches out for a small child (*Lexicon*, "Herakles"

1674–79; Vollkommer 32). Though Herakles kills his first wife, Megara, and is instrumental in the death of Deianira, he also marries, upon his apotheosis, the goddess Hebe (cf. Homer, *Odyssey* 11.604–05; Hesiod, *Theogony* 950; Pindar, *Nemean* 1.110, 10.15–18, and *Isthmian* 4.101). The vase-painting motif occurs as early as the late seventh century, and Herakles is associated with the wedding ceremony on the island of Cos. Hebe is the daughter of Hera, a goddess closely connected with marriage. Hera's relationship with Herakles can be highly destructive, as we see in the *Herakles*, but its full expression is much broader and more multidimensional. (see Loraux, "Herakles" 48; Padilla *Myths* 26–27). In a religious concept rooted in Attic cult (see Price 128, 192; Kearns 35–36), Herakles possesses the epithet "Caregiver of Children" (*kourotrophês*), in the capacity of which office he nourishes and protects children of both sexes—a topic, again, rendered thematic in Euripides's *Children of Herakles* (see Wilkins, "Young"). Associated, therefore, with children's healthy development, Herakles also oversees the concerns of young men: Athenian boys, about to become ephebes, poured a libation to him (at the *oinistêria*); similarly, in rival Sparta, ephebes both sacrificed to him and engaged in ritual combat in his honor. Herakles overlaps with Hermes as a patron of the *gymnasion*, and *gymnasia* are commonly located near his shrines, a connection thematized in a poetic tradition that the play clearly evokes (Pindar, *Nemean* 10.53; for the Attica cultic evidence, see Woodford 214). Euripides may have returned to the juxtaposition of the familial and antifamilial Herakles in his tragic *Auge* (Nauck, fragments 265–81), perhaps produced about the same time as the *Herakles*. Euripides thus clearly invested in plumbing the domestic ties of Herakles for their tragic potential (see Padilla, "Heroic Paternity").

The *Herakles*, if produced after the *Trachiniae*, thus allowed Euripides the opportunity to refashion the figure of Herakles in ways that return to some of his themes in the still earlier *Alcestis*. In that "prosatyric" play, Herakles emerges from his folkloric- and satyric-based home of dramatic presentation to develop sensitivity to the nature of *philia* and the *oikos*, and in a way that incorporates tragic and philosophical sentiments. Though this project is both reinforced and undermined by Sophocles's Herakles, a Herakles that hearkens to a rawer and mysterious heroic persona, the "populist" Euripides recovers the more humane and philosophical capacities of the hero and also distances Herakles from the Olympian gods through their own harsh and condemning treatment of him. Though tragically unable to make a successful transition from warrior to father-husband, it is the hero's intent to do so in the course of the play, and it is the measure of this failure that proves its most poignant message. Herakles remains an outsider, but in a fashion that is less dependent on the overindulgent and haphazard hero of comedy or the mediator and *sôtêr* figure of tragedy. Euripides recovers Herakles for the full drama of human relations.

Tragedians in fifth-century Athens followed, and diverged from, established narratives by adapting inherited myths to suit their specific thematic interests in them for the production of dramas. But the process of adaptation was hardly a straightforward one. When relocating figures from established narratives into new narratives, the resonances that a playwright caused in the minds of his audience, whether consciously or unconsciously in his artistic reasoning, were multilayered. The significance of a motif, theme, or event may belong to a "saga" or "cycle" accepted as independent of a particular medium; it may lie in an allusion to an iconographic milieu; it can serve as an allusion to an earlier poem or tragedy; it may be a link to another dramatic genre; and it may evoke nondramatic material of a sacred-cultic nature.

To attempt, at end, an assessment of how audiences might have responded to this style of presentation of multiple referencing, one must be wary of basing a judgment on Aristotle's *Poetics* (which emphasizes plot structure and other formal elements) and the Platonic dialogues, such as *Republic* 10 (which condemns the emotionality of tragedy): these texts were composed by their authors decades after the tragedies we are considering had been produced on the Athenian stage. Rather, when we look at Aristophanic Old Comedy, plays that were produced in the same period, we see a poetics that openly delights in allusions and creative lampooning of other dramas, cultic practices, and historical personages. The graphic arts could also include this aesthetic. Tragedy, by generic convention, cannot usually be self-conscious about allusions to material outside the text or to a creative use of the narrative tradition. However, a striking exception to this rule is found in Euripides's *Electra* (524–46, when Electra appears to mock an early scene of Aeschylus's *Libation Bearers*), a passage indicating that Euripides enjoyed pushing this envelope to the near breaking point. Thus a tragedian's ability to demonstrate creative adaptation of the mythical traditions and to engage in subtle allusions may have constituted a central—if now underappreciated—component of audiences' judgments of a tragedian's artistic talents and sophistication. Though we remain largely in the dark about the aesthetic quality of tragedy produced in the fourth century BCE, it is possible that these dramatic works were less organic than the tragedies of the fifth century—thus leading to Aristotle's "primer," in the form of the *Poetics*, to guide aspiring dramatists in their dramaturgy. Playwrights no longer needed to rough-hew tragic stories from nontragic materials, and their now recycled tragic narratives perhaps suffered from a rhapsodic (vs. bardic) quality of "the rerun."

NOTE

[1]All translations of Greek passages are my own.

The Art of the Deal: Teaching Folktale Types and Motifs in Euripides's *Alcestis*

Monica Silveira Cyrino

Teaching Euripides's *Alcestis* can be something of a challenge, since this seemingly short and sweet drama about the heroic hospitality of King Admetus and the heroic self-sacrifice of his wife, Alcestis, has elicited more than its fair share of controversy. Critics have argued over every aspect of the play, except perhaps its date (438 BC). Questions arise in the classroom about Alcestis's ostentatious devotion to her husband: Is it not rather self-congratulatory to deliver one's own eulogy during a funeral procession? And how should we explain Admetus's apparent cowardice and passivity in the face of all the decisive actors around him? Does he really deserve all the rewards gods and people keep heaping on him? And what of the curious role of the superhero Herakles? Is he a typical Euripidean "rescuer" figure, a true deus ex machina, or just a comically obnoxious guest bearing an unwanted housewarming gift? Even the genre to which this play belongs is debated, due in part to the controversial status of the grotesquely "happy" ending, a tidy, compact finale that can hardly be justified by the wrenching and complicated action that precedes it: is the *Alcestis* a true tragedy of human fate, a satyr play because it occupies the fourth position in its tetralogy, or some hybrid of the two, a sort of tragicomedy, which, as my students have suggested, evokes a tone located somewhere between medieval fairy story and modern television sitcom?

Among all these questions, and interwoven into any successful teaching strategy, is the issue of the extensive presence of folktale elements permeating the dramatic action and how to understand them in the context of Euripides's tragic play. Students should be encouraged to investigate the ways in which Euripides employs folktale types in the *Alcestis* and how he recharges these several motifs with new dramatic and psychological power. Ever since Albin Lesky (*Alkestis*) first asserted that the core of the Alcestis story had its origin in popular fairy tale rather than in the literary tradition, few critics have denied the structural and thematic importance in the play of the folktale type, wherein human anxieties about our mortality are alleviated through simple tales of cheating death by cunning, piety, or love. Yet critics have struggled to understand the reasons why Euripides chose to introduce such folksy elements into his dramatization of the consequences that accrue to accepting the gods' friendship. John Wilson notes that the fairy-tale theme is "unusual, even unique, in extant Greek drama" and attributes its prominence to the play's "prosatyric function" (3); D. J. Conacher argues that the insertion of Herakles as savior within the folktale motif of wrestling with a personified Death allowed Euripides to explore the "psychological and ethical possibilities" of Admetus's inactivity and Apollo's irresponsibility ("Myth" 18); and D. M. Jones believes Euripides used the folktale as a backdrop against which to "develop the human side of the story," suggesting that the supernatural quality of the play's fairy-tale location in Thessaly may be compared with a modern writer's use of a mystical locale such as Tibet or Ireland (57–58). While many of these interpretations are attractive, what emerges from a careful reading of the *Alcestis* is that Euripides decided to compose a multilayered and problematic play by blending folktale elements with the literary myth of divine-human friendship. What I propose to my students is that Euripides is asking his audience to experience the dramatic tension between the tragic view of death's inevitability and the folktale type of wish fulfillment where death is tricked and even defeated.

Of course, classical Greek tragedy draws mainly from the literary and mythological traditions of epic and other narrative poetry, where members of the Olympian family of gods are shown to interfere in the lives of human beings through a strict divine economy of reward for piety and *arete* (excellence) and punishment for wrongdoing and hubris (prideful overstepping of set boundaries). These myths almost invariably end with a reaffirmation of the rule of Zeus, with its law-and-order, family-values, zero-tolerance slogan ringing in the ears of the audience: "And there is nothing here that is not Zeus." Students of Greek mythology recognize that the story in Euripides's *Alcestis* also relies on this mythical background of Olympian familial conflict, as Apollo reminds us in the prologue (Lattimore, *Alcestis* 1–21).[1] Asklepios, the half-mortal son of Apollo, becomes so skilled in the arts of medicine that he succeeds in bringing the dead back to life. To penalize this subversion of the cosmic order of life and death and to ratify the allotted *timê* (sphere of honor) belonging to Hades, immortal First Brother and Lord of the Dead, Zeus kills Asklepios with a thunderbolt, symbol of his incontrovertible, masculine-phallic authority (3–4). No wish fulfillment here, no celebration of cleverness, no Sisyphean comeback, just the iron will of Zeus: like the culture hero Prometheus, Asklepios becomes a casualty of Zeus's inexorable power-maintenance plan, just another statistic among the hundreds of divine punishment myths in the corpus of Greek legend.

The myth continues with the reaction of Apollo to the murder of his son, and here we see the familiar theme of father-son rivalry so prevalent in the Hesiodic account of Zeus's rise to dominion (as told in the *Theogony*). Furious at his son Asklepios's death, but not daring to attack Zeus himself, Apollo gets his revenge by shooting arrows at the Cyclopes, forgers of the big man's thunderbolt (5–6): although not a direct-threat succession myth along the lines of Ouranos-Cronos-Zeus, Apollo does target the major Olympian weapons installation and therefore the very substance of Zeus's strategic power base. Yet Zeus again reasserts his paternal authority, this time by punishing Apollo with a term of indentured servitude to the Thessalian king Admetus (6–7). A god being sent to the mortal world for a term of bondage would be the divine equivalent of a death sentence, so Zeus's punishment of his son Apollo replays his execution of Apollo's own son Asklepios and confirms his Olympian control over the cosmic cycle of living and dying. Scholars have noted the analogy between the name *Admetus* and Hades's frequent epithet, Adamastos, "the unconquerable one"; they have also noted the correspondence between the famous hospitality of Admetus and the notorious hospitality of Hades Polydegmon, "he who welcomes all." In any case, Apollo submits to Zeus's will and goes down from Mount Olympus to the House of Admetus, even if it means his temporary "death" away from the bliss of his immortal existence. The father curbs the son's rebellion; Zeus's law is upheld; death cannot be avoided.

It is during this period of earthbound service that a threat to Admetus's life occurs and Apollo intervenes, in gratitude for being well treated by his human host. It is at this point, too, that Euripides intervenes by introducing into his drama some provocative elements of the folktale fantasy of defeating death. Here students may be asked to think about how the two traditions of mythology and folktale interact within the context of tragic drama. Conacher notes that the myth of Apollo's servitude to Admetus appears to be of quite separate origin from the tale of Alcestis's substitute death for her husband: the latter, he says, "with its bargains and struggles with the monster Thanatos, that pathetically simple incarnation of human fears, suggests the primitive, superstitious and infinitely more urgent preoccupations of folk tale" ("Myth" 17). Lesky's study, using comparative material from German, Greek, and Armenian folk songs, identifies the kernel of the folktale in what he deduces to be its oldest and barest form: on the king's wedding day, Death comes for the bridegroom; although Death is persuaded to accept an alternate soul, the aged parents of the king both refuse to sacrifice themselves; but then, the young bride volunteers to die to save the life of her doomed lover (*Alkestis* 36–42). Lesky also lists some variations and developments of the tale, including the physical combat with Death in which the husband himself is always the brave challenger. In Euripides's play, several separate strands of this love-and-death folktale are connected and interwoven onto the mythical story of the friendship between Admetus and Apollo, which arose from the god's term of bondage after Zeus's righteous punishment of Asklepios's hubris. So the play juxtaposes the ways in which the two different genres, myth-based tragedy and popular folktale, deal on a narrative level with the theme of human fear of death's inevitability.

The idea that a person might foil death by means of a deal or swindle, or because of someone's skill or goodness, is a ubiquitous European folktale type, where death is sometimes personified as a devil, ogre, or other evil spirit (Aarne and Thompson 329–32). A common motif within this folktale type is the use of deception to escape death, through disguise, shamming, or even by substituting another person in place of the intended victim (Thompson K500, K520, K527). Students will note that the "deception of death" story pattern appears at key points and in subtly varied guises throughout the Alcestis story. At the opening of the drama Apollo boasts that he hoodwinked the Moirae, or Fates, into letting Admetus escape the appointed day of his death (*Alcestis* 10–11). We recall from the trial scene in Aeschylus's *Eumenides*, the final play of the *Oresteia* trilogy, that Apollo's preferred mode of persuading the Moirae to spare the damned is by getting them drunk; this act of trickery may correspond to the folktale deception motif whereby the evil spirit is magically enclosed in a bottle (Thompson D2177.1). Apollo here represents the power of light over darkness, and he is resplendent in his role as Python slayer, tamer of the monstrous Furies, fighter of deadly irrational chthonian forces par excellence, and therefore the right man for the job of saving his new friend Admetus from his date with gloomy destiny. Unlike the myth of Asklepios's superhuman medical skill, an act of hubris that attracts punishment, in the folktale version the bright, clever god succeeds in outwitting grim Death. If we look at this story from a different angle, another well-known folktale type emerges, wherein human hospitality is rewarded by a god (Aarne and Thompson 750A–B). In this folktale type, the reward manifests itself in the motifs of the granting of magical powers or wishes used both foolishly and wisely by a husband and wife (Thompson D2172.2, J2071–79). In the play, Admetus gets to avoid his death as a reward for his honorable entertainment of his servant-guest, Apollo. Thus the piety of Admetus, which in the play is set beside the art of the musician Orpheus (*Alcestis* 357–63), is strong enough to suspend the powers of death, at least for a time. These folktale-tinged events, Admetus's hospitality and Apollo's trick, since they occur before the action of the drama, serve to attach the myth of divine friendship to the fairy-tale salvation from death, which is enacted in "real time" during the course of the play.

Certainly the most powerful expression in the play of the "rescue from death" story pattern is Alcestis's dying in place of her husband, an act Euripides highlights by separating it chronologically from the original bargain: the play opens on the very day that Alcestis's death is fated. Marriage folktales often emphasize a wife's faithfulness even in death (Thompson T211.1), which in the Alcestis story then intersects with the folktale wish to postpone death if a substitute can be found (Thompson D1855.2). In the folktale type of the "love sacrifice," where the bride or wife of the doomed man volunteers to die on his behalf, the bravery and nobility of the young woman is also set against the cowardice and meanness of the husband's elderly parents, who refuse to help him in his hour of need (Aarne and Thompson 899). Euripides elaborates this contrast in his brutal portrait of Admetus's father, Pheres: in their savage exchange of insults and attacks, the theme of father-son rivalry evident from the conflict between Zeus and Apollo is replayed, but this time paternal authority is shown to be discredited. Admetus even goes so far as to reject his blood relationship to his parents, naming Alcestis his "only parent" (*Alcestis* 646–47) and counting himself to be her child because of her ultimate expression of love. Nancy Rabinowitz comments on the Oedipal quality of Admetus's hostility toward Pheres and his fetishization of Alcestis as the mother-wife, the one who literally gives him life a second time (*Anxiety* 79–80). So when Euripides introduces the figure of the unwilling father, he not only magnifies Alcestis's dramatic deed of self-sacrifice but also confirms the structure of the folktale type, in which, as Plato states in the *Symposium*, "only lovers are willing to die for one another" (179B).

In offering herself to die as a substitute for Admetus, Alcestis also enacts the ambiguous figure of the fairy-tale bride of Death (Aarne and Thompson 365). Students of Greek literature remember that bridal imagery occurs regularly in Greek tragedy to describe in particular the sacrificial deaths of virgins: one example is Sophocles's depiction of Antigone's funeral march as a wedding procession in the play *Antigone*. As Nicole Loraux has noted, the tragic text draws the virgin as an intrinsically incomplete figure, allowing her to find the erotic fulfillment she missed in life only through the sexualization of her death-marriage (*Tragic Ways* 36–41). But in our drama, because Alcestis is already a wife, the theme is developed more along the lines of folktale and is dovetailed into the "substitute death for love" story pattern. Since Alcestis's death originates in her marriage to Admetus (Adamastos), she can be compared to Persephone, whose union with Hades symbolizes her death away from the upper world (Rabinowitz, *Anxiety* 70). Moreover, just as Persephone's return brings about the renewal of life in the springtime, the Alcestis who comes back from the dead is described as a young woman, newly rejuvenated and girlishly dressed (*Alcestis* 1049–50). As a bride who returns from the dead, Alcestis can also be likened to the figure of Eurydice: that is, the musical skill of Orpheus, like the piety of Admetus, is powerful enough to resurrect his wife. Both stories exhibit several folktale motifs: the encounter with the other world to secure one's bride (Thompson F87), the attempt of the husband to resuscitate his wife (Thompson E165), and the theme of testing, where conditions are set up as barriers to the hero's conjugal reward (Thompson H310–59). But Orpheus fails the test and breaks the folktale taboo of looking back at his wife (Thompson C331) and so loses Eurydice again to the underworld; but when the veiled Alcestis is first brought back to the world of the living, she is disguised as a trophy of Heraklean prowess and is thus protected from the potentially murderous gaze of her husband while her savior, Herakles, puts Admetus's famous hospitality to the test once again. Even the hero's gesture of unveiling the "mystery woman" and revealing Alcestis to her surprised husband reinforces the bridal imagery at work in the wedding ceremony aspect of this scene (Rabinowitz, *Anxiety* 87, 95). The supernatural ambience surrounding Alcestis's appearance at the end of the play is emphasized by the folk motif of ritual disenchantment by the three-day term of silence imposed on her under the threat of punishment (*Alcestis* 1144–46), establishing her liminal status as a bride dangerously exposed to death (Thompson D758.1). Alcestis's muteness and the otherworldly stillness of her person also may indicate that for three nights she will play the role of the statue, the "cold consolation" her husband longed for as a replacement of her (*Alcestis* 348–54), after which time, like Galateia and other figures of folktale, she will magically come to life (Thompson D435.1.1).

Finally, students see how the rescue of Admetus by his wife, Alcestis, comes full circle in the parallel rescue of Alcestis by the superhero, Herakles. In the folktale where the mortal struggles with the monster Death to save his bride (Thompson R185), the heroic challenger is almost always the husband himself, not an outside agent, as Lesky and others have found. But here it is Herakles who, after being entertained chez Admetus without knowing that the house was in mourning for the dead mistress, returns the favor to his host by restoring Alcestis to life. Some students may want to interpret this event by suggesting that Euripides introduced the figure of Herakles into the story to impart a negative ironic or psychological focus on the character of Admetus, and they may perhaps offer derogatory explanations about why Admetus is represented as forfeiting the role of the folktale savior-groom. Clearly the dramatic reassertion of Admetus's heroic hospitality at the end of the play and the motif of his successfully passing the test both involve his reluctant acceptance of Herakles's gift of the veiled girl, which looks a lot like a betrayal of his promise to his dying wife to touch no other woman (*Alcestis* 330–31). Thus it appears that Admetus has benefited from both folktale options of escape from mortality, his wife's performance of the love sacrifice and his friend's exertions as the "hero who fights with Death," while contributing sweat equity to neither. How do we explain the apparent tensions at work in the plot of this play?

In the end I encourage my students to consider the important function of Herakles himself in mediating between the two different narrative strategies presented in this drama about one man facing the threat of death: the tragic view of death's inevitability and the folktale wish fulfillment of defeating death. In the legends of Herakles, the hero straddles the boundary between the mortal and immortal worlds: many of his famous labors show him victorious over the supernatural forces of death and returning unscathed to the human sphere of the living (e.g., the story of retrieving the cattle of Geryon). The figure of Herakles also recalls the earlier role of Asklepios, since both heroes succeed in raising the dead, and this connection serves to join the folktale part of the story to the myth of Olympian father-son rivalry; we might even conclude that Apollo enlists the superhero as his agent to help Admetus in honor of his dead physician son. Furthermore, as Zeus's son, Herakles seems to be granted special allowance to subvert the law of death, which Zeus himself upheld earlier by his execution of Asklepios, at the same time that the hero is seen to reaffirm Zeus's law of hospitality in rewarding the piety of Admetus. The double nature of Herakles, both human and divine, is therefore tied to his dual role in the drama: he is present throughout the play as the human recipient of the custom of *xenia*, reciprocal guest-friendship, and then at the end he appears as godlike savior who has the power to change the course of life-and-death cosmic events. So the character of Herakles, the hero who both dies and conquers Death, may be demonstrated both to represent and to resolve the tensions between the different ways tragedy and folktale deal with the fear of human mortality. Students discover that Euripides chose to explore both views in his drama, which may account for the discrepancy between the rather unrealistic "happy ending" and our feeling that it is not completely justified by the plot that precedes it. Admetus, with Apollo's help, is awarded the Good Housekeeping Seal of Approval, but some of Zeus's earlier resistance surfaces when Herakles declines his host's invitation to extend his visit (1151–52). No doubt he knows that the house of Admetus is headed for some chilly times, and as my students surmise, the hero doesn't want to be around when Alcestis recoveres her voice. Cold consolation, indeed.

NOTE

[1]Line numbers from Lattimore's translation in the Chicago series correspond fairly well to those in A. M. Dale's edition of the Greek text.

Women and the *Medea*

Laurel Bowman

Honour now comes to womankind.
—Chorus, *Medea*

Women are useless at good deeds, but skilled workers at every kind of evil.
—Medea, *Medea*

The representation of women in Euripides's *Medea* often seems contradictory. The characters speak at length and frequently with sympathy about the nature of women, women's role in society, and even the representation of women in Greek literature. At the climax of the play, however, the female protagonist commits an outrageous crime, the murder of her own male children.

Both the complexity of Euripides's *Medea* and the central position of women in the play make it a natural starting point for the study of the representation of women in Greek tragedy. The play is also a rich source of information on Athenian attitudes toward women and their role in society. The reader must take care, however, to avoid importing into the text modern cultural assumptions about women's nature and social role. Interpretation of the play requires knowledge of its ancient context, including the cultural and legal role of women in Athenian society, the mythical background of the story presented in the play, and the role of women in Athenian drama. This essay briefly summarizes the cultural, dramatic, and mythical contexts of the play with which its intended audience would have been familiar. It then examines the representation of women and of Medea herself in the play.

Mythical Background

Euripides's audience would have been familiar with the figure of Medea, who appears in myth long before the production of his play. Every myth in which she figures portrays her as a dangerous witch, with magical powers. In the stories familiar to fifth-century Athenians, Medea was the daughter of Aeetes, king of Colchis on the Black Sea, and granddaughter of Helios, the sun god. She fell in love with the Greek Jason, used magic to assist him in stealing the Golden Fleece from her father, and eloped with him back to Greece. When her father tried to stop their flight, she murdered her brother and threw his dismembered body overboard to delay the pursuit (Bremmer; Gantz 363–64). On their arrival in Greece, she again used magic to arrange the murder of King Pelias of Iolcus by his own daughters, in an attempt to put Jason on the throne. She and Jason were then forced to flee Iolcus for Corinth (Gantz 366–68).

Euripides several times reminds the audience of the *Medea* of the mythical background to the play. Medea explicitly recounts what she has done to help Jason and complains that, thanks to the crimes she herself enumerates, she cannot return as an exile to Iolcus or to her father (Warner, *Medea* 475–83, 502–05). She admits to the murders of Pelias and her own brother and to the abandonment of her city and her father (486–87, 167, 166). In Euripides's version, Medea herself killed the serpent that kept guard over the Golden Fleece, instead of simply assisting Jason in doing so (480–82). This alteration in the traditional story makes Euripides's Medea seem even more powerful and increases Jason's debt to her.

In every telling of the story, Jason and Medea's children die in Corinth. In earlier versions of the myth, however, either the Corinthians kill the children to avenge Medea's murder of their king or the children die accidentally, as a consequence of Medea's attempt to make them immortal (Gantz 368–69). Ever since the production of Euripides's play, the compelling image of Medea as tortured murderer of her own children has superseded all other versions of the myth. Euripides's play is the earliest extant text to make Medea herself the killer and may be the earliest representation of Medea as an infanticide. (See, most recently, Graf 35; Gantz 370; Rabinowitz, *Anxiety* 146. For an opposing view see Michelini, *Euripides.*) In every version of the myth, Medea expresses some form of the "reproductive demon," a type of supernatural figure blamed for the death of children in many cultures. Such a figure is often described as the ghost of a mother who has lost—and sometimes murdered—her own child (Johnston). Medea's act of infanticide, in Euripides's version, is not out of character for a reproductive demon figure. Dramatically, however, Euripides's decision to represent Medea as the killer of her own children, rather than as an innocent sufferer at their deaths, makes a striking difference to any reading of the play. Interpretation of the *Medea* must consider why Euripides chose to show its protagonist as guilty of such a monstrous crime.

Life of Athenian Women

Medea's description of women's lives in her address to the chorus of Corinthian women is an accurate and sympathetic summary of cultural expectations for the life of a middle-class Athenian woman from a citizen family (230–51). Such a woman's father would be wealthy enough to give her a dowry, and her husband would have the wealth and standing to demand one. The males of this class of citizens were the assumed audience of the play, and it is the values, customs, and expectations of this class that are held up to question in Medea's address.

Women of this class were usually married in their early teens to men in their thirties. The woman had no say in the choice of her husband. Marriages were arranged by agreement between the father and the groom. The bride's father would provide her with a dowry. Once married, the woman moved from her father's to her husband's household and became subject to her husband's legal authority. She was responsible for running the household, a duty that her youth, inexperience, and lack of familiarity with her new environment could have made difficult. If she and her husband were unhappy together, he could seek companionship outside the household, but she was more dependent on her husband for company, as even to be seen too often outside the house could damage a woman's reputation. Public space, outside the household, was considered the male domain. Custom forbade a woman to leave her own house and enter public space too often, even with a legitimate excuse, such as attendance at a women's religious festival or a neighbor's childbed (Just 118–25). Her husband's greater freedom extended to the sexual realm. He could take a mistress without penalty, but law made divorce mandatory if a wife was discovered to be unfaithful (MacDowell 88).

The foremost duty of an Athenian wife was to bear legitimate citizen children to continue her husband's household. Infertility was probably the most common grounds for divorce (Blundell 127). Childbearing was not only painful but also dangerous. Without antibiotics, modern anesthetics, or an understanding of the importance of hygiene, the risk of death or lifelong debility as a result of pregnancy and childbirth was much greater than it is now. Care of young children was also the wife's duty, with all the emotional hazard that entailed in a society where at least one child in two died before the age of five (Demand 22). Medea recalls these risks when she says she would rather go into battle three times than give birth once (251; Easterling, "Infanticide" 182). The chorus further articulates the hazards of child rearing (1081–115).

Medea reverses all expectations of women's role and function in an Athenian marriage. She chooses her own mate instead of being given to one. Instead of binding together her natal and conjugal households, she ruins both. Instead of perpetuating Jason's family through the production of male children, she murders his sons and eliminates his chance to have more by murdering his new wife as well. Insofar as her relationship with Jason resembles a marriage, it is a signal failure (Visser). There are, however, several indications in the play that Medea's position in Jason's household could be taken by an Athenian audience as that of a concubine rather than a wife.

A foreign concubine would have no citizenship rights or family support in Athens. Since a union with a foreign woman would offer the man neither useful in-laws nor the chance of legitimate children, it would have been inherently less stable than a marriage to an Athenian citizen, which offered both. Such a relationship would be at risk of dissolution or at least subordination to marriage to the daughter of a citizen if the opportunity for such a marriage arose. An abandoned foreign concubine lacked the network of family on which an Athenian woman could rely to provide her a place to live, the necessities of life, and a measure of social status. Without such support, she would have no recourse if, like Medea, she was left destitute.

Athenian Marriage and Citizenship Laws

Of the Athenian laws that related to women, the ones that affect an interpretation of the *Medea* are primarily those governing marriage. Every Athenian citizen woman, of any age, had a male guardian in authority over her. A woman's marriage was arranged by an oral betrothal contract between her legal guardian—usually her father—and the groom, in which the guardian consented to give the woman to the groom for purposes of marriage. The woman's consent to this agreement was not legally necessary and not sought. If no betrothal agreement between the woman's guardian and the prospective groom had been made, their union, however long-lived or fertile, was not a marriage (Just 43–45). Even in a legal marriage, a man could divorce his wife simply by sending her back to her father (Blundell 127).

Athenian male citizens were, by the Periclean citizenship law of 451–50 BC, only legally permitted to marry women who were themselves the daughters of Athenian citizens. If an Athenian male citizen formed a domestic relationship with a foreign woman, even with her guardian's consent, the relationship did not constitute a legal marriage. Children of such a union were not legitimate and did not have Athenian citizenship (MacDowell 86).

The word most often used to describe a legal marriage, *gamos*, is used in the *Medea* only to describe Jason's marriage to Kreon's daughter (the one exception, at line 1388, is ironic). Medea was not betrothed to Jason by agreement between Jason and her legal guardian. Jason swore oaths to Medea herself (495–98), but we are not told that these oaths specifically concerned marriage, and in any event, oaths sworn to the bride were irrelevant in Athenian marriage law. The bride did not have the legal authority to make a marriage, or any other contract, on her own behalf. Consent of her legal guardian was required, and her father in the myths was notoriously opposed to the match.

The relationship between Jason and Medea, as Greek to barbarian, is represented in the play as being in several respects parallel to a nonmarital relationship between an Athenian citizen and a foreign woman. Jason emphasizes his status as a Greek versus Medea's as a barbarian (e.g., 536–41). Medea accuses Jason of abandoning her because his "barbarian bed" is not respectable enough as he grows older (591–92). An Athenian citizen's irregular union with a foreign concubine would similarly not seem "respectable," in that it would not strengthen the social position of his family or produce legitimate children, as a legal marriage could. Medea complains that she could understand his behavior if she had been barren, but she has borne sons for him (490), which would protect an Athenian wife from the most common reason for divorce. If she is a foreign concubine, however, her sons are illegitimate. Jason claims that he is marrying the king's daughter to produce royal sons (596–97). To an Athenian audience, Jason's desire to sire royal children, who would have rights in their native city, would seem analogous to the desire of an Athenian man for legitimate sons with the rights of Athenian citizenship (Rabinowitz, *Anxiety* 141).

It must be added, however, that Euripides does not give the audience a certain guide as to the legitimacy of Jason and Medea's union. As Patricia Easterling points out, no overt stress is laid on the legal status of their relationship, whatever it is ("Infanticide" 180). Moreover, fifth-century Athenian marriage laws would not technically hold force in *Medea*, as it is set not in fifth-century BC Athens but in Bronze Age Corinth, and neither Jason nor Medea is a Corinthian native. Medea certainly places great importance on Jason's oaths to her, and she considers their relationship marital. However, the Athenian audience's perception of Medea's position would have been colored by the marriage and citizenship laws to which it was accustomed. The distance between Medea's, Jason's, and the audience's view of their relationship would have heightened the tension of the drama.

Women and the Production of Athenian Tragedy

Although the protagonist of *Medea* was a barbarian woman, the play was performed by and for Athenian men. *Medea* was originally performed at the City Dionysia, a festival held each year in Athens to honor the god Dionysus. The three-day period of the festival reserved for tragic performances began with a number of civic ceremonies, performed in the presence of the audience gathered for the dramas. The ten generals elected for the year performed a libation, or a drink offering, to the gods. The tribute collected that year from the subject states was carried in and displayed. The names of men who had performed great services for the Athenian state were read out and crowns or garlands granted to them. Finally, the sons of Athenian men who had died in battle were brought before the crowd in full armor, paid for by the state, when they were themselves of age for military service. The ceremonies that preceded the first performance each year thus stressed Athenian wealth, power, and civic responsibility. They honored the men who had benefited the state in life and death. These displays would have encouraged in the audience a sense of civic pride and unity and a desire to emulate those who had been honored (Goldhill, "Great Dionysia").

Tragedy was itself a form of civic display. The plays were performed in a dramatic competition, funded by the state. Each year three playwrights were chosen by a city official to produce plays at the City Dionysia. On each day of the tragic competition, three tragedies and a satyr play by one playwright were performed. At the conclusion of the three days of the tragic competition, judges chosen by lot voted on the performances. The victorious playwright was awarded an ivy crown (Csapo and Slater 108). The reward for winning the dramatic competition was the same kind of public recognition that was awarded men who had served the state in some other outstanding way. Tragedy must be understood in the context of this civic display (Goldhill, "Great Dionysia" 127).

The participants in the preplay ceremonies were all men, and the activities honored there, service to the state in warfare and governance, were all part of the public sphere, which was in Athens almost exclusively reserved for men. The religious festival—the City Dionysia—of which the dramatic performances formed a part was largely a male festival, in which women were at most onlookers. The playwright, Euripides, like all Athenian playwrights, was also male. The tragedies themselves, in that they were performed before an audience of Athenian citizens, were part of the public—and thus the masculine—sphere. The intended audience of tragedy was the group of male Athenian citizens gathered together in the theater, from whose number the judges of the dramatic competition were also drawn. Women may or may not have been present at dramatic performances (Csapo and Slater 286; see also Goldhill, "Audience" 62–66), but the reactions or opinions of the women in the audience would have carried no more weight than those of the slaves and foreigners who would also have been present.

Since the City Dionysia was a male public festival, all performers in the tragedies were male. This included the actors playing female roles. In the *Medea*, a male actor in female dress and wearing a mask would have played Medea herself. A group of singing, dancing adolescent boys, also in stylized female dress and masks, would have performed the role of the chorus of Corinthian women.

The fact that the actors playing female roles were cross-dressing men is perhaps of more consequence in the *Medea* than it is in other tragedies. The *Medea* explicitly foregrounds and calls into question the nature of women and their role in Athenian society. That it was (in reality) a man, not a woman, who spoke Medea's lines and performed her onstage deeds made the questions more pointed. It is impossible to say what message the audience would have taken from this. Perhaps the men, or at least the women, in the audience would have been reminded by the male actor that they were watching not a "real story" but a masculine construction, the presentation of a male-told myth. Perhaps the strength of Medea was only tolerable because she was "really" a man, as Nancy Rabinowitz suggests ("How Is It Played?").

Medea could safely be used by Euripides to explore antisocial extremes of conduct because her behavior is ascribed to a character who is both female and "barbarian." She thus stood at two removes from the possible conduct of the intended audience of male Athenian citizens. The staging of the final scene of the play further distanced her from the audience. Medea's final appearance in the play is overhead in a winged chariot supported by the *machina*, a cranelike device ordinarily reserved in Greek theater for appearances of divinities. In the original production Medea probably appeared in Oriental costume for this scene (Sourvinou-Inwood 289). In her final appearance, Medea thus would have appeared not only as female but also as emphatically barbarian and quasidivine rather than mortal, triply distanced from the self-definition of the mortal, male, Athenian audience.

Representation of Women in the Medea

Given the masculine, public context of the performance of tragedy, it is not surprising that although a female character may be central to a play, women's concerns never are. Female characters are frequently vividly and sometimes sympathetically represented in tragedy, but their function is always as adjunct in one way or another to the male character whose fate is the subject of the play (Zeitlin, "Playing" 69). The audience, whatever the gender of its individual members, is encouraged to identify with this (male) perspective (Rabinowitz, "Tragedy" 51).

In the *Medea*, women's lives are sympathetically portrayed as dependent, restricted, and lacking in freedom of choice. However, the behavior of Medea herself, as an independent woman who makes her own choices, is no argument in favor of loosing the restrictions on ordinary women's lives. The destructive potential of a woman like Medea is illustrated primarily by her catastrophic effect on the males she is associated with: Jason, Kreon, her father, her brother, and her sons. Even the death of Kreon's daughter is only the tool Medea uses to murder Kreon and ruin Jason. The audience is encouraged to view Medea's behavior as monstrous and to identify with the betrayed and murdered males.

In her opening address to the chorus of Corinthian women, Medea describes the lot of women as comprehensively wretched (230–51). The conditions of life she describes are those of women of the citizen class who fulfill Athenian cultural norms and whose conduct is virtuous, or at least attracts no blame. Virtuous women are portrayed in this speech as isolated, passive, helpless, dependent on male authority, and lacking all control over the decisions that will define their lives. Their greatest hope of safety is to agree with their husbands in all things (13–15). The only positive action possible to them is childbearing, and even that is described as dangerous and the bringer of sorrow (251, 1081–115).

Several characters, however, comment on women's capacity for destructive behavior. Medea says that women are cowards unless wronged in sexual matters, when there's no bloodier spirit (263–66). Later she claims that women are useless for any good deed but very skilled at evil (408–09). Kreon fears and distrusts clever women (319). Jason accuses women of giving first priority to their sex lives (570), to which Medea seems to assent (1368). Even the chorus blames women's beds for causing mortal evils (1291–92).

Virtuous women are then portrayed as passive and helpless, and the only constructive activity ascribed to them, child rearing, is described as likely to bring pain. Any other female action is depicted as actively destructive and undertaken only in the service of immoderate sexual desire. Behavior defined as feminine is thus either passive and powerless or active and destructive. There is no model for positive feminine action.

The action of the drama reinforces this negative paradigm. The chorus of Corinthian women is powerless to perform the positive action of persuading

Medea not to kill her children. Medea, however, the incarnation of the model of destructive feminine activity, easily carries out four murders. Her only serious opposition is her own maternal love, which she ultimately overcomes.

Representation of Medea

The depiction of Medea in the play undermines the sympathetic portrayals of women and reinforces the negative stereotypes voiced by various characters. Medea includes herself in her description of women's lot to elicit the sympathy and support of the Corinthian women whom she addresses, saying, "Of all things that live [. . .] we women are the most miserable" (230–31). However, the nurse's prologue (6–12) has already reminded the audience that the description does not suit Medea's life. Instead of being given to a husband by her father, she chose her own husband. Once she had eloped with Jason, she did encounter new customs and laws, but unlike an Athenian woman, she chose this of her own free will. She is a mother, but a dangerous and ultimately murderous one (90–95).

That this sympathetic account of women's lives comes from Medea calls the account itself into question, for the Athenian audience and for us. Medea has given a pathetic description of women's lot in life to elicit sympathy for herself, but the audience is aware that Medea herself does not deserve the sympathy she asks for. In denying Medea their sympathy, the audience cannot help holding her description of women's life suspect also.

Medea's description of her own situation (252–58), a sympathetic account of the hazards of life for foreign women, is again undermined by her own career. When Medea says that she has no brother to turn to, the audience remembers that she murdered her brother, as she herself has admitted (167). She is cityless (255) and, unlike the chorus members (253), cannot return to her father's household, because she herself betrayed her father. The audience's sympathy for Medea, and the credence it gives her speech, is diminished by the details of her previous career that the speech recalls.

In her ability to garner sympathy and support from the chorus and others through her rhetorical skill, Medea is precisely the sort of intelligent woman Kreon distrusts (319). The events of the play prove his distrust well-founded. Medea bears out the negative model of women's nature constructed in the play in other respects as well. She does not perform any positive actions of which we are informed; she is spurred into action by an injury in the sexual sphere of her life; and her actions are astoundingly destructive.

Were this all there was to say about Medea, Euripides's play would be one-sided and much less interesting. However, Medea has many virtues. She is loyal and helpful to her friends; she has courage and determination; and, unlike Jason, she keeps her word. In Athenian terms, however, all her virtues are "masculine." That is, her virtues are those ascribed to and praised in men rather than women. Bernard Knox points out that Medea adheres closely to the paradigm of the Sophoclean (male) hero, especially in her determination to help her friends and harm her enemies, the essence of the heroic code ("*Medea*"). He suggests that she is best understood as a masculine character, a (male) hero in a woman's body, and that she demands to be taken seriously because she is a hero. The argument that Medea is female by sex but masculine by gender has many ramifications (Rabinowitz, *Anxiety* 153). Medea's debate with her heart over the murder of her children, for example, can be read as a gendered debate between her feminine maternal love and her masculine heroic pride (Foley, "Medea's Divided Self"). However, although there is no model for positive female action in the play, even action that follows a masculine paradigm is ultimately destructive, if a woman undertakes it.

From the point of view of the Athenian audience, Medea was a marginal character in every way that mattered. She was female; she was foreign; she might well have been seen by an Athenian audience as a concubine rather than as a member of a legitimate household. The action of the play is further marginalized by its setting in Corinth and, at that, not in the palace but in an ordinary house, far from the center of power. Euripides uses Medea's marginalized figure to ask questions about Athenian social norms that a character who fit those norms could not. Medea's character and actions call into question the treatment of women and foreigners in Athenian society. Her later behavior seems to justify every doubt expressed about the nature of women and foreigners and also to justify the tight controls kept on them. The masculinization of her character makes it easier for an Athenian male to understand and sympathize with her motives, even as he condemns her acts. It is difficult to say what ultimate judgment the Athenian audience may have reached about the play. Knowledge of the cultural, legal, and dramatic context in which the play was originally performed can cast light on the questions it posed for its ancient audience.

Reading the *Medea* in the classroom must take into account the civic and religious function of tragedy in the Athenian city-state. In particular, the entirely masculine context of the play's performance needs to be kept in mind. Medea is a vividly portrayed character, and the lives of women are sympathetically represented in the play. However, the *Medea* was performed by a male actor who delivered lines written by a male playwright, for the benefit of a male citizen audience. The play was performed at a largely masculine festival with political as well as religious implications. Under these circumstances, it is folly to expect or see in the *Medea* a naturalistic representation of the lives, hopes, or innermost thoughts of real Athenian women. Medea, like every other female character in Greek drama, represents the hopes, dreams, nightmares, and in sum the Athenian male *imaginings* about women. Dramatically, the female characters are foils to the males. They are whatever the plot and the fate of the male characters who are its focus require them to be. The playwrights who created the female characters may have been keen and sympathetic observers of women's lives, but their observations and their sympathy would have been subordinated in their plays to the dramatic needs of the art they practiced. Classical Greek tragedy was an art form of the Athenian male citizenry, and the *Medea* must be read with that in mind.

Euripides in the *Medea* is the first extant poet to suggest that myths about women would be different if women were telling them. On hearing the tale of Jason's perfidy, Euripides has the chorus sing that it is men, not women, who are faithless. If women had been poets, they add, there would be as many tales sung against men as there are against women (410–30). Whether Euripides, a male poet, has produced such a woman's tale in the *Medea* is doubtful. Why he chose to suggest such poetry as a possibility is, like the reason for the sympathetic portrayal of women's lives in Medea's address to the chorus, an open question that will well repay class discussion.

Hecuba and the Political Dimension of Greek Tragedy

Justina Gregory

Introducing students to Greek tragedy requires attention at once to text and to context. Instructors might begin by explaining the structure of tragedy, drawing attention to its basic pattern of actors and chorus who alternate speech and song and pointing out, as well, variations on that basic pattern. They will want to remind students of tragedy's visual and aural aspects and encourage them to imagine the plays as a feast for the eyes and the ears even though all that survives to us is a bare text. They will undoubtedly choose to discuss the emotional experience purveyed by tragedy, its paradoxical capacity to entertain and delight while recounting stories of atrocious suffering. It is equally important that they alert students to tragedy's political dimension and explain that in fifth-century Athens tragedy was perceived as an instructional genre that at once reflected and promoted discourse pertaining to the Athenian polis (Gregory 2–4).

Some scholars downplay the political dimension of tragedy, insisting that for the contemporary audience the aesthetic experience was paramount (Heath, *Poetics* 5–17; Griffin, "Social Function" 55). Such a stance discounts, however, the important testimony of Aristophanes. As a contemporary of the great tragedians and a playwright himself, Aristophanes was ideally situated to comment on tragedy's role in his own society. There is no warrant for assuming that because Aristophanes composed comedies he was therefore incapable of earnestness, and drama's political and instructional function was evidently one of the principles he took seriously (Taplin, "Tragedy" 333). In *Frogs* Aristophanes stages a mock debate between "Aeschylus" and "Euripides" that takes place in the underworld, where the two are competing for the title of best tragedian. "Aeschylus" demands: "On what grounds should we admire a tragedian?" The response of his rival, "Euripides," is unequivocal: "For his skillfulness and his admonitions, because we [i.e., the tragedians] improve the people in the cities" (*Frogs* 1009–10; unless otherwise specified, all translations in this essay are my own). "Aeschylus" concurs with his rival on the didactic function of tragedy, noting: "Boys have a schoolteacher who provides explanations; grownups have the poets" (*Frogs* 1054–55).

A glance at the plays' circumstances of production helps students bring into focus the distinctive political role of tragedy in fifth-century Athens. Tragedy was an institution unique to Athens; although it was not an invention of the Athenian democracy, by the fifth century it had become closely identified with the official life of the democratic polis. The plays were presented annually on the occasion of a state-sponsored festival of Dionysus and performed in a theater that was situated in the heart of civic and religious Athens. Their production depended on some of the democracy's most characteristic institutions and incorporated some of its most cherished principles. The playwrights who would compete for prizes at the festival were selected in advance by Athens's chief political magistrate, the eponymous archon. Reflecting the democratic principle of accountability, an assembly held after the festival offered a chance to investigate any irregularities connected with the event. Tragedies were expensive to produce, for each tragedian presented not a single offering but three tragedies followed by a satyr play, each of which required the services of a musician, two or three professional actors plus sundry extras, and twelve or (later) fifteen nonprofessional chorus members. Not only did the participants need to be outfitted with masks, costumes, and props, they also needed to be maintained during the period of rehearsal. The city provided the salaries of the actors and (probably) the musician; all remaining expenses, however, were met by a wealthy private citizen who was appointed, again by the eponymous archon, to underwrite the production as a *leitourgia* or public contribution. This circumstance suggests that the tragedies were understood to make a contribution to the public welfare on the same order as other significant public expenditures that were financed through *leitourgiai*: outfitting a warship, for example, or donating the prizes for an athletic competition.

The composition of the chorus, the judges, and the audience contributed to the democratic ambience. Ordinary Athenians (extraordinary, to be sure, in their skill at singing and dance) made up the chorus. Like many other Athenian institutions, the tragic festivals were competitive. Each year three tragedians vied for first prize, and the ranking was determined by a panel of judges chosen by lot, that favorite instrument of the democracy. The plays were viewed by an audience whose attendance, after a fund was established to offset the price of admission, was subsidized by the state. As a further inducement to attend, city business was suspended for the five days' duration of the festival.

A religious as well as a civic celebration, the festival of Dionysus attracted the same broad constituency that participated in the many other religious festivals that articulated the Athenian year. There is good reason to believe that the theater audience spanned the full spectrum of society: men, women, and children; aristocrats, commoners, and slaves; city dwellers and rustics; citizens, resident aliens, and foreigners (Csapo and Slater 286–87). The theater seems to have been inclusive of the entire population in a way that the assembly and the law court, those other great Athenian gathering places, were not. Accordingly, the plays presented at the festival of Dionysus offered an ideal context for civic self-examination. The setting afforded the dramatists a chance to address themselves to representatives of the entire population on ethical and political issues—often volatile and divisive—that concerned them both as individuals and as members of the community. If such was the dramatists' charge, however, they approached it circumspectly, for the tragedies did not reflect the contemporary world in any obvious manner. To the contrary, they featured gods and heroes as characters and were set in the remote past of the heroic age.

Dramatists had not always confined themselves to the mythical repertory. Early in the fifth century they experimented with tragedies centering on historical events of the recent past, but this practice proved too risky to be continued. When in 492 BCE Phrynichus presented his *Capture of Miletus*, which took as its subject the conquest only two years earlier of a city in Asia Minor allied to Athens, "the entire theater audience burst into tears, and Phrynichus was fined a thousand drachmas for reminding them of a calamity that struck close to home" (Herodotus 6.21.2). The practice of composing historical tragedies did not disappear overnight—indeed, the single specimen that survives today, Aeschylus's *Persians*, was produced in 472—but by the time Euripides composed *Hecuba* in the late 420s, mythical rather than historical plots had become the rule. It was not that the subject matter of these plays was any less germane to the contemporary situation but that the tragedians had devised a means of examining contemporary concerns at a safe remove, through the prism of the mythical past.

Once students discover that the tragedians were regarded as the political instructors of their fellow citizens and that the production of tragedies was sponsored and partially financed by the polis, they may tend, not unreasonably, to equate Greek tragedy with "state art" of the twentieth century and assume that the tragedians were expected to produce propaganda that would glorify the polis. A more sophisticated interpretation based on the same evidence identifies the tragedians as intellectual resisters who produced works that were at odds with their celebratory context and subversive of the city's values (Goldhill, "Great Dionysia" 114).

Each of these hypotheses contains a grain of truth. Euripides certainly composed his share of patriotic tragedies (for example, *Children of Heracles*, which celebrates Athens as the protector of helpless suppliants) and introduced patriotic passages into other plays (for example, the chorus's celebration of Athens in *Medea* [824–45]). *Hecuba* gives the lie, however, to the notion of the tragedian as propagandist. If the play does not overtly condemn the imperial policies of fifth-century Athens, it uses analogy to call them into question. Yet there is nothing underhanded or subversive about this critique; the playwright combines an admiring and affectionate evocation of Athenian institutions and principles with an urgent warning against abuse of power.

When viewed against the backdrop of its times, *Hecuba* at once confirms the political dimension of tragedy and illustrates the complexity of the instruction offered by the playwrights. Athens in the late 420s was a democracy at home but an empire abroad. The Greek cities that after the Persian Wars had joined with Athens to form the Delian league, a defensive alliance intended to deter any future threats emanating from Persia, subsequently experienced a gradual change of status. They found themselves transformed from Athens's allies into Athens's subjects; discontent ran high, and we hear of repeated attempts by cities to secede from the league. During the Peloponnesian War, in consequence, Athens often found itself waging war on two fronts: not only against its official adversaries, Sparta and its allies, but also against the restless cities of its own empire.

There is no question that *Hecuba* can profitably be read from a variety of perspectives—as centrally concerned, for example, with the stability of human nature (Nussbaum, *Fragility* 399), or with the quality of justice (Mossman 169–203). My discussion draws together text and context by examining how the play moves between past and present, between the heroic age and the fifth century. Beginning with the anachronisms that figure in the opening episodes of *Hecuba*, I suggest that the play's political import is not limited to isolated terms and concepts but encompasses issues of major consequence to Athens in the late 420s: consistency in public policy, the sacrifice of young lives to benefit the community, alternatives to triumphalism, and finally, the morality of power. To demonstrate the topicality of these issues for Euripides's contemporary audience I often have occasion to appeal to Thucydides's *History*, a work that constitutes an indispensable guide both to the historical events of the last decades of the fifth century and to the prevailing intellectual climate of those years.

One study has drawn attention to the pervasive but discreet use of anachronism in Greek tragedy, demonstrating how the tragedians unobtrusively integrate references to such technological innovations as writing or coinage into tragedy's heroic-age setting (Easterling, "Anachronism"). The anachronistic political references in *Hecuba*, however, are of a different order, for they are designed to be noticed and pondered. In the opening scenes of the play Euripides repeatedly introduces allusions to fifth-century Athenian ideas and institutions, thereby setting up a resonance with the contemporary context that reverberates throughout the play.

Anachronistic references abound in the chorus's account of the assembly of Greek soldiers, convened by the generals to devise a response to the ultimatum issued by Achilles's angry ghost. Having hastened forth in search of Hecuba, the chorus of Trojan women begins in good reportorial fashion by announcing the assembly's outcome: "They say that in the full assembly of the Greeks it has been resolved to make your daughter a sacrificial victim to Achilles" (107–09). Their language alludes to the standard Athenian "enactment formula" attested in fifth- and fourth-century inscriptions, which introduced decrees of the Athenian assembly with the phrase, "resolved by the council and the people" (Rhodes 64). The echo of technical language cannot be accidental, for paraphrases of the "enactment formula" turn up twice more with reference to the assembly's decision to sacrifice Polyxena (195, 220). Presumably Euripides aims to put the contemporary audience in mind of Athenian political procedure. At this juncture the anachronism serves primarily to promote narrative intelligibility, for the Trojan women's account of the assembly is highly compressed, and it omits or elides important information. For example, the women do not explain how Polyxena came to be designated as the Greeks' sacrificial offering—a not inconsequential detail if Hecuba and the audience are to assess the legitimacy of that decision.

Odysseus claims that Achilles demanded Polyxena and only Polyxena (305, 389-90); his implication is that the Greeks had no choice but to sacrifice the girl, since the directive issued from a superhuman source. It must be remembered, however, that Odysseus is characterized as a "glib and wily talker, a smooth-tongued demagogue" whose account of events is not necessarily reliable (131–32). Indeed, the chorus's narrative reveals that far from demanding a human sacrifice or specifying Polyxena as the victim, the ghost confined himself to a sarcastic question about the Greeks' neglect of his tomb (113–15). The crucial developments culminating in Polyxena's sacrifice seem to take place in the course of the Greek assembly. Initially the soldiers debate "offering a blood sacrifice to the tomb" (118–19), yet the resolution emerging from their conclave designates Polyxena as the chosen victim (108–10, 220–21). The anachronistic language in the chorus's account cues the spectators on how to span these narrative gaps; by drawing an analogy to Athenian assembly procedure, they can infer that Polyxena's name was introduced in a rider or amendment to the original motion once Odysseus had won the assembly over to the principle of human sacrifice. This inference in turn guides the audience in evaluating Polyxena's sacrifice, for it suggests that the girl's death was the result of rhetorical and parliamentary manipulation and that the ghost could conceivably have been mollified by other means.

Anachronisms can do more, however, than close the interstices of a narrative. A skillful playwright can deploy them to move in two directions; one temporal context is not sacrificed at the expense of the other, but each is deepened and enriched through juxtaposition (Pelling 217). An instance from the first episode of *Hecuba* illustrates how chronological violations can sharpen the audience's awareness of both the time frames adumbrated by the play, both the heroic age and the fifth century.

When Odysseus arrives to fetch Polyxena for the sacrifice he encounters Hecuba's fierce resistance. Toward the close of a lengthy speech combining abuse, argument, supplication, and warning, Hecuba implores him, "Go to the Argive army and talk them around, explaining that it is invidious to put to death women whom previously you did not kill after you had dragged them away from the altars, but to whom you showed pity" (287–90). When Hecuba asks Odysseus to "talk [the soldiers] around" to rescinding their earlier decision, she appears to have in mind the fifth-century procedure known as *anapsêphesis*, which allowed for bringing a decision of the Athenian assembly to a vote for a second time (Dover, *Greeks* 187). This was an unusual maneuver (it is mentioned only twice in Thucydides) that apparently carried some risk of opprobrium for the speaker who proposed it (cf. Thucydides 6.14). Such a move might be expected to focus attention not only on the specific decision under review but also on the principle of consistency in public policy. Whether such consistency is a virtue is a question that the play raises on two occasions, but without offering any definitive answer; indeed, Hecuba finds herself arguing on both sides of the issue. As we have seen, she pleads with Odysseus to reverse himself in the case of her daughter Polyxena and save the girl's life. In her later attempt to requite her son Polydorus, however, she urges Agamemnon with equal intensity to uphold the laws that have been set in place to protect victims of injustice (798–805).

If *Hecuba* was produced in or around 424, as evidence internal to the play suggests, the audience might well recall that consistency in public policy had recently surfaced as an issue in the Athenian assembly. Mytilene, a city on the island of Lesbos, revolted from the Athenian alliance in 427. After the insurrection was put down the Athenian assembly voted to kill all the men of Mytilene and enslave the women and children; subsequently, however, the citizens had second thoughts and convened another assembly to reconsider their decision. Thucydides portrays the Athenian demagogue Cleon, who represents the Athenian hard-liners, as arguing on the occasion of the second assembly that "bad laws which are never changed are better for a city than good ones that have no authority" (3.37.3; unless otherwise specified, all translations from Thucydides are from Crawley), while his adversary, Diodotus, advocated a more flexible and pragmatic approach. On this occasion the *anapsêphesis* was successful; the assembly rescinded its earlier decision and instead of punishing the Mytileneans without discrimination voted to put to death only those implicated in the revolt.

Not only the procedure implicit in Hecuba's words but also their substance would strike a familiar chord with Athenian spectators. Hecuba attempts to persuade Odysseus that the Greeks have no justification for killing Polyxena now, since they had already spared her life at the time of the fall of Troy (287–90). Her more general point is that prisoners of war should not be put to death. This is one of a number of passages in the play bearing on the conquerors' treatment of the conquered. Elsewhere Polyxena describes the life of slavery that would be her alternative to sacrificial death, a life characterized by demeaning manual labor and sexual humiliation (357–67). When Agamemnon unexpectedly offers Hecuba her freedom, his words reveal that the Trojans' enslavement is ascribable not to impersonal fate but to the whim of the conquerors (754–55). Finally, Polymestor lays bare the rationale for killing the male children of the defeated enemy: it is a measure intended to preclude any resurgence of power by the conquered and eliminate any possibility of future vengeance (1138–39).

The play's portrayal of the Trojans is sympathetic throughout, and this tilt in dramatic perspective encourages the audience to question the Greek conquerors' harsh treatment of the vanquished. But why should Euripides choose to raise this issue in this particular play? *Hecuba* is set, after all, in Homeric times, when it was taken for granted that the victors would kill the male inhabitants of a conquered city and sell the women and children into slavery (*Iliad* 4.237–39). There is evidence to suggest, however, that in the 420s the treatment of the conquered was a live issue for the Athenians, that during the Peloponnesian War Athenian policy toward defeated populations was not fixed but fluid, inconsistent, and evolving. At Mytilene, as we have seen, the Homeric precedent was adopted only to be rescinded; indeed, Thucydides characterizes the punishment that initially threatened the Mytileneans as "strange, unusual" (*allokoton*; 3.49.4). A few years later Thyrea in the Peloponnese suffered a different fate; on taking the town in 424, the Athenians dealt with the residents according to their place of origin. Some hailed from the island of Cythera; these were assessed four talents' tribute but were permitted to remain on their land. Other residents, however, came originally from the island of Aegina, and these the Athenians put to death "on account of the old inveterate feud" between Athens and Aegina (4.56.5).

The principle of differentiated treatment of the conquered, variously observed at Mytilene and Thyrea, was abandoned in the case of Scione. When Scione in Chalcidice revolted from the Athenian alliance in 423, Cleon, who will be remembered as the hard-liner in the debate over Mytilene, successfully moved a decree stipulating death for all the inhabitants (4.122.6). Not only did this penalty target rebels and loyalists without discrimination, but it was passed prospectively, before the Athenians had even invested Scione, let alone conquered it. Moreover, the decree was subsequently put into effect without afterthoughts or modifications: Thucydides reports that in 421 "Athens succeeded in reducing Scione, put the adult males to death, and making slaves of the women and children, gave the land for the Plataeans to live in" (5.32.1). If we take these incidents together, it seems possible to discern a gradual hardening of Athenian policy with respect to conquered populations. Yet public opinion may well have remained divided on this issue, as we know it was in the case of Mytilene. Euripides's presentation of the aftermath of conquest in *Hecuba* would accordingly have elicited powerful and diverse reactions from the spectators.

The discussion thus far has suggested that *Hecuba* carries on a political dialogue with the present, without compromising its integrity as a drama set in the heroic age, on the level of terminology (for example, the Athenian "enactment formula"), political procedure (for example, *anapsêphesis*), and public policy (for example, the treatment of the conquered). As we shall see, the dialogue with the present is extended through references to the cherished democratic principles of equality before the law and freedom, and finally, it is sustained at the play's thematic level.

When Hecuba begs Odysseus to use his influence with the assembly on Polyxena's behalf, her penultimate argument includes a twofold anachronism: "In your country there is established a law (*nomos*), applying equally (*isos*) to free men and slaves, concerning the shedding of blood" (291–92). Not only does she here allude to fifth-century Athenian legislation on homicide, but the collocation of *nomos* and *isos* evokes *isonomia* or "equality before the law," a cherished Athenian political principle that guaranteed all Athenian citizens equal access to the political process and the impartial protection of the laws. Technically, of course, Polyxena as a non-Athenian, a woman, and a slave has no claim to *isonomia*, and Odysseus does not dignify Hecuba's argument with a response. But if Hecuba's attempt to extend an Athenian citizen's privilege to a wider constituency does not convince Odysseus, it may well have enlisted the sympathy of the spectators and inspired some to question the standards of justice prevailing in fifth-century Athens: *isonomia* within the polis, but the politics of power without.

Freedom or *eleutheria* is another principle that had become a byword for Athenian democracy and that is insistently evoked in the play. Polyxena takes satisfaction in banishing the light of day "from [her] eyes while they are still free" (367) and insists on kneeling "freely" before her executioner "so that [she] may die a free woman" (550). Although Polyxena is concerned to assert her personal status as a free individual rather than as a slave, her language might also put the audience in mind of the political freedom that had emerged as crucial to the Athenian self-image in the wake of the Persian Wars (Hall 193). Indeed, when Hecuba at a later point in the play makes the claim that "no man is [truly] free" (864), she puts an overtly Athenian and political gloss on her assertion: "Either he is enslaved to money or to fate, or the city's masses or its written laws prevent him from acting according to his inclination" (865–67). It is characteristic of the play's political complexity that the concept of "freedom" is invoked in contexts that encourage the audience to consider not only its positive associations but also its ambiguities and limits. For despite her brave words Polyxena is dying an involuntary death as a slave, and as Hecuba points out, the very democratic safeguards that are afforded Athenian citizens also constrain their individual freedom of action.

The political aspect of *Hecuba* extends to the thematic level. The first half of the play, which concerns the death of Polyxena, is one of those sacrifice actions that figure so frequently in the work of Euripides. Generally, although not invariably, the sacrifice involves the voluntary death of a young woman, and it may well be asked why this theme held such attraction for the playwright. It was not because human sacrifice had ever been the norm in Greece or because there was any possibility of its being practiced in the future (Henrichs, "Human Sacrifice" 232–34). Rather, the playwright seems to have used the motif of voluntary self-sacrifice as a vehicle for investigating—in vivid, powerful, but safely distanced form—"the conflicting demands of the state and the private individual" (Wilkins, "State" 177). This was a topic of obvious significance to any city that, like fifth-century Athens, found itself perpetually at war, for a community at war necessarily demands the sacrifice not, to be sure, of its young women but of its young men. The displacement of sex and situation allows the playwright to explore this recurrent and troubling demand in a way that is pointed without being provocative or seditious.

The analogy between the sacrificial death of young women and the death in battle of young men is not a matter of speculation; the link is drawn explicitly in a fragment of a lost Euripidean tragedy. In *Erechtheus* (apparently contemporary with *Hecuba*), the queen of Athens assents to her daughter's sacrifice as a means of saving the city. She explains her reasoning as follows:

> It is for this that we bear children, to safeguard our altars and our home-
> land. The city as a whole has just one name, but its inhabitants are many;
> how can it be right for me to destroy them, when it is possible to give
> one girl to die on behalf of all? [. . .] If our family had a crop of male
> children instead of females, and the flame of war had the city in its grip,
> would I refrain from sending them forth to battle out of fear that they
> would perish?   (Nauck, fragment 360.14–25)

Here a mother speaks for her daughter. Other Euripidean sacrificial victims (for instance, Heracles's daughter in *Children of Heracles*) speak for themselves, carefully expounding the connection between their own death and the anticipated benefit to the community. Polyxena is anomalous, to be sure, in affirming her sacrifice as a private rather than a patriotic choice; she embraces her death not to save her people but to avoid the degradations of slavery. Polyxena's circumstances preclude her from describing her sacrifice as a civic benefit: since she is a prisoner of war who is being offered to the ghost of Achilles to assuage his anger at the Greeks, the community that will profit from her death is not her own but that of the enemy.

For the most part, however, Polyxena adheres to the typical reasoning of Euripidean sacrificial victims. Conscious of her status as the sister of Hector and other brave heroes (361) and presumably anxious to emulate their example, she equates her own readiness for sacrifice with the alacrity that was expected of soldiers going into battle. "If I am not willing to die," she explains to Hecuba, "I shall appear a coward, a woman who clings to life" (347–48). Polyxena here draws the standard connection between the sacrificial death of a young woman and the death in battle of young men: like a brave soldier, she accepts her death and even welcomes it (346–47). Offsetting Polyxena's stoutheartedness, however, and providing another perspective on her choice, is her mother's unyielding resistance to the sacrifice. It is true that Hecuba appears to achieve a measure of resignation after the fact, finding a measure of comfort in Talthybius's account of her daughter's noble end. The Greek messenger concludes his narrative by eulogizing Polyxena as a woman "of extraordinary courage and supreme spirit" (579–80) and Hecuba herself as "the most blessed of all women in your children, as well as the most unfortunate" (581–82), and Hecuba responds that his account has assuaged the worst of her anguish (590–91). Her formulation makes it clear, however, that a significant residue of grief subsists, as it must similarly have subsisted for the relatives of the soldiers who died in the Peloponnesian War. It is these bereaved relatives who constitute the audience of Thucydides's Funeral Oration and to whom Pericles has the temerity to suggest that a noble death is no cause for sorrow: "Comfort, therefore, not condolence, is what I have to offer to the parents of the dead who may be here. Numberless are the chances to which, as they know, the life of man is subject; but fortunate indeed are they who draw for their lot a death so glorious as that which has caused your mourning" (2.44.1). There is no telling how this senti-

ment was received; even Pericles admits that his words sound harsh and rebar-
bative (2.44.2). Both the dramatist and the historian draw attention to the
dilemma created by the differing valuations that individuals, families, and the
community place on a single human life, and both recognize the problem as
insoluble.

The political tonality of *Hecuba* is not confined to the episodes but also
makes itself felt in the choral odes, never more clearly than at the close of the
second *stasimon*. The strophe and antistrophe identify the judgment of Paris
as the source of the Trojans' misfortunes. In the epode, the chorus of Trojan
women describes the consequences of Paris's choice: "The result was war and
bloodshed and ruin for my home. But there also weeps near the fair-flowing
Eurotas River some Spartan girl, sobbing in her house, while the mother, now
that her sons have perished, beats her hand against her grey head and tears at
her cheeks, making her nails bloody with the flaying" (650–56).

The passage is striking in its evocativeness: the playwright makes vivid the
abstract notion of loss by embodying it in two individuals whose physical man-
ifestations of grief the audience is made to hear and see. Less immediately
striking but equally significant is the identity of the illustrative individuals, for
with the "also" of the second sentence the ode's focus shifts from the suffering
of the Trojans to the suffering of their enemies. The change of direction conveys two points simultaneously. The first is that the enemy too has human connections; the Trojan chorus recognizes that every Greek soldier who died at
Troy has a wife, sister, or mother waiting at home to grieve his loss. This observation is in itself neither startling nor unique; Homer, for example, notes that
the death of the Greek commander Protesilaos left his wife "with both her
cheeks torn" (*Iliad* 2.700) in the same traditional gesture of mourning that is
described by Euripides. Yet the observation gains power from its context, as it
juxtaposes grief experienced at Sparta to grief experienced at Troy. Furthermore, by identifying his two exemplary mourners as Spartan Euripides
reminds his audience that the suffering of wartime is not confined to one side.
It spares neither losers nor winners, neither Trojans nor Greeks; from the perspective of Euripides's contemporary audience, it encompasses both Athenians
and Spartans. There can be no differentiation, then, when it comes to mourning the dead; both sides share the experience of grief and loss. Once again, the
same conclusion is to be found in the *Iliad*, most remarkably in book 24 with
its meeting of Priam and Achilles, archenemies who discover a sense of companionship in their mutual bereavement. It is an insight that contrasts with the
rhetoric of battlefield exhortations, which typically pits "us" against "them" and
distinguishes sharply between victors and vanquished. In an example of the
battlefield perspective, Homer's Agamemnon rallies his brother against the
Trojans: "O brother Menelaus, why do you care so much for these people? Did
you in your house get treated very well by the Trojans? Not a single one of
them must escape sheer destruction at our hands, not even the boychild that
the mother carries in her womb, but let all of Troy's people perish together,

uncared for and unmourned" (*Iliad* 6.55–60). In Euripides's play the Greek
commanders adopt the same perspective as they exhort their soldiers to get on
with the task of taking Troy: "O men of Greece, when, oh when, will you sack
Troy's high citadel and go home?" (*Hecuba* 929–32). By incorporating both
points of view into their works, the humanitarian and the militaristic, the epic
poet and the dramatist seem to invite the audience to compare the two and
adjudicate between them.

The final topic that draws together the world of the play and the world of the
audience is that of the responsible exercise of power. A major theme of *Hecuba*
is the obligation of the conquerors to act in accordance with justice, an obligation that they flout at their peril (282–83, 798–805, 850–53, 1233–35). The
most succinct expression of this theme is contained in Hecuba's warning to
Odysseus: "Those who have power should not exercise it in the wrong way, nor,
when they are fortunate, should they assume that their fortune will last forever" (282–83). Hecuba here combines the concept of moral responsibility
with the traditional Greek principle of the mutability of destiny (see Herodotus
1.32): she cautions Odysseus that the Greeks should rule with discretion now
so as not to incur reprisals in the future, when their fortune has shifted and
their former victims have them at their mercy. The end of the play seems to
echo Hecuba's warning, for a premonition of change is built into the closing
lines. The wind that is rising as the play draws to an end foretells the Greeks'
reversal of fortune. It will enable them to leave Thrace behind, to be sure, but
only to shipwreck them on the high seas or to carry them to troubled destinies
in Greece (see Kovacs, *Heroic Muse* 110).

The Athenian spectators must have listened attentively to Hecuba's warning,
for the maintenance of their empire required them to ponder the relation of
power and justice. This relation is a frequent theme of Thucydidean politicians. Defending Athenian imperialism before the Spartan assembly before
the outbreak of the Peloponnesian War, Thucydides's Athenian ambassadors
maintain that Athens has ruled with moderation, adding that "praise is due to
all who, if not so superior to human nature as to refuse dominion, yet respect
justice more than their position compels them to do" (1.75.4). In contrast Pericles, speaking to the Athenian assembly, confronts his fellow citizens with the
blunt warning that "what you hold is, to speak somewhat plainly, a tyranny; to
take it perhaps was wrong, but to let it go is unsafe" (2.63.2). One could multiply Thucydidean examples, but all point to the same conclusion: the Athenians sitting in the theater of Dionysus would have recognized the problem of
reconciling power with justice as pertinent not only to *Hecuba* but also to
themselves.

Once alerted to the political aspects of *Hecuba*, students will undoubtedly
cease to envisage the tragedians as the designated spokesmen of the establishment. To the contrary, they may evince astonishment that a dramatist whose
productions were sponsored by the polis was permitted to hold up to such per-

sistent scrutiny ideas and institutions that the spectators presumably held dear. Three factors help explain this license. The first is the allusiveness of the political commentary. As we have seen, Euripides in common with the other tragedians eschews direct references to contemporary events; he writes about the heroic age and leaves it to the members of the audience to make the requisite connections. The second factor bears particularly on *Hecuba* and other Trojan War tragedies: all reflect the influence and atmosphere of the *Iliad*, whose focus on the costs of war and critique of the heroic ethos constitutes a powerful precedent (see Mossman 22–26). Spectators would not be surprised that the play shares with the epic poem not only the same milieu and the same cast of characters but also the same tendency to call into question prevailing verities and assumptions. The final factor that helps explain the dramatist's boldness is the institution of free speech (*parrhêsia*), like *isonomia* and *eleutheria* a privilege enjoyed by Athenian citizens that became a byword of the democracy (see Plato, *Republic* 557b4–5). This principle seems to have been generally extended to the dramatic poets, although there were significant exceptions: Phrynichus was fined, as we have seen, for his *Capture of Miletus*, and Aristophanes was prosecuted for denigrating Athens in his comedy *Babylonians* (Aristophanes, *Acharnians* 377–82). There was, moreover, a prevailing attitude of tolerance toward the critical tone characteristic of traditional didactic poetry (Dover, *Greeks* 153), an attitude that the dramatists could presumably count on in their turn. Fifth-century audiences seem to have accepted that tragedy would explore controversial issues of the day and may even have regarded such questioning as intrinsic to the genre.

A recent study objects to such an account of tragedy's role as itself anachronistic, arguing that poetic instruction as the Greeks conceived it was "straightforward and unproblematic" rather than open-ended and questioning (Griffin, "Social Function" 49). This description certainly fits, for example, the archaic poet Tyrtaeus, whose elegies encapsulate simple directives for virtuous conduct. Not only, however, was Tyrtaeus working in a different genre with its own distinctive patterns of form and thought, but he was also a Spartan; Spartans and Athenians held notoriously different views on the uses of language and on the relation between "words" and "deeds"—that favorite polarity of Greek thought (see Parry). The difference is set forth by Thucydides's Pericles. Comparing the laconic Spartans to the Athenians with their passion for the cut and thrust of disputation, Pericles explains: "We do not consider discussion an impediment to action, but rather consider it harmful not to take instruction in advance by means of discussion before proceeding to do what is necessary" (2.40.2; my trans.). Discussion was both informal and formal and unfolded in many different venues: in the marketplace, in the lawcourts, in the citizens' council, and in the assembly. If we judge by the tragedies that survive, an important part of the "instruction in advance" that Pericles considered indispensable to effective action also took place in the theater of Dionysus.

On Reading Euripides's *Hippolytos*

Ian Storey, Martin Boyne, and Arlene Allan

There are nine and sixty ways of constructing tribal lays,
And every single one of them is right.
          —Kipling, "In the Neolithic Age"

Aristophanes of Byzantion calls Euripides's *Hippolytos* "one of his best plays" (Halleran, *Euripides:* Hippolytus 62–63), and critics have made it and *Bacchae* the exemplars of Euripides's work, displaying as they do his keen interest in psychology, the gods, and the characters of women. *Hippolytos* is a tragedy that often appears in anthologies of ancient drama, in classical literature syllabuses, in surveys of Greek social attitudes, and even in courses on comparative literature. In this essay we present various ways of reading this play, readings that will differ depending on whether it is read in the original Greek or in translation, in courses on literature or drama and theater or social history. We include in our discussion textual criticism, the text as literary unity, genre and intertextuality, drama and ritual, structuralism, the psychoanalytical, and text as theater. Each approach is equally valid. The choice depends on the background of the teacher and the students and on the nature and goals of the course.

Textual Criticism and Commentary

In the time-honored philological tradition, the text of a play is a quarry to be excavated, a manuscript tradition for the editor to establish, a collection of cruces to be solved, to determine as far as possible what Euripides actually wrote. For the commentator it is an aggregation of problem passages to annotate and explicate, adduce parallels and weigh conflicting views. Students approaching *Hippolytos* in this way will profit greatly from James Diggle's Oxford Classical Texts series; from W. S. Barrett's classic commentary and the more recent one of Michael Halleran (the Aris and Phillips edition, written with the Greekless reader in mind); and from the textual studies of David Kovacs (*Heroic Muse*; "Shame"), Godfrey Bond ("Chorus"), and Alan Sommerstein. There is no shortage of major cruces for the student of the text. When Phaidra exclaims that "there are two kinds, one not bad, but the other a burden on the house," is she talking about "pleasures" (*hedonai*; 383) or "respect" (*aidos*; 385)? If the latter, how can *aidos* be both good and bad (see Conacher, *Euripidean Drama* 54–55; Craik; Kovacs, *Heroic Muse*; C. Segal, "Shame")? The received text at 1102–50 suggests that here we may have a very unusual choral ode with a subchorus of male hunters singing in response to and perhaps together with the main chorus of servant women. And finally who are the "three destroyed by Love" (1403)?

But most students and instructors are going to meet the play in a course on literature or theater and will want to read it as a unified text. Here we encounter the New Criticism, reading the play "as a self-sufficient object in itself" (Goldhill, "Modern Critical Approaches" 329) with attention to the structure and form of the play, to its ironies and tensions. Thus students can explore the characters and interactions of the three (four?) main characters (Knox, "*Hippolytus*"; Winnington-Ingram, "*Hippolytus*"); the great tension in Euripides between gods and men—"You should be wiser than men, being Gods" (120; see Knox, *Hippolytus*; Conacher, *Euripidean Drama* 27–55; Hartigan, *Ambiguity* 37–67); the theme of sexuality and gender (Burnett, "Hearth"; Rabinowitz, *Anxiety* 155–69; Zeitlin, "Power"); the play as a tragedy of human knowledge (Luschnig, *Time*; C. Segal, *Euripides* 89–153); the play as a commentary on the Socratic dictum, "no-one does wrong knowingly" (Snell 47–69; Michelini, *Euripides* 297–309); or the play as the interaction of speech and silence (Knox, "*Hippolytus*"; Goff). One may focus on key words and concepts, such as *aidos* ("reverence," "respect"); *sophrosyne*, which will be translated as anything from "virtue" to "moderation" to "chastity"; and *semnos*, with its positive ("aweful") and negative ("arrogant") meanings (Conacher, *Euripides and the Sophists* 26–41; Halleran, *Euripides: Hippolytus* 43–49; C. Segal "Shame"), and on the rich imagery of the play with powerful repeated images of water, escape, animals and the hunt, and a polarization of indoors and outdoors (Burnett, "Hearth"; C. Segal, "Tragedy"; Zeitlin, "Power"). *Hippolytos* features the great Athenian hero Theseus in an atypical role, deceived father rather than cultural archetype, and comparison with *Herakles, Suppliant Women*, and Sophokles's *Oedipus at Kolonos* provides an interesting look at this figure and allows the student a link with contemporary Athens and the audience (Gregory 51–84; Mills 186–221; H. Walker 113–27). Theseus and Hippolytos also lead the student into the crucial father-son motif (Rabinowitz, *Anxiety* 173-88).

Unlike "problem plays" such as *Alkestis, Bacchae*, and *Orestes, Hippolytos* will not spark great disagreements about the overall interpretation of the play, but certain useful debates may occur. For instance, how do we take the characters themselves? Does Phaidra "protest too much"? Is Hippolytos a prig whose devotion to Artemis is symptomatic of an unhealthy repression (Dimock; Griffin, "Characterization" 137–38; Sale)? Is his opening scene with the huntsmen (58–120) to be played straight or off the wall? Does Euripides intend a real tension between two unpleasant anthropomorphic deities (Aphrodite, Artemis) and the realities that they represent? Here structure may help, since a double-ring composition may be observed: false Love (1–57) + true Chastity (58–120) :: true Love (1268–83) + false Chastity (1284–1465). More than one critic has called attention to the final act of forgiveness between father and son, an act impossible for gods (Knox, "*Hippolytus*" 31). The ending can also be usefully debated, with its apparent irony that "unwedded maids before the day of marriage will cut their hair in your honor" (1425), a seemingly inappropriate *time* for one who was devoted to Chastity (Burnett, "Hearth"; Rabinowitz, *Anxiety* 155–69). The best general studies and one's recommended first reading are those by Bernard Knox ("*Hippolytus*"), Desmond Conacher (*Euripidean Drama*), and David Kovacs (*Heroic Muse* 22–77).

The "Potiphar's Wife" Theme

A more particular way of looking at *Hippolytos* is as an instance of the repeated literary motif known as the "Potiphar's Wife" theme. This ancient theme with Eastern roots goes as far back as the "Tale of the Two Brothers" (c. 1500 BC) and is best known in the story of Joseph and the wife of Potiphar in Genesis 39. In its full form the story involves these elements: an older man and his wife, an attractive and virtuous younger male who is usually a stranger in the older man's country and subject to his authority, the love (or lust) of the woman for the younger male, her advances and his rejection because of virtue and respect, her fear of disclosure and subsequent false accusation to her husband that the younger male tried or succeeded at raping her, the punishment inflicted by the older man on the younger man, the rescue of the younger male often by miraculous means, the revelation of the truth, and punishment of the woman. Euripides used this motif often in his early plays. It appeared in his lost *Peleus*, *Phoinix*, and *Stheneboia* (of this last play, produced probably in 430, we have the first thirty lines, which show startling parallels with the extant *Hippolytos*, not to mention the first *Hippolytos*). It quickly becomes clear that in the second *Hippolytos* Euripides is inverting the Potiphar's Wife theme. The play is set in Hippolytos's home (Troizen), not in Theseus's Athens. The older woman is in love against her will and will die to protect her reputation (400–21); the younger man refuses, not out of virtue, but because he hates women. Jasper Griffin notes that the two great encounters in this theme are missing in our play: the one between the woman and the youth and the one between the woman and her husband ("Characterization" 132). Phaidra dies before rather than after she is found out, and in this story alone the young man dies.

We turn now to the matter of the first version and the concept of intertextuality, or "text talking to text," for both author and ancient audience would have had the first *Hippolytos* very much in their minds. One of the most important words in the study of Greek tragedy is "version," and here perhaps more than anywhere else in Greek drama, version and authorial intent loom large. Students can usefully explore two problems: exactly what can we say about the lost *Hippolytos*, and why did Euripides rewrite the play this way?

The first *Hippolytos* seems to have been an orthodox Potiphar's Wife play, with an aggressive and lustful Phaidra and an innocent Hippolytos (see the comments of Aristophanes about *pornai* ["prostitutes"] such as Phaidra [*Theseus* 497; *Frogs* 1043–54]). Only forty-three lines and various ancient testimonia remain; these fragments have been collected by W. S. Barrett (15–45) and Michael Halleran (25–37; Aris ed.) in their editions of the play, with good critical comment by each. Other recommended studies of the first *Hippolytos* and of Sophokles's *Phaidra* include those by S. R. Cavan; Sophie Mills (195–207);

Bruno Snell (23–46); and T. B. L. Webster (*Tragedies* 64–76). An interesting exercise with a good class is to take the material as presented in the Aris and Phillips edition by Halleran and see what can be gleaned from the individual fragments. Note fragment 443, which, if spoken by Phaidra in the prologue, suggests that there was no deity to open the play; fragment 440 (who would call Theseus by name and tell him not to believe a woman?); and fragment 446, where the chorus sing of the honors of Hippolytos, since a god at the end is surely necessary to reveal those honors.

In assessing the reason for the revision, most critics accept the statement of Aristophanes of Byzantion, "that which was unseemly and worthy of condemnation has been corrected in this play" (Halleran, *Euripides:* Hippolytus 62–63), but this description hardly fits the Euripides that we know, who like Shaw or Wilde would not have been worried by bad press. We should rather conclude that Euripides took the unusual step of revising the play because he thought he could "write a play on that age-old theme which would be better" (Griffin, "Characterization" 132), a play in which Phaidra meets neither her husband nor the man she loves, a play in which the characters and their psychology are reversed from their usual presentation. If, as Griffin ("Characterization" 130) and others assume, Sophokles's *Phaidra* lies between the two versions by Euripides, then the second *Hippolytos* would be talking to that play also. Cavan reaches the attractive conclusion that the second *Hippolytos* was Euripides's last go at the Potiphar's Wife theme (40).

Drama, Myth, and Ritual

Myth and ritual theorists have attempted to answer the difficult question of the origin of tragedy by locating the origins of drama in ritual. Drama is the enacted myth that explains or accounts for the ritual itself. Given that *Hippolytos* concludes with the establishment of a cult ritual, the play can be read as a performance of the etiological myth that sustains the historical practice. While this approach to *Hippolytos* can lead to a much broader investigation of "drama as ritual," a more directed study of the play can be accomplished through the "ritual in drama" approach (Friedrich, "Everything" 269–70). Reading *Hippolytos* with the knowledge of the rituals performed by and for its original audience in the city beyond the theater can provide students with insights into both the religious consciousness of that audience and the ways in which ritual elements operate within the drama itself. The secondary material on tragedy and ritual is enormous, but a preliminary guide would include the following topics and authors: drama and ritual, Rainer Friedrich; weddings, funerals, and tragedy, Rush Rehm (*Marriage*), Richard Seaford ("Tragic Wedding," "Structural Problem," *Reciprocity*); funerary rituals and tragedy, Margaret Alexiou, Gail Holst-Warhaft; supplication, John Gould ("Hiketeia"); maturation rituals, Susan Cole, Jean-Pierre Vernant and Pierre Vidal-Naquet; Greek religion generally, Walter Burkert.

Within the play world of *Hippolytos* there are a number of allusions to ritual proceedings with which the audience would have had first-hand experience, including, but not limited to, the rituals of maturation, marriage, and death. In developing an appreciation of the maturation rituals of the young men and women of fifth-century Athens, students are able to gain a deeper understanding of the significance of Hippolytos's refusal to partake in these rituals for himself and for the community. Likewise, an introduction to marriage and funerary ritual will enhance students' sensitivity to the many allusions both to rituals in the play and to their contextual significance. For instance, knowing that the song sung by the double chorus of men and women at Hippolytos's exit (1102–50) takes its inspiration from the processional hymns sung at both weddings and funerals enables students to see Hippolytos's departure as imitating two opposed but symbolically similar rites of passage.

Other rituals and ritualized elements are also to be found in this play. Oaths and curses have real force both within and outside the play world as powerful speech acts with divinely sanctioned consequences. An oath, in fact, is a curse on oneself for failure to fulfill the promise made between parties with the gods as witnesses. Breaking his oath would create a no-win situation for Hippolytos in that, while he would exonerate himself before his father, he would be shown to be "base" before the gods and thus subject to their punishment. A further ritual form appears in the opening of the choral passage (525–29), the hymn of praise to a god—in this instance, Eros and Aphrodite. Familiarity with the praise-prayer formula will permit the students to recognize where Hippolytos's address to the goddess (61–87) varies from the standard model and thus alerts them to potential inconsistencies in Hippolytos's self-characterization.

The ritual of supplication is used to great effect in *Hippolytos*. Because this ritual is sanctioned by Zeus, a failure to honor a suppliant's appeal could have dire consequences for the supplicated. Understanding the dynamics involved in supplication will enable students to recognize how its use in this play (324–35, 605–15) perverts the ritual and to see the significance of these perversions for the dramatic action.

Structuralism

In fifth-century Athens rituals were thought to be essential in the maintenance of order within the polis and between gods and men. If a ritualist approach to *Hippolytos* enriches students' understanding of the dramatic action, a structuralist reading will deepen it by revealing a whole complex of dyadic oppositions that structure the thought world of the fifth-century Athenian, a complex of polarities that the rituals themselves were designed to both mediate between and mitigate against. For structuralist approaches generally, see Charles Segal (*Interpreting*), Jean-Pierre Vernant and Pierre Vidal-Naquet; as applied to *Hippolytos*, see Anne Burnett ("Hearth"), Barbara Goff, Simon Goldhill (*Reading* 117–39), Segal ("Pentheus"), and Froma Zeitlin

("Power"). A structuralist approach can follow two paths: the anthropological or the linguistic.

An anthropologically informed structuralist reading will engage students in the task of identifying both the various polarities that constitute "reality" for the audience and producers of the play and the patterns that they form. Additionally, the students can be asked to "map" these patterns within the various codes—dietary, sexual, familial, and spatial—through which that culture constructs its world.

First, to identify some of the terms that form half of the dyadic pairs, students can be asked to describe Hippolytos as he is first presented in the play. This task will yield terms such as *male, young, hunter, pure,* and so on. Students can then be asked to provide appropriate opposing terms (*female, old, city dweller, impure*). As they proceed further, some of these oppositions will not prove to be as important to the action as others are. When this task is performed for Phaidra as well, certain polarities will start to emerge: culture-nature, civilized-wild, male-female, *polis-oikos* ("city"-"house"), exterior-interior, public-private, visible-concealed, speech-silence.

With the list set out in this way, students are usually quick to recognize that the pairs can be seen as gendered constructs that privilege the spheres of male activity over those associated with the female. But for both Phaidra and Hippolytos this gendering becomes problematic as, over the course of the play, each comes to be associated with the terms that normally belong to their sexual opposite. This change in subject position threatens the civilized order of both the *polis* and the *oikos* and thus necessitates some form of corrective action. Additionally, from the structuralist perspective, these inversions reveal the underlying tensions and contradictions that must be suppressed, denied, or concealed for the "reality" produced through the polarities to be maintained.

In Phaidra's case, the contradictions that she embodies appear to be resolved when she disappears from public view back into the interior of the house, permanently silenced by death. Her last act before dying, however, reactivates the tensions by giving her a "voice" that speaks beyond the grave. The letter that shouts its message (877) combines with the mute testimony of her corpse (971)—which is also made visible again to the public (810, 905)—to condemn Hippolytos before his father. Final resolution of the tensions revealed through both Phaidra and Hippolytos is ultimately achieved through the institution of the commemorative ritual declared by Artemis. It is Phaidra's love, and not her "manly" resistance to it, that is to be remembered, while Hippolytos himself will be commemorated as a victim of that love and honored for his nobility in the face of an untimely death. Through his deathbed recognition of Aphrodite's powers, his farewell to Artemis, and his forgiveness of his father, Hippolytos moves from being a threatening youth on the margins of society to being the honored recipient of a ritual cult that marks the rite of passage of as yet "untamed" maidens (1425) into adulthood and marriage.

This simplified application of a structuralist approach to the tragedy of

Hippolytos brings to the attention of students the complexity of the play and of the culture that produced it. Moreover, it can lead to a more critical appreciation of the "structures" that support their own culture and to a consideration of the ways in which knowledge itself becomes a cultural product.

Psychoanalysis

Another, and currently very popular, approach to Greek tragedy is the psychoanalytical. Based largely on the theories of Freud and Jung, psychoanalysis is most readily connected to ancient literature through Freud's (in)famous Oedipus complex. But there is much more to this approach, and most of it is popular, especially among readers of younger generations, mainly because psychoanalytical approaches to literature tend to deal with secrets and lies, with dark and distant pasts, and—most frequently—with sex. Psychoanalysis opens up the characters to reveal what lies beneath their surface, allowing the reader to infer from the character's words and actions things that are not explicitly stated in the text. Not all of Euripides's plays are suitable for psychoanalytical treatment, but *Hippolytos* is certainly one of the best. Along with *Bacchae* this play has possibly received the most attention from psychoanalytically oriented critics, no doubt because, like Pentheus, Hippolytos is a complex figure whose traits and behavior make us question what is going on inside his head. While most of the main characters in the *Hippolytos* could be studied psychoanalytically, we focus here on the title character as a model.

William Sale and Charles Segal are the best-known exponents of the psychoanalytical approaches to Greek tragedy. Sale, in his work on Euripides, focuses on existential psychoanalysis, while Segal adds more Jungian and Freudian elements in his work. Existential psychoanalysis relies heavily on the theories of Heidegger, which, when applied to *Hippolytos*, reveal a title character whose *Dasein* (Heidegger's term for "being-in-the-world") involves complete devotion to Artemis and the total exclusion of Aphrodite. Sale tells us that sex, or sexuality, is an "existential," an "ontological" component of the world (8); Hippolytos's rejection of this existential defines his sense of "being" in the world that he has carved out for himself. An examination of the text confirms what kind of world Hippolytos wants. He tells his servant that he worships Aphrodite "from a long way off" (103), which is clearly what irks Cypris, not his devotion to Artemis (20–22). Later, in his tirade against women (616), he tells the Nurse of the wickedness of women and that he will "never have enough of hating" them (664). And in his response to Theseus's accusations, he affirms his virginity, noting that "Save what I have heard or what I have seen in pictures, / I'm ignorant of the deed" (1004–06). Clearly, then, our Hippolytos prefers to exist without sex and without women.

An existentialist would call Hippolytos's rejection of sexual desires "neurotic" (Sale 54). This is where the more traditional psychoanalytical approaches blend with the existential. As Sale tells us of Hippolytos, "to feel sexual desire would

entail a significant expansion of his world—would entail growing up" (52).
Indeed, Hippolytos acts like a prepubescent who has yet to develop an interest
in girls; as Goldhill says, Hippolytos is unnatural in rejecting what should be the
normal course of adolescent development (*Reading* 117–36). He is repressing
normal sexual impulses in what Segal calls his "failure to confront the reality of
adult sexuality" ("Pentheus" 278). A Freudian approach would wonder if something in Hippolytos's past led to this situation, and any analysis of Hippolytos
must consider his family background. As the bastard son of the Amazon
woman, one of his father's many affairs, Hippolytos must have had anything but
a stable life. In fact, Sale suggests that Hippolytos might even despise his
father's own sexuality and, as a result, his illegitimate birth. These feelings cause
him to hate women as he does, perhaps because he associates women with wan-
tonness and lust; after all, he wants someone to "teach them to be chaste" (667).
At the same time, he probably feels cheated by Theseus of his true mother, and
Phaidra as stepmother is a poor substitute for the dare-we-say "Oedipal"
impulses that seem unconsciously to influence Hippolytos's behavior.

Consequently, Hippolytos's rejection of sex and of women further suggests,
from a Jungian perspective, his failure (or inability) to acknowledge the feminine aspects of his own psyche. This failure leads to an extreme masculinity, one
in which Hippolytos takes great pride, but at the same time it is one that ironically is not fully developed, mainly because he is a virgin. Robin Mitchell notes
that, paradoxically, Hippolytos's femininity is a result of this virginity, something
that was acceptable for women in ancient times, but hardly for men. This complication makes Hippolytos's relationship with Artemis—supposedly the foundation of his existence—the very thing that brings him down. Segal sees
Artemis as a "sexually pure maternal figure, [. . .] a replacement for the Amazon mother he has lost," but notes that the places they frequent together, "the
uncut meadow" and the shore, are "symbols of unresolved sexual conflicts"
("Pentheus" 279). Where, in fact, does Hippolytos's devotion to Artemis begin
and end? Does he desire her sexually? Everything he tells us suggests that he
does not, but Sale would have us believe that Hippolytos actually has aspirations to be divine. These aspirations founder on the rock of Artemis's being able
to encompass childbirth, while he cannot. They founder because she can ignore
sexuality, while he cannot. They founder because the gods are by nature less
complex than we are and their worlds more unified than ours can be (44).

In fact, Hippolytos's inability to engage fully with Artemis or Aphrodite
appears to parallel his inability to be satisfactorily masculine or feminine. As
Segal suggests, he rejects the "ineluctable [and] dangerous wholeness" of both
the Artemis-Aphrodite and the masculine-feminine dualities ("Tragedy" 167).
Despite his admitted devotion to Artemis, he is caught in limbo and is thus vulnerable to destruction, much like Pentheus in the *Bacchae*. The fact that
Artemis "allows" her follower to die, as well as the fact that he is destroyed by
two cornerstones of masculinity in this myth cycle—his father, Theseus, and
the bull—suggests that the deity with whom he is most allied cannot save him.

While a psychoanalysis of *Hippolytos* based on the text is useful, it tends to raise more questions than it answers. An authentic psychoanalysis would involve delving deeper into Hippolytos's psyche to answer the questions that a modern audience would have. The true nature of his relationship to Artemis would be one issue, but we could also ask the following: Is Hippolytos, who hates women so much, a homosexual? Does he have any sexual fantasies? What actually happens in the "uncut meadow"? The text might not tell us, but an exploration of these provocative questions can lead to a better understanding of what the play actually does represent.

Staging Hippolytos

Finally, studying Greek tragedy as performance raises the central question of authenticity, the distinction made between ancient staging conventions and the choices available to the modern producer. The issue of authenticity is particularly useful pedagogically, since the ancient perspective permits insight into the traditions underlying the dramatic festivals in fifth-century Athens, while the modern perspective allows students to examine the themes of the plays from a contemporary point of view. There are many excellent treatments of ancient staging (see Taplin, *Greek Tragedy*, and Wiles, *Tragedy*, in particular); our focus here is on modern performance options.

When we staged the *Hippolytos* with the Classics Drama Group at Trent University in 1994 (details in Boyne; Storey), the Artemis-Aphrodite "opposition" was the pivot on which the production was based. The acting space allowed a clear distinction to be made between Aphrodite's "side" and that of Artemis, a physical framing that gave shape to the entire production. Not only did the goddesses speak their respective parts, positioned as they are at the beginning and end of the action, but they also drifted in and out of view depending on the particular action on stage. During the long first episode involving Phaidra and the Nurse (176–524), Aphrodite was in full view; but when Hippolytos was expounding his chastity and feelings toward women (e.g., 601–68, 902–1101), Artemis slipped silently into view, retreating when she was no longer "in command" of the words on stage. Such a staging technique can accentuate the effect that the two divine figures have over the mortal figures, illustrating either the helplessness of the humans or the sheer power of the gods (or both). Examining other staging options concerning the goddesses—for example, does Aphrodite appear as a regular character in the prologue, with only Artemis making her entrance ex machina?—can allow a thorough exploration of the intentions underlying Euripides's attitudes toward the divine-human relationships in this play.

Furthermore, much can be done with the important conflicts that constitute the main "action" of this play. Each of the central confrontations—Phaidra and the Nurse, Hippolytos and the Nurse, Hippolytos and Theseus—can be staged to allow the audience to understand the dynamics of the various relationships.

Emphasizing these confrontations can also make more conspicuous the absence of scenes between Phaidra and Hippolytos and between Phaidra and Theseus in this version. The weakness of Phaidra in her opening scene can be used to stress the "sickness" that Aphrodite has imposed on her; by contrast, the importance of the Nurse to the action that follows can be made clear through her domination of the physical space in that scene. Similarly, the shock and incredulity that accompany Hippolytos's reactions to the Nurse's revelations and to Theseus's accusations can be accentuated through the way in which he acts (on stage) toward the other characters. In short, the growing area of performance theory, which is encouraging a discussion of ancient drama in its original context—that is, not as literature but as theater—is exciting and full of potential for students. At the same time, as Goldhill suggests ("Modern Critical Approaches" 337), it is an area about which we know so little. The speculative nature of any discussion of the performance of ancient theater, however, can be as liberating as it is restricted; any thorough discussion requires an equally thorough understanding and appreciation of the text in question.

So while there might not be "nine and sixty ways" of reading and interpreting the *Hippolytos*, there are certainly numerous options available to instructors and students and, indeed, to anyone who chooses to engage with the text. Some of these are traditional, others more controversial; in any case, they are sure to generate discussion, debate, and disagreement—an outcome true, of course, to the essential spirit of Euripidean tragedy.

Teaching Euripides's *Bacchae*
Stephen Esposito

> We sit within our net, we spiders, and whatever we catch
> in it, we can catch nothing at all except that which allows
> itself to be caught in precisely *our* net.
> —Friedrich Nietzsche, *Daybreak*

Arguably the darkest and fiercest tragedy ever produced, Euripides's *Bacchae* was written during the dramatist's self-imposed exile in Macedonia and was staged posthumously by his son (c. 406–05 BC). It is the only surviving Athenian tragedy about Dionysus. This youngest god in the pantheon was the only Olympian born of a mortal woman, one of the few Olympians with no divine consort, the only Olympian who did not treat mortal women as erotic objects, the only Olympian to suffer death, the only Olympian with no fixed site of worship, the only god whose worshiper could be called by the same name as the god himself (*Bacchae* 491), the most popular god in the townships of Attica, the god with the largest following of any Greek divinity, and *the* god of the Hellenistic Age. As the god of epiphany (*der kommende Gott*) Dionysus lacks, more than any other Greek deity does, a consistent identity, since he is characterized by duality, contrast, and reversal (Otto; Burkert; Detienne, *Dionysos*).

The *Bacchae* itself is the only extant tragedy in which two characters go mad, the only one to present a god in human disguise, the one most closely tied to the setting of ritual and sacrificial feast, and the richest literary source of Dionysian imagery to survive from the fifth century. It is one of only two tragedies in which the protagonists die at the end (*Hippolytus*), one of only three tragedies to begin and end with divine appearances (*Hippolytus*, *Ion*), one of only three tragedies in which the gods who appear onstage are malevolent and destroy the protagonist (*Hippolytus*, *Heracles*), and the one tragedy that, more than any other, plays with the theatrical and dramatic potential of disguise, by presenting a man dressed as a god disguised as a man, a man dressed as a young military king who then dresses as a woman, and old men dressed as young women dressed in animal skins and other exotic Bacchic trappings (Dodds, *Euripides:* Bacchae; Taplin, "Comedy"; Seaford, *Euripides:* Bacchae; B. Simon; Carpenter and Faraone; Michelini, *Euripides*). All these features make Euripides's last complete play unique and "deeply untypical" (Taplin, "Comedy" 191).

This essay examines that untypical uniqueness in two distinct ways. First, I present a diachronic literary analysis of the narrative, focusing on the salient themes as they emerge. Second, I discuss critically two major interpretive problems: namely, how to "read" the chorus and how to "read" Dionysus's vindictiveness. This two-part approach is intended to mimic a procedure that I have found helpful in the classroom: that is, to analyze the story's unfolding and then to study important thematic cruxes.

The prologue (1–63) begins with the entrance of a male actor dressed as a god disguised as a man. Dionysus has come from Asia to Greece where he intends to spread his cult. He will reveal to Thebes his divinity as the son of Zeus and Semele and initiate the city into his mysteries. Why Thebes? Because it is here, his birthplace, that his aunts have denied that Zeus was his father. They insist that Semele was seduced by a mortal. Dionysus punishes this slander by inflicting madness on them and all Thebes's women and then driving them onto nearby Mount Cithaeron, where they become his devotees. This opening act of war is designed to vindicate his mother and prove his divinity.

The prologue, then, discloses Dionysus's identity (1–22), his reason for coming (23–46), and his intent (47–63). Several key themes emerge. The *Bacchae* will be a drama of revelation—of how this androgynous god of wine, dancing, and illusion manifests himself in the world. But the epiphany will be oblique: by indirection he will find direction, disguising himself as an effeminate Asian stranger and testing Pentheus, the rebel "god-fighter" (*theo-machos*), through a series of miracles. As the god of madness his weapon of revenge is the imposition of a frenzy on his victims; he attacks the mind. The first miracle is the frenzying and driving of the Theban women onto the mountain. So the prologue establishes the play's spatial coordinates and from this dichotomy (city versus mountain) emerge the other crucial oppositions: male versus female, nature versus culture, reason versus madness, mortal versus immortal.

Act 1 (170–369) sets the stage for the confrontation of the protagonist and antagonist that occurs in acts 2, 3, and 4 (434–976). Thebes's two most prominent authorities, Tiresias and Cadmus, city seer and city founder, attempt to convert Pentheus. This contest between age and youth is carefully structured, with two short outer scenes framing the main event: lines 170–214 (45 lines) featuring Tiresias and Cadmus; lines 215–329 (115 lines) featuring Pentheus and Tiresias; and lines 330–69 (40 lines) featuring Cadmus, Pentheus, and Tiresias. The central scene (Pentheus's first monologue, 215–62) serves as a second prologue, "a counter-manifesto to the first [prologue]—having heard the god's programme of action, we now listen to man's" (Dodds, *Euripides: Bacchae* 97). Pentheus believes that Thebes's women have abandoned the city for the pleasures of Aphrodite and Dionysus. Even Tiresias and Cadmus have been seduced by this Bacchic revelry. The city is falling apart. Having already jailed many of the women, Pentheus plans now to hunt down and decapitate the Lydian quack.

In act 2 (434–518) the "showdown" finally begins. The apparent defeat of the Stranger is presented in three stages: lines 434–50 (17 lines), Dionysus bound; lines 451–502 (52 lines), Dionysus unbound; lines 503–18 (16 lines), Dionysus rebound. One of Pentheus's soldiers brings the captured Stranger before the king and reports that the jailed Theban Bacchae have escaped: "The chains, of their own accord, came loose from the women's feet and the keys unlocked the jailhouse doors without a human hand. This man has come here to Thebes *full of many miracles*" (447–49; all quotations are from my edition of the play). This is the first of several miracles by which Dionysus explicitly attempts to reveal himself to Pentheus. Confronted with his bound enemy, Pentheus asks, "Who are you and from what family?" (460). The Stranger explains that his home is Sardis, where he was initiated into Dionysus's rites. Since those rites are forbidden knowledge to all except the initiated, the Stranger teases Pentheus with hints. Pentheus calls Dionysus a Sophist (489) and threatens to cut off his hair, take his thyrsus, and lock him up. Dionysus, in his role as the god of liberation, replies, "The god himself will set me free whenever I wish" (498). An angry Pentheus orders his guards to seize Dionysus for his insults: "I have more power than you" (505). The Stranger replies, "You don't know who you are?" Pentheus fires back with pride: "I am Pentheus, son of Agave and of my father Echion." "Indeed you are," says the Stranger, "and that name spells your misfortune" (506–08). But Pentheus has no clue, because he is unable to see beyond the narrow world of his walled city and its attendant illusions of male power. Like Nietzsche's spider he catches nothing "except that which allows itself to be caught" precisely in his web. This act, then, introduces the problem of human perspective, of how we see and do not see.

Act 2 ends with Pentheus locking Dionysus up again and then taking notice of the chorus of Bacchae for the first time: "And as for these women you've brought as collaborators in your evil deeds, either we'll sell them or I'll keep them as family possessions, slaves at my looms, after, that is, I've stopped their hands from banging out that rat-a-tat-tat on their drums" (511–14). Stage convention precluded Pentheus's execution of his extraordinary threat, but the harshness of his words reveals his intimidating modus operandi. Indeed, his emphatic last word here, *kektēsomai*, "I shall possess (them)," encapsulates his myopic perspective on what constitutes power.

Act 3 (576–861), the play's structural and thematic center, has three parts: lines 576–656 (81 lines), Dionysus's epiphany by way of the "palace miracles"; lines 657–786 (130 lines), the first messenger scene; and lines 787–861 (75 lines), Dionysus's persuading Pentheus to dress up as a woman to spy on the mountain-roaming maenads. The long messenger scene describing the magical powers of the Bacchae on Mount Cithaeron is clearly the centerpiece, framed as it is by the two shorter scenes. When act 3 begins, the stage is empty. Suddenly we hear from offstage a voice:

THE VOICE:	Io! Hear my voice, hear it! Io Bacchae, io Bacchae!
CHORUS-LEADER:	Who is here, who is it? From where does the voice of Euios summon me?
THE VOICE:	Io! Again I speak, the son of Semele, the son of Zeus!
CHORUS-LEADER:	Io! Master, master! Come into our revelling band, O Bromios, Bromios!
THE VOICE:	Shake the very foundation of this world, august goddess of Earthquakes!

CHORUS-LEADER: Ah, ah! Look how quickly Pentheus' palace will be shaken to its fall! Dionysus is in the palace. Worship him!   (576–90)

For twenty-eight lines (576–603) the god's voice sings from offstage while the chorus sings from the orchestra. The effect must have been stunning in the original performance. Oliver Taplin observes that "nowhere else in Greek tragedy is a god heard calling from off-stage, let alone accompanied by thunder and lightning" (*Greek Tragedy* 120). The earthquake that shakes the palace is the first of four supernatural events that constitute the "palace miracles"— all of which seem designed to answer the prayers of the preceding choral song. The other three miracles, in the aftermath of the quake, are Pentheus's *hallucinations* about the bull, the burning palace, and the light (615–31); the blazing of Zeus's lightning at Semele's tomb (594–99, 623–24); and the offstage collapse of the stable in which the Stranger had been jailed (633–34). The following passage sets forth the "palace miracle" sequence:

CHORUS-LEADER: But didn't he bind your hands in tight nooses?
THE STRANGER: In just this I mocked him. He *thought* he had
        bound me
    when in fact he never even laid a hand on us but
        fed on his hopes.
    Finding a bull in the stables where he had led me
        as a prisoner
    he threw nooses around its knees and hooves,
    breathing out fury, sweating profusely from his body,
    gnashing his teeth into his lips. But I, sitting calmly
        nearby,
    just watched. In the meantime Bacchus came
    and shook the palace, kindling a flame on his
        mother's tomb.
    When Pentheus saw this, *thinking* the palace was
        burning,
    he rushed to and fro, ordering his servants to bring
        water.
    Every slave helped in the task but they all labored
        in vain.
    Imagining that I had escaped, he gave up this toil
    and darted into the dark house with his dagger
        drawn.
    Then Bromios, as it seems to me at least, since I
        speak only my opinion,
    made a light in the courtyard. Chasing eagerly after
        it, Pentheus rushed forward

and tried to stab the shining [image], *thinking* he
was slaying me.
In addition to these humiliations, Bacchus outraged
him in other ways too.
He smashed the building to the ground. Everything
lies shattered
so that now he sees the most bitter consequences
of trying to chain me.
From weariness he has dropped his sword and lies
exhausted.
Though only a man, he dared to fight a god. Calmly
leaving the palace,
I have come to you, giving no thought to Pentheus.
(615–37; emphasis added)

The young king's arduous ordeals as he attempts to tie up the bull (i.e., Dionysus) resemble those of the initiand in the Eleusinian mysteries as described by
Plutarch, who had himself, some five hundred years later, been initiated into
the Dionysiac mysteries. At the moment of death, Plutarch informs us that

the soul suffers an experience like those who celebrate the great initia-
tions [. . .] in the beginning wanderings and wearisome running around
in circles and some unfinished journeys half-seen through darkness; then
[just] before the consummation [come] all the terrors—panic and trem-
bling and sweat and amazement. And after this a certain miraculous light
comes upon you [. . .].   (107; "On the Soul," fragment 178; my trans.)

Analogous to the key features (wandering, terror, bright light) of this Plutarch
passage are Pentheus's initiation-like sufferings in the Dionysiac mysteries:
panting, sweating, shuddering (620–21); wild rushing about (625–28); darkness
(628; cf. 510, 611); the sudden epiphany of miraculous light (630–31) symbolizing the presence of the god; and finally, the initiand's exhaustion (635). These
markers all point to the initiand's ignorance, fear, and confusion. In contrast to
Pentheus, whose rite of passage into the joy and knowledge of the Dionysiac
mysteries fails, the chorus succeeds here, progressing from fear (604), trem-
bling (607), loneliness (609), and despair (610)—all the result of the earthquake and fire at Semele's tomb—to joy (609) at seeing the great light (608),
which they identify with the liberated god (Seaford, "Dionysiac Drama"
255–57 and *Euripides:* Bacchae 201).

This initiation scene is followed by the centerpiece of act 3, the first messenger's report (677–774; 98 lines). Laden with an air of mystery, this gripping
eyewitness account describes the magical powers of the Theban Bacchae on
the mountain. At one point the messenger explains what happened when he
and some shepherds attempted to ambush the Bacchae:

The whole mountain and all its wild creatures
joined the Bacchic revelry and everything was roused to running.
Agave happens to jump close by me
and I leapt out hoping to seize her,
deserting the thicket where I was hiding myself.
But she shrieked:
    "O my running hounds,
    we are being hunted by these men here. Follow me!
    Follow me, armed like soldiers [*hôplismenai*] with your thyrsi at hand!"
Only by fleeing did we avoid
being torn to pieces [*sparagmos*] by the Bacchae;
but they attacked our grazing calves and not with swords in their hands.
You could have seen one of them, apart from the others, mauling
    with both hands
a young heifer with swelling udders, bellowing all the while;
and other women were ripping apart mature cows, shredding
them up [*sparagmos*].   (725–39)

The frenzied maenads are "armed like soldiers" (hoplites, Greek armored warriors), and their weapons are *thyrsi* (fennel stalks topped with ivy, carried by
worshipers of Dionysus) rather than spears (733). This sex-role reversal
(female as hunter and hoplite) anticipates Pentheus's sex change in the next
scene and underscores the androgynous powers of Dionysus, whose very
nature is to confuse and defy the traditional dichotomies that polarized Greek
culture. And the subsequent *sparagmos* (ripping apart) of the "hubristic" bulls
(*tauroi hubristai*; 743) by the Bacchae foreshadows Agave's much more grue-
some rending of her son (1125–28). But Pentheus sees in this miracle on the
mountain nothing but hubris and humiliation:

You there, go to the Electran gates. / Order all the shield-bearing foot-
soldiers / and riders of swift-footed horses to meet me there. / Call up my
light infantry, too, and the archers. / We're going to march against the
Bacchae / since this is too much to bear, that we suffer / what we suffer
at the hands of women.   (780–86)

Still "kicking against the prick, a man at war with god" (794–95), the young king
refuses to recognize these repeated proofs of Dionysus's divinity and again
resorts to his weapons (809). Dionysus must devise a new strategy. And so at
line 810 the following exchange begins:

THE STRANGER: Ah!
                Do you want to see those women sitting together in the
                mountains?

PENTHEUS: Indeed I would. I'd give a vast weight of gold for that.

THE STRANGER: But why have you fallen into so great a passion [*erôs*] for seeing them?

PENTHEUS: I would be pained to see them drunk with wine.

THE STRANGER: But still you would see with pleasure things that are bitter to you?

PENTHEUS: Certainly I would—but in silence and sitting under the fir trees.

THE STRANGER: But they will track you down even if you go secretly.

PENTHEUS: Good point. I'd better go openly.

THE STRANGER: Shall we lead you then? Will you really venture on the journey?

PENTHEUS: Lead me as quickly as possible. I begrudge the time you're wasting.

THE STRANGER: Then put on this long dress of fine oriental linen.

PENTHEUS: What are you saying? Instead of being a man shall I join the ranks of women?

THE STRANGER: Yes. I fear they would kill you if you were seen as a man there.

PENTHEUS: Another good point. You're a pretty clever fellow and have been right along.

THE STRANGER: Dionysus instructed us fully in these matters.

PENTHEUS: How could your advice be successfully carried out?

THE STRANGER: I myself will dress you up once we've gone into the house.

PENTHEUS: In what kind of costume? A woman's? But I would be ashamed [*aidôs*].   (810–28)

The "Ah!" at line 810 is the play's "monosyllabic turning point," the beginning of the end for Pentheus (Taplin, *Greek Tragedy* 158). He now comes under the god's power and loses much of his ability to reason. His *erôs* (813) to spy on his mother, a sexual desire hitherto disguised, begins to assert itself, however ambivalently (814–15). This is the engine that drives Dionysus's new stratagem. He coaxes Pentheus to spy on his mother; in order to do this, however, Pentheus must be dressed up as a maenad. The proud king baulks: "Instead of being a man shall I join the ranks of women?" (*es gunaikas ex andros*; 822). Shame (*aidôs*; 828) inhibits him: "Anything is better than being laughed at (*engelan*) by the Bacchae" (842). Laughter is the most lethal of weapons in a shame culture like that of the Greeks. In their intensely competitive society one man's victory came at another's expense. Losing the contest (*agôn*) meant "losing face" before one's peers. And even worse than losing face was doing so at the hands of women. The centrality of this concern is indicated by the appearance of "laughter" (*gelôs*) words ten times in the *Bacchae*, more than in any other play by Euripides (Dillon). So Pentheus is torn between his *erôs* and his *aidôs*, his passion and his shame. As act 3 ends, he is uncertain whether to march to the mountain with his weapons or dress as a maenad (845–46). But Dionysus, addressing the chorus, is certain:

> Women, the man stands within the cast of our net.
> He will come to the Bacchae and pay the penalty of death!
> Dionysus, now the deed is yours—for you are not far off.
> Let us punish him! First put him outside his mind.
> Instill a light-headed frenzy [*lyssa*]. Since, if he reasons well,
> he definitely won't be willing to dress in a woman's costume.
> But if he drives off the road of reason, he will dress up.
> I want the Thebans to mock him
> as we parade him through the city in his dainty disguise,
> after those terrifying threats of his.
> I'll go and dress Pentheus up in the very adornments
> he'll wear to Hades after being slain by his mother's hands.
> He will come to know Dionysus, the son of Zeus,
> that he is, in the ritual of initation [*en telei*], a god most terrifying,
> but for mankind a god most gentle.   (848–61)

This thematic prologue to the play's second half summarizes Dionysus's plan of revenge. The god will instill a frenzy to induce Pentheus to cross-dress. As transvestite the young king will obliterate his old identity and assume a new, Dionysiac one. In this ambivalent, disorienting rite of passage Pentheus "takes on the very attributes of his alter ego that he most scorns [. . .] and acts out the opposite of the values of his male peer group: effeminacy instead of masculinity; emotionality instead of rationality; illusion, magic, and trickery instead of realistic clarity, forthrightness, and martial discipline" (C. Segal, *Dionysiac Poetics* 171). Thus as the initiand immerses himself into the cult group (*thiasos*), the individual dies in order to be "born again" into the communion of devotees. It is this Dionysiac experience of ritual death (Pentheus's humiliation and status reversal) that makes Dionysus "a god most terrifying" (860). To others—the uninitiated masses who know the god only through his invention of wine, the stopper of sorrow (278–83)—he is "a god most gentle."

Act 4 (912–76; 65 lines) reverses the situation of act 2 (85 lines) where the physically bound Stranger was ushered in and out by Pentheus. Now the mentally bound Pentheus, wearing "the costume of *a woman, a maenad, a bacchant*" (915; emphasis added), is ushered in and out by the Stranger. Dionysus's crescendo of sarcastic feminine nouns registers the immensity, intensity, and vengefulness of the conversion. As act 4 is a mirror of act 2, so Pentheus is now the mirror (at least in physical appearance) of his cousin Dionysus. But Pentheus's divestiture of his regalia symbolizes the physical dissolution of his kingship as well as the psychological dissolution of his mind.

Hence his astonishing first words as a bacchant: "And truly I seem to myself to see two suns and a double Thebes, that fortress of seven mouths. And you seem to be *a bull* leading us in front and *horns* seem to have sprouted on your head. But were you a *beast* before? Because certainly you are a bull now" (918–22; emphasis added). Scholars suggest various explanations for Pentheus's surrealistic double vision: that his "light-headed frenzy" (851) has distorted his eyesight; that he is drunk with the god's wine; that he is looking into a ritual mirror; that the suppressed duality of his psyche has broken loose. These interpretations all, perhaps, contain some element of truth. On a more literal level, Pentheus's two suns and two Thebes evoke the play's antithetical double topography: mountain (Theban females led by the mother) versus city (Theban males led by the son). This is a play, after all, that takes place in a city (virtually) emptied of women. As ironfisted Greek king in the costume of an effeminate Asian bacchant, Pentheus now straddles both these worlds of Dionysus, but as androgynous voyeur, eager to "witness sexual acts without being ensnared in the complexities of his own desires," he fits in neither (Nussbaum, Introduction xxxiv). Pentheus's altered vision includes the Stranger *incarnate* as a horned bull. This is the same beast he vainly tried to tie up earlier, "breathing out fury, sweating profusely from his body, gnashing his teeth into his lips" (618–21). Like a mystagogue leading his anxious initiate, this horned bull, symbol of male virility, will now escort Pentheus to the mountain to spy on his mother's sexual proclivities. The arresting image suggests that Pentheus's own unleashed *erôs* will, at last, escort him into the strange realm of Dionysiac secrets he so desires to see. It turns out, then, that in his weird hallucinations there does indeed lie an ambiguous element of truth (Kirk, *Bacchae* 100). Proud of his fashion-modeling skills, the preening Pentheus asks the Stranger, "How do I look, then? Don't I carry myself like Ino or like Agave, my mother?" (925–26). So completely does he resemble his mother that probably the actor playing Pentheus will return as Agave (1168), needing only to change his mask (Seaford, *Euripides:* Bacchae 224). The irony, of course, is that she will be carrying the head of her son, thinking he is a beast. Such is the violent grace of this most terrifying god.

Act 5 (1024–152) has as its highlight the second messenger's speech (1043–152) describing the tearing apart (*sparagmos*) of his master by Agave:

> Seizing his left arm with her forearms
> and pressing her foot against the doomed man's ribs
> she tore off his shoulder, not by her own strength—
> no, the god gave a special ease to her hand. [. . .] The ribs were laid bare
> by the tearing apart. All the women, with blood-spattered hands,
> were playing ball with Pentheus' flesh. [. . .] But the pitiful head, the
>   very one
> which his mother just then happened to take with her hands,
> *she impales on the tip of her thyrsus and carries it,*

as if it were the head of a mountain lion, through the middle of
   Cithaeron,
leaving behind her sisters in the choruses of dancing maenads.
Rejoicing in her ill-fated prey she comes inside these city walls
calling upon the Bacchic god as the fellow huntsman,
the comrade in the chase, the triumphant victor
but for her he brings only tears as a victory-prize.
                    (1125–27, 1134–36, 1139–47; emphasis added)

About this horrific climax one scholar has written that "Euripides creates a
Pentheus who is transformed visually into a symbol of Dionysus. Pentheus
becomes the *thyrsus* of the god: first he is crowned with long hair and a *mitra*
[headband], then he himself crowns the tip of a fir tree raised by the maenads
on the mountain, and finally he becomes the literal crown of the *thyrsus* carried by his mother" (Kalke 410).

   The epilogue (1165–392) begins with the entry of the frenzied Agave, "sacred
priest" of the slaughter of the mounted beast (1108-14), dancing with Pentheus's
bloodstained head/mask impaled on her *thyrsus*. She bids the chorus to join her
feast. Though these Asian maenads celebrate their enemy's murder, cannibalism
is beyond even their limits. Eventually Cadmus, in the first psychotherapy scene
in Western literature (1263–300), coaxes his daughter out of madness. Suddenly
the god appears "out of the machine" to announce the fates of Cadmus and
Agave, to proclaim his Olympian ancestry, and to chastise Thebes's founder:

DIONYSUS:	You were late to understand us. When you ought to have known us, you did not.
CADMUS:	We have realized our mistakes now. *But your punishment is too severe.*
DIONYSUS:	Yes, but I am a god and was treated with hybris by you.
CADMUS:	*Gods ought not be like mortals in their passions* [*orgê*].

                             (1345–48; emphasis added)

The god's vengeful passion leaves us so frozen in horror and sadness that we
can only wonder if Gloucester was not right: "As flies to wanton boys are we to
th' gods, / They kill us for their sport" (*King Lear* 4.1.37–38). Dionysus's wrath
has progressively ripped apart the polis, the psyche, and the body (C. Segal,
"Menace"). As William Arrowsmith writes, "So terrible is his demonstration of
force majeure, so indiscrimate his revenge, that in the end Dionysus proves
that he is no god at all—if by god one means something that can be prayed to
or that feels pity or concern" ("Euripides' *Bacchae*" 66)

This judgment leads me, in the second portion of this essay, to take up two central problems of interpretation that have been hotly debated in recent years. As
a springboard here I use the introduction to Paul Woodruff's translation

because, even though I often disagree with his interpretations, he focuses on the important questions.

The first question regards the chorus of Asian Bacchae. Woodruff claims that the "message of the play, as delivered by the chorus, is that peace, order, and control come through cult, and not through force of weapons (Pentheus' choice) or through the New Learning (which Tiresias represents)" (xvi). And as true initiates into Dionysus's mystery religion they link "two feelings that strike noninitiates as contrary—ecstasy and moderation—but these are in fact united in the experience of the initiate and they are united without a residue of tension. The chorus is at peace with itself" (xxxvi). Well, this chorus may initially preach that peace, order, and control come through cult, but that preaching regresses significantly over time. And while these Asian Bacchae may be at peace with themselves, it is not at all clear that we should be at peace with them (Kirk, *Bacchae* 10).

As the Stranger leads Pentheus off to Mount Cithaeron to spy on the Theban Bacchae, the chorus sings this chilling refrain: "Let justice go openly. Let sword-bearing justice go forth, *slaying Pentheus right through the throat*—the godless, lawless, unjust earth-born offspring of Echion" (991–96, 1011–16; emphasis added). And a few lines later: "Go, Bacchus, and with a laughing face *cast the noose of death* on the hunter of the Bacchae when he attacks the herd of maenads" (1020–23; emphasis added). Then, after the second messenger reports Pentheus's death (1030), "the radical, antipolis spirit of this chorus emerges most powerfully" (C. Segal, "Chorus" 75). Charles Segal elsewhere notes, "In the *Bacchae* the communal, civic voice has disappeared. The chorus of Lydian maenads who make up the chorus occupy a situation almost unique in Greek tragedy, namely hostility to the city. [. . .] They interact with the citizens of the polis far less than do most choruses in Greek tragedy, and in fact they speak only thirteen iambic trimeters in the extant portion of the play" ("Classics" 19). The chorus-leader sings in a meter of excitement: "O lord Bromios, you have revealed yourself a mighty god!" The messenger is astonished: "What do you mean? Why do you say this? Do you truly rejoice, woman, in the misfortunes of one who was my master? [. . .] It is not honorable, women, to rejoice at the evils that have been done" (1032–40). After the messenger has described the tearing apart of Pentheus by Agave, the whole chorus cries out: "Let us lift up our feet and dance for Bacchus! Let us lift up our voices and shout for the doom of Pentheus. [. . .] Cadmean Bacchae, you have made your victory hymn renowned, but it ends in a dirge of wailing, of tears. *A fine contest*—to plunge your hands in the blood of your child so that they drip with his blood" (1153–55, 1160–64; emphasis added). *A fine contest*? Their "triumphant sarcasm" reveals that for Dionysus's devotees justice means revenge which, in this case, means virtual murder (992–94; Seaford, *Euripides:* Bacchae 241). To be sure, the standard Greek moral code was to help one's friends and harm one's enemies. Punishment is one thing, but their Medea-like desire for such savage revenge is not what one would expect from religious initiates who had earlier sung the praises of "the tranquil life and prudent thinking" (389–90). Their vindictive spirit, echoing that of Dionysus, does not tally with Woodruff's claim about this chorus as the embodiment of peace, order, and moderation. If the devotees of this god can enthusiastically rejoice in the brutal ripping apart of a son by his frenzied mother and her Dionysiac revelers ("All the women, with blood-spattered hands, were playing ball with Pentheus' flesh" [1135–36]), one wonders what benefits this kind of religious fanaticism would bring to the polis. One could claim that it is natural for the chorus to want to see their would-be enslaver punished by Dionysus (Seaford, *Euripides:* Bacchae 219). But their praise of Agave's impaling of her own son's head on her thyrsus is ignoble at best (1141).

In sum, the progression of the odes toward a celebration of such violence raises, in my estimation, fatal objections to much of Woodruff's interpretation of the chorus. Although he recognizes that we must not be seduced by the chorus because "their religion is not all sweetness and light" (xxvi), the preponderance of his discussion privileges the peaceful aspect of the Bacchae. Yet it is their darker side, "the animal horror of their 'black' maenadism," that is emphasized in the latter half of the play (Dodds, *Euripides:* Bacchae xlvii, 159).

A second, related question is raised by these considerations and is well articulated by Woodruff: "Any fully adequate interpretation, however, must deal in some way with the moral problem posed by Dionysos' excessive anger against his human family, and it should explain why Euripides puts his emphasis on this excess" (xxxii).[1] This is indeed a crucial question, but as best I can tell Woodruff does not answer it. After raising this important question, Woodruff reviews various interpretations of the play before stating his own conclusions (xxxviii–xlii), which are, in sum, that the play is an attack on the "New Learning" (i.e., Sophistry) that flourished in the late fifth century and that the "point of the play is not that we should be content with mystery and give up our ambition for a clear understanding. [. . .] The point, rather, is that clear understanding comes only by way of initiation, and not by active intellectual efforts" (xli–xlii). These observations, whether one agrees with them or not, do not address the issue of Dionysus's vindictiveness. In my own translation, I suggest a double answer (psychological and sociopolitical) to this question, following the leads of William Arrowsmith, Charles Segal, and Bernard Knox. On the one hand, there is a crucial psychological element to Dionysus's taurine ferocity. As an androgynous boundary-crossing god, he embodies a repressed part of Pentheus, especially the feminine side of the young king that remains largely inaccessible to him. As Nietzsche said, "The degree and kind of a man's sexuality reach up into the ultimate pinnacle of his spirit" (*Beyond* 81; aphorism 75). Pentheus's suppression of this natural part of the human psyche leads to an eruption of volcanic proportions as his *erôs* (812) explodes, tearing him to pieces as he struggles unsuccessfully to release, through voyeurism, his passion for seeing the "feminine other" on the forbidden wild mountain.

Pentheus's failed rite of passage into manhood is caused partly by his procrustean perspective on what constitutes social order, which, as Segal observes, is in his case "a warrior-society of obedient, disciplined male citizens in hoplite ranks who protect the enclosed, walled space of the city in which the women are safely secluded and secured" ("Menace" 204). Pentheus's tragedy of the self implies a tragedy for the city not least because the self in question is the king. Just as we witness the progressive fragmentation of Pentheus's palace, psyche, and body, so we witness the fragmentation of Thebes as the women are driven to the wild mountain so that the city contains only men. It may well be that this splitting of the palace and polis in Euripides's play represents a larger cultural *sparagmos* as revealed in the brutal power politics of the Peloponnesian War. In other words, as Knox suggests, it may be that

> Euripides, in his presentation of divine intervention in human affairs, had in mind the conduct and the language of the imperial city-states of his own day. [. . .] The prime concern of the city-state is maintenance of its prestige, manifestation of its power as a warning to potential rebels or ambitious neighbors. As with Euripides' gods, no insult, offense or threat to that power can be allowed to pass unnoticed. Honor must be maintained.   ("Divine Intervention" 228–29)

Woodruf criticizes this interpretation, as articulated by me (Esposito 18), for "reading into fifth-century attitudes the harsh judgments of Thucydides" (xxxvii). Given that Thucydides's *History* and Euripides's (contemporaneous) tragedies explore similar themes (Finley 1–54), I do not understand Woodruff's criticism. Because historical contextualizing of "late" Euripides is crucial to the present argument, I quote at length here what seems to me the most incisive account of the matter. Arrowsmith argues that Euripides's last plays (*Phoenician Women*, *Orestes*, *Iphigeneia at Aulis*, and *Bacchae*), all written in the closing decade of the fifth century, represent a searching critique of Athenian culture. Why does Euripides undertake this project?

> The cumulative disaster of the Peloponnesian War [431–04], the plague [c. 430–27], the rise of demagogues, and the emergence of radical self-interest became the determinants of both public and private life. So that as the delicately adjusted mutual relations of moral density attenuated, centrifugal forces more and more prevailed over the centripetal. This is the desperately anomic [lawless] Athens so graphically depicted in the last plays, all socialized tragedies, and all unmistakably apocalyptic (in the dissonance of their cadence). The themes are persistent from play to play: the absence of leadership or leadership committed to political bad faith; the active corruption of the citizenry, deemed incapable of responding morally, and to that degree morally incapacitated by its own immoral leaders; the dissolvent strife of selfish individualism; the perversion of *arete* [excellence, prowess] and the general inversion or voiding of moral terms; the disappearance of moderates and modera-

tion alike by the polarization of political life; and, last but far from least, the convergence of brutal divine behavior embodied in myth with political brutality in human affairs. In the *Phoenissae* heaven, through an oracle, demands the sacrifice of the innocent Menoikeus; Dionysus in the *Bacchae*, in quest of his own *philotimia* [coveting of honor], makes a mother kill her own son; in the *Orestes* a god commands a boy to murder his mother; in the *Iphigeneia at Aulis* the goddess Artemis commands a father, already enslaved to his own lifelong politics of bad faith, to kill his daughter in order to free his fleet from Aulis and prosecute the war of the "free Greeks" against Trojan "barbarians" and "slaves." The convergence between myth and behavior has of course been heightened by the dramatist in order to confront the audience with its own social and cultural reality, to make it respond *morally* to the immoral spectacle which is created by, and imitates, its own politics, the narrowing but still sizeable gap between its received and operative values. Dramaturgically, the plays have all been shaped to enable that moral response by stating the situation in its extremest form. Thus the myths have all been even more violently anachronized than in the early plays; the setting is not merely fifth century, but the century's final, desperate decade.

(Lecture 2; emphasis added)[2]

Arrowsmith's analysis, I believe, helps situate Dionysus's vindictiveness in a larger dramatic and cultural context and thereby provides an instructive supplement to the psychological reading that I discussed earlier. From a contrary point of view, Richard Seaford reads the end of the play in a positive light, arguing that the demise of the oppressive Pentheus represents Thebes's liberation by Dionysus and that the god, in his final epiphany, establishes himself and his cult as a vital and cohesive force for the city (*Euripides:* Bacchae 44–52). But it is difficult to see how a mother desiring to cannibalize her son (1184) or, at the play's emotional climax, a mother and grandfather struggling to reassemble Pentheus's corpse onstage could be sources of civic cohesion (Esposito 89, 97). The text, the stage action, and the emotional impetus of the epilogue do not support such a consoling reading (C. Segal, *Dionysiac Poetics* 382–85; Griffin, "Social Function" 52–54). The emphasis is not on the salvation of the city but on the lamentation, desolation, and pity of the human characters. As Oliver Taplin observes:

Bakchai pointedly closes with the break-up of both family and polis. It might easily have ended with a triumphal Dionysiac departure by the chorus, off to spread the blessings of the god to another city—even to Athens! It might, that is, have ended with metatheatrical celebration, but it doesn't; and in that it epitomizes tragedy's refusal to take the *easy* or *comforting* way out of the terrors it enacts.   ("Comedy" 197)

The pathetic image of a Bacchic mother, driven mad by the angry son of Zeus, raising the impaled head of her own son on a cultic *thyrsus* in honor of her Bacchic god—this horrific image translates the dramatist's final prophetic vision. It is not difficult to imagine that after watching for twenty-five years the savage *sparagmos* of Athens and Sparta, all the aging playwright could summon was pity and fear. It was too late now for anything else: too late for Pentheus and Agave, too late for Athens, and perhaps even too late for the genre of clas-sical tragedy itself, with its stage building shattered by a Dionysiac earthquake, its protagonist torn to pieces by his own mother, and its royal mask disembodied by the theater god's most zealous devotee.

NOTES

The epigraph from Nietzsche's *Daybreak* is aphorism 17, p. 73.

[1]Martha Nussbaum asks a similar question—"Can Dionysus really become civilized?" (Introduction xxxiv)—and answers it from a very insightful "trans-Aristotelian" perspective.

[2]This passage is from the second of Arrowsmith's four Bampton lectures on Euripides delivered at Columbia University in 1984. The first Bampton lecture, "Euripides and the Dramaturgy of Crisis," has been published. All four Bampton lectures, as well as Arrowsmith's collected essays on Greek drama, will be forthcoming in a volume entitled "Euripides and the Dramaturgy of Crisis" (ed. S. Esposito). For similar observations on Euripides as cultural critic, see Arrowsmith, "The Criticism of Greek Tragedy," and, focusing more specifically on the *Bacchae*, Arrowsmith's introduction (148–49) to his translation in the University of Chicago Press series The Complete Greek Tragedies.

NOTES ON CONTRIBUTORS

Arlene Allan has a PhD from the University of Exeter, where she is completing her dissertation on Hermes in myth and drama. She has extensive experience in acting and in directing Greek drama, as well as considerable expertise in teaching classics to a wide range of groups. She is currently a sectional lecturer at Northwestern University.

Laurel Bowman is assistant professor of Greek and Roman studies at the University of Victoria. She has published articles and reviews on Sophocles and Greek poetry. She teaches a range of courses on Greek and Roman myth and literature. Her current projects involve prophecy in Greek literature and Heracles in Greek and Roman myth.

Martin Boyne is a PhD candidate at the University of Toronto and has been an adjunct faculty member in the Department of Ancient History and Classics at Trent University, where he has taught courses in Latin, as well as in classical drama in translation. He is director of Trent's Classics Drama Group, which has produced nine Greek plays since 1994. His research interests include modern versions of classical drama, especially in opera.

Monica Silveira Cyrino is associate professor of classics and department chair at the University of New Mexico, Albuquerque. She has authored *In Pandora's Jar: Lovesickness in Early Greek Poetry* (1995), as well as articles on Greek lyric poetry, Euripidean tragedy, and Greek mythology. Her main research interest is the construction of the erotic in Greek and Roman poetry and mythology, as reflected in her forthcoming book, "Celebrating Aphrodite." In 1998 she received the Excellence in Teaching Classics Award from the American Philological Association.

Stephen Esposito is associate professor of classical studies at Boston University. He has translated Euripides's *Bacchae* (1998). In addition to articles and reviews on Greek tragedy, he has written *Sophocles Agonistes: The Struggle between Reason, Faith, and Chance in* Oedipus the King (forthcoming). Current projects include editing a collection of essays by William Arrowsmith, a new translation of Sophocles's *Ajax*, and "Understanding Greek Drama: A Student Casebook to the Themes and Problems of Eleven Masterpieces." In 1999 he was a semifinalist for the Metcalf Award for Excellence in Teaching at Boston University.

Mary-Kay Gamel is professor of classics, comparative literature, and theater arts at the University of California, Santa Cruz. She has directed productions of ancient drama, Eugene O'Neill, Carl Orff, and new scripts, and she has written on ancient drama and on Roman texts in performance. Her translation, with introduction and commentary, of Euripides's *Iphigenia at Aulis* appeared in Ruby Blondell et al., *Women on the Edge: Four Plays by Euripides* (1999). In 2000–01 she was Flora Stone Mather Visiting Professor at Case Western Reserve University.

Justina Gregory is professor of classical languages and literatures at Smith College. Her principal publications are *Euripides and the Instruction of the Athenians* (1991) and *Euripides:* Hecuba, edited and with an introduction and commentary (1999). She is primarily interested in Greek tragedy and fifth-century intellectual history; her current focus is on representations of education in Greek tragedy.

Dale Grote is associate professor of classics at the University of North Carolina, Charlotte. He has written articles and reviews on Greek drama and Aristotle's *Poetics*. As a one-person classics department, he teaches a variety of courses, from elementary Latin to a senior-level course for the English department on ancient drama. He has published on Sophocles, Plato. and Aristotle's *Poetics*. He has recently completed *A Comprehensive Guide to Wheelock's Latin* (2000).

Adele J. Haft is associate professor of classics at Hunter College, City University of New York. Her interests are ancient Greek tragedy, epic, and novel; Homeric studies; ancient Greek sports and Roman spectacles; and maps in literature and history. In addition to writing numerous articles on Homeric poetry, she has coauthored *The Key to The Name of the Rose* (1999) and written articles on medieval maps in *The Name of the Rose* and on maps in twentieth-century poetry; this last area is the subject of a book in progress.

Michael R. Halleran is professor of classics and divisional dean for the arts and humanities at the University of Washington. He has written *Stagecraft in Euripides* (1985), as well as volumes of translation and commentary on Euripides's *Heracles* (1988; rev. 1993) and *Hippolytus* (1995, 2001). His interests include Greek literature, especially tragedy, and intellectual history. Currently, he is working on a commentary on Euripides's *Alcestis* for the series Cambridge Greek and Latin Classics.

Laura McClure is associate professor of classics at the University of Wisconsin, Madison. Her primary areas of research are Athenian drama, the classical tradition, and women in the ancient world. She is the author of *Spoken like a Woman: Speech and Gender in Athenian Drama* (1999) and the coeditor of *Making Silence Speak: Women's Voices in Greek Literature and Society* (2000). She has also published articles on Greek tragedy, pedagogy, and the classical tradition. In 1999 she won the University of Wisconsin Distinguished Teaching Award. Her current work focuses on courtesans in the Greek literary tradition.

Marianne McDonald is professor of theater and classics at the University of California, San Diego, and member of the Royal Irish Academy. Her books include *Euripides in Cinema: The Heart Made Visible* (1983), *Ancient Sun, Modern Light: Greek Drama on the Modern Stage* (1992), and *Sing Sorrow: Classics, History, and Heroines in Opera* (2001). She writes about ancient theater and women's issues, as well as the presence of the classics in opera, theater, and film. Current projects include new translations for performance of *The Trojan Women* and *Antigone*, as well as an introduction to Greek drama for "theater people."

Gary S. Meltzer is associate professor of classics at Eckerd College. He has published articles on Euripides, Sophocles, Homer, and the classical tradition. His research and teaching mainly involve Greek tragedy, Greek and Roman literature, and the humanities. His work in progress on Euripides is titled "The Poetics of Nostalgia: The Longing for the 'Just Voice' in Euripidean Drama."

Ann N. Michelini is professor of classics emerita at the University of Cincinnati. She is the author of a book and articles on Aeschylean tragedy; *Euripides and the Tragic Tra-*

dition (1987); and a number of articles. Her current research is on literary approaches to Platonic dialogues and on the expansion of myth to epic dimensions in several late plays by Euripides.

Paul Allen Miller is director of comparative literature and associate professor of classics at the University of South Carolina, Columbia. In addition to many articles and essays, he has written *Lyric Texts and Lyric Consciousness* (1994) and edited *Rethinking Sexuality: Foucault and Classical Antiquity* (1998). He is currently writing a book using post-Lacanian psychoanalysis to examine the historical conditions of possibility for love elegy.

Robin Mitchell-Boyask is associate professor and chair in the Department of Greek, Hebrew, and Roman Classics at Temple University and the editor for the American Philological Association's World Wide Web site. He has published a number of articles on Euripides and Greek tragedy and on Vergil's *Aeneid*, as well as a study of Freud's reading of classical literature and scholarship. Currently he is finishing a monograph on the relation between the Asclepius cult and Athenian drama. He teaches mainly Greek and Latin literature and languages and courses in Temple's core undergraduate program.

Mark W. Padilla is professor of classics and interim dean of Arts and Sciences at Bucknell University. His publications include *The Myths of Herakles in Ancient Greece: Survey and Profile* (1998) and numerous articles on Greek drama and Plato. He is the editor of *Rites of Passage in Ancient Greece: Literature, Religion, and Society* (1999). His teaching includes Greek literary genres and classical myth. He is now working on a monograph on Sophocles's *Women of Trachis*.

Deborah H. Roberts is professor of classics and comparative literature at Haverford College. Her most recent publications are a translation of Euripides's *Ion* in *Euripides 4*, Penn Greek Drama Series (1999), and the coedited volume *Classical Closure: Reading the End in Greek and Latin Literature* (1997). She is currently working on a book (with Sheila Murnaghan) on twentieth-century women writers and Greco-Roman antiquity. Plans for further work include translations of Greek tragedy and a study of archaism, colloquialism, and intertextuality in translations of ancient literature.

Ian Storey is professor of ancient history and classics at Trent University. His publications include the introduction to Peter Meineck's translation *Aristophanes I* (1998). His research interests focus on Greek drama, Athenian prosopography, and the writings of C. S. Lewis. Current projects include a monograph on the dramas of Eupolis and a prosopography to Old Comedy, as well as work on C. S. Lewis's novel *Till We Have Faces*.

CONTRIBUTORS AND SURVEY PARTICIPANTS

Arlene Allan, *University of Exeter*
Karen Bassi, *University of California, Santa Cruz*
Laurel Bowman, *University of Victoria*
Martin Boyne, *Trent University*
Nancy Ciccone, *University of Colorado, Denver*
Thomas Cooksey, *Armstrong Atlantic State University*
Owen Cramer, *Colorado College*
Monica Silveira Cyrino, *University of New Mexico, Albuquerque*
Juana Celia Djelal, *Penn State University, University Park*
Stephen Esposito, *Boston University*
Owen Ewald, *University of Washington*
Mary-Kay Gamel, *University of California, Santa Cruz*
Barbara Goff, *University of Texas, Austin*
Justina Gregory, *Smith College*
Dale Grote, *University of North Carolina, Charlotte*
Rima Gulshan, *University of Maryland, Eastern Shore*
Adele J. Haft, *Hunter College, City University of New York*
Michael R. Halleran, *University of Washington*
Judith Hallett, *University of Maryland, College Park*
Susan Hussein, *Montclair State University*
David Kilpatrick, *Polytechnic University, Brooklyn, NY*
David Konstan, *Brown University*
Donald Lateiner, *Ohio Wesleyan University*
Bruce Louden, *University of Texas, El Paso*
Wilfred Major, *Saint Anselm College*
Laura McClure, *University of Wisconsin, Madison*
Marianne McDonald, *University of California, San Diego*
John McMahon, *Le Moyne College*
Gary S. Meltzer, *Eckerd College*
Ann N. Michelini, *University of Cincinnati*
Paul Allen Miller, *University of South Carolina, Columbia*
Robin Mitchell-Boyask, *Temple University*
Mark W. Padilla, *Bucknell University*
Sheila Rabillard, *University of Victoria*
Deborah H. Roberts, *Haverford College*
Louis Roberts, *State University of New York, Albany*
Ian Storey, *Trent University*
Gonda Vansteen, *University of Arizona*
Froma Zeitlin, *Princeton University*

WORKS CITED

Aarne, Antti, and Stith Thompson. *The Types of the Folktale: A Classification and Bibliography*. Folklore Fellows Communications 184. Helsinki: Suomalainen Tiedeakatemia, 1973.

Adkins, Arthur. *Merit and Responsibility: A Study in Greek Values*. Oxford: Oxford UP, 1960.

Alexiou, Margaret. *The Ritual Lament in the Greek Tradition*. Cambridge: Cambridge UP, 1974.

Apollodorus. *The Library*. 1921. Ed. and trans. James George Frazer. 2 vols. Loeb Classical Lib. Cambridge: Harvard UP, 1976. Dual lang. ed.

Appollonius. *Argonautica*. Trans. R. C. Seaton. Loeb Classical Lib. London: Heinemann; Cambridge: Harvard UP, 1912. Dual lang. ed.

Aristophanes. *The Frogs*. Trans. Benjamin Bickley Rogers. *Aristophanes*. Vol. 2: *The Peace. The Birds. The Frogs*. Cambridge: Harvard UP, 1961. 291–437.

———. *The Knights. Peace. The Birds. The Assemblywomen. Wealth*. Trans. D. Barrett and A. Sommerstein. London: Penguin, 1978.

———. *Lysistrata. The Acharnians. The Clouds*. Trans. A. Sommerstein. London: Penguin, 1973.

———. *The Wasps. The Poet and the Women. The Frogs*. Trans. D. Barrett. London: Penguin, 1964.

Aristotle. *The "Art" of Rhetoric*. Trans. John Henry Freese. Loeb Classical Lib. Cambridge: Harvard UP, 1926. Dual lang. ed.

———. *Poetics. The Basic Works of Aristotle*. Ed. Richard McKeon. New York: Random, 1941.

Arnott, Peter. *Greek Scenic Conventions in the Fifth Century B.C.* Oxford: Oxford UP, 1962.

———. *Introduction to the Greek Theatre*. London: Macmillan, 1959.

Arrowsmith, William, trans. *The Bacchae*. Grene and Lattimore, *Euripides V*: 141–228.

———. "The Criticism of Greek Tragedy." *Tulane Drama Review* 3 (1959): 31–57.

———, trans. *Euripides:* Alcestis. New York: Oxford UP, 1974.

———. "Euripides and the Dramaturgy of Crisis." Ed. Stephen Esposito. *Literary Imagination* 1.2 (1999): 201–26.

———. "Euripides' Bacchae." *Greek Drama: A Collection of Festival Papers*. Ed. Grace Beede. Vermillion: Dakota, 1967. 61–74.

———. "A Greek Theater of Ideas." *Arion* 2.3 (1963): 32–56. Rpt. in E. Segal, *Euripides* 13–33.

———, trans. *Hecuba*. Grene and Lattimore, *Euripides III*: 1–68.

———. Lecture 2. Unpublished manuscript, 1984.

———. "The Lively Conventions of Translation." *The Craft and Context of Translation*. Ed. Arrowsmith and Roger Shattuck. Austin: U of Texas P, 1961. 122–40.

———, trans. *Orestes*. Grene and Lattimore, *Euripides IV*: 105–208.

Athenaeus. *The Deipnosophists*. Trans. Charles Burton Gulick. 7 vols. Loeb Classical Lib. London: Heinemann; Cambridge: Harvard UP, 1927. Dual lang. ed.

Bagg, Robert, trans. *The Bakkhai*. Amherst: U of Massachusetts P, 1978.

———. *Euripides:* Hippolytos. New York: Oxford UP, 1973.

Baldry, H. C. *The Greek Tragic Theatre*. New York: Norton, 1971.

Barlow, Shirley A., ed., trans., and comm. *Euripides:* Trojan Women. Warminster: Aris, 1986. Dual lang. ed.

———. *The Imagery of Euripides: A Study in the Dramatic Use of Pictorial Language*. 2nd ed. Bristol, UK: Bristol Classical, 1986.

———. *The Gospel at Colonus*. Video. 1987. Films for the Humanities.

Barrett, W. S., ed. and comm. *Euripides:* Hippolytus. Oxford: Oxford UP, 1964. Text in Greek.

Barthes, Roland. *Mythologies*. Trans. Annette Lavers. New York: Noonday, 1972.

Belfiore, Elizabeth S. *Murder among Friends: Violations of* Philia *in Greek Tragedy*. New York: Oxford UP, 2000.

———. *Tragic Pleasures: Aristotle on Plot and Emotion*. Princeton: Princeton UP, 1992.

Bews, J. P., et al., eds. *Celebratio: Thirtieth Anniversary Essays at Trent University*. Peterborough: Trent U, 1998.

Bieber, Margarete. *The History of the Greek and Roman Theater*. 2nd ed. Princeton: Princeton UP, 1961.

Blondell, Ruby, ed. and trans. *Medea*. Blondell, Gamel, Rabinowitz, and Zweig 147–215.

Blondell, Ruby, Mary-Kay Gamel, Nancy Sorkin Rabinowitz, and Bella Zweig, trans. *Women on the Edge: Four Plays by Euripides*. New York: Routledge, 1999.

Blundell, Sue. *Women in Ancient Greece*. Cambridge: Harvard UP, 1995.

Boardman, John. "Herakles in Extremis." *Studien zur Mythologie und Vasenmalerei*. Festschrift Konrad Schauenburg. Mainz am Rhein: von Zabern, 1986. 127–32.

———. "Herakles, Peisistratos, and Eleusis." *Journal of Hellenic Studies* 95 (1975): 1–12.

Boardman, John, Jasper Griffin, and Oswyn Murray, eds. *The Oxford History of Greece and the Hellenistic World*. Oxford: Oxford UP, 1986.

Boedeker, Deborah. "Becoming Medea: Assimilation in Euripides." Claus and Johnston 127–48.

Bond, Godfrey W. "A Chorus in *Hippolytus*: Manuscript Text versus Dramatic Reality." *Hermathena* 129 (1980): 59–63.

———, ed. *Euripides:* Heracles. Oxford: Clarendon, 1988. Text in Greek.

Bonnet, Corinne, Colette Jurdain-Annequin, and Vinciane Pirenne-Delforge, eds. *Le bestiaire d'Héraclès: IIIe Rencontre héracléenne*. Kernos Suppléments 7. Liège: Centre International d'Etude de la Religion Grecque Antique, 1998.

Boyne, Martin R. "Old and New Directions: 'Translating' Euripides on a Modern Stage." Bews et al. 122–33.

Bremmer, Jan N. "Why Did Medea Kill Her Brother Apsyrtus?" Clauss and Johnston 83–100.

Breuer, Lee, and Bob Telson. *The Gospel at Colonus*. Theatre Communications Group. Lunt-Fontanne Theater, New York, 1988.

———. *The Gospel at Colonus*. Video. 1987. Films for the Humanities.

Brockett, Oscar G. *History of the Theatre*. 7th ed. Boston: Allyn, 1995.

Brommer, Frank. *Heracles: The Twelve Labors of the Hero in Ancient Art and Literature*. Trans. and rev. Shirley J. Schwarz. New Rochelle: Caratzas, 1986.

Brown, John Russell, ed. *The Oxford Illustrated History of Theatre*. Oxford: Oxford UP, 1995.

Browning, Robert. *Agamemnon, La Saisiaz and Dramatic Idyls*. London, 1877. Boston: Houghton, 1882.

———. *Aristophanes' Apology; Including a Transcript from Euripides: Being the Last Adventure of Balaustion*. London, 1871. Rpt. in *The Poems*. Ed. John Pettigrew. Vol. 1. New Haven: Yale UP, 1981. 867–942.

———. *Balaustion's Adventure; Including a Transcript from Euripides*. London, 1875. Rpt. in *The Poems*. Ed. John Pettigrew. Vol. 2. New Haven: Yale UP, 1981. 185–329.

Burian, Peter, ed. *Directions in Euripidean Criticism*. Durham: Duke UP, 1985.

———. "Tragedy Adapted for Stage and Screens: The Renaissance to the Present." Easterling, *Cambridge Companion* 228–83.

Burkert, Walter. *Greek Religion*. Trans. John Raffan. Cambridge: Harvard UP, 1985.

Burnett, Anne Pippin. *Catastrophe Survived: Euripides' Plays of Mixed Reversal*. Oxford: Oxford UP, 1971.

———. "Hearth and Hunt in *Hippolytus*." Cropp et al. 167–85.

———. *Revenge in Attic and Later Tragedy*. Sather Classical Lectures 62. Berkeley: U of California P, 1998.

Buxton, R. G. *Persuasion in Greek Tragedy: A Study of* Peitho. Cambridge: Cambridge UP, 1982.

Cacoyannis, Michael, trans. *Euripides*: The Bacchae. New York: Meridian, 1982.

———, dir. *Iphigenia*. Videocassette. Columbia Tristar Home Video, 1977.

———, dir. *The Trojan Women*. Videocassette. USA Home Video, 1971.

Calame, Claude. "Héraclès, animal et victime sacrificielle dans les *Trachiniennes* de Sophocle?" Bonnet, Jurdain-Annequin, and Pirenne-Delforge 197–215.

Campbell, David A., ed. and trans. *Greek Lyric*. 5 vols. Loeb Classical Lib. Cambridge: Harvard UP, 1982–93. Dual lang. ed.

Carpenter, Thomas, and Christopher Faraone, eds. *Masks of Dionysus*. Ithaca: Cornell UP, 1993.

Cartledge, Paul, ed. *The Cambridge Illustrated History of Ancient Greece*. Cambridge: Cambridge UP, 1998.

Cavan, S. R. "The 'Potiphar's Wife' Motif in Euripidean Drama." Bews et al. 29–41.

Chapman, George. *Chapman's Homer: The* Iliad, *the* Odyssey, *and the Lesser Homerica*. 1611–16. Ed., introd., and comm. Allardyce Nicoll. Bollingen Series 41. New York: Pantheon, 1956.

Chappell, Fred, trans. *Alcestis*. Slavitt and Bovie, *Euripides 3*: 1–59..

Clauss, James J., and Sarah Iles Johnston, eds. *Medea: Essays on Medea in Myth, Literature, Philosophy, and Art*. Princeton: Princeton UP, 1997.

Cohen, Beth. "From Bowman to Clubman: Herakles and Olympia." *Art Bulletin* 76 (1994): 696–715.

Cohen, Robert. *Acting One*. Mountain View: Mayfield, 1991.

Cole, Susan G. "The Social Function of Rituals of Maturation: The Koureion and the Arkteia." *Zeitschrift für Papyrologie und Epigraphik* 55 (1984): 233–44.

Collard, Christopher. *Euripides*. Greece and Rome. New Surveys in the Classics 14. Oxford: Oxford UP, 1981.

———, ed., trans., and comm. *Euripides:* Hecuba. Warminster: Aris, 1991. Dual lang. ed.

———. "Formal Debates in Euripides' Drama." *Greece and Rome* 2nd ser. 22.1 (1975): 58–71.

Collard, Christopher, Martin J. Cropp, and Kevin H. Lee, eds., trans., and comms. *Euripides: Selected Fragmentary Plays*. Vol. 1. Warminster: Aris, 1995. Dual lang. ed.

Conacher, Desmond J. *Euripidean Drama: Myth, Theme, and Structure*. Toronto: U of Toronto P, 1967.

———, ed. and trans. *Euripides:* Alcestis. Warminster: Aris, 1988. Dual lang. ed.

———. *Euripides and the Sophists*. London: Duckworth, 1998.

———. "The Myth and Its Adaptation." Wilson, *Twentieth Century Interpretations* 14–21.

Craik, Elizabeth. "AIDVS: *Hippolytos* 373–430. Review and Interpretation." *Journal of Hellenic Studies* 113 (1993): 45–59.

Croally, N. T. *Euripidean Polemic:* The Trojan Women *and the Function of Tragedy*. Cambridge: Cambridge UP, 1994.

Cropp, Martin, ed. and trans. *Euripides:* Electra. Warminster: Aris, 1988. Dual lang. ed.

Cropp, Martin, et al., eds. *Greek Tragedy and Its Legacy: Essays Presented to Desmond J. Conacher*. Calgary: U of Calgary P, 1986.

Cropp, Martin, Kevin Lee, and David Sansone, eds. *Euripides and Tragic Theatre in the Late Fifth Century*. Illinois Classical Studies 24-25. Champaign: U of Illinois, 2000.

Csapo, Eric, and William Slater. *The Context of Ancient Drama*. Ann Arbor: U of Michigan P, 1995.

Dale, A. M., ed. and comm. *Euripides:* Alcestis. Oxford: Clarendon, 1961. Text in Greek.

Damen, Mark. "Actor and Character in Greek Tragedy." *Theater Journal* 41 (1989): 316–40.

Dassin, Jules, dir. *A Dream of Passion*. Videocassette. New Line Home Video, 1978.

Davie, John, trans. *Euripides:* Alcestis *and Other Plays*. Introd. and comm. Richard Rutherford. New York: Penguin, 1996.

———, trans. *Euripides:* Electra *and Other Plays*. New York: Penguin, 1999.

Davies, Malcolm, ed. *Epicorum Graecorum Fragmenta*. Göttingen: Vandenhoeck, 1988. Text in Greek.

———. "Lychas' Lying Tale—Sophocles, Trachiniae 260ff." *Classical Quarterly* 34 (1984): 480–83.

Dean, Alexander, and Lawrence Carra. *Fundamentals of Play Directing*. 4th ed. New York: Holt, Rinehart, 1980.

De Jong, Irene. *Narrative in Drama: The Art of the Euripidean Messenger-Speech*. Leiden: Brill, 1991.

Demand, Nancy. *Birth, Death, and Motherhood in Classical Greece*. Baltimore: Johns Hopkins UP, 1994.

———. *A History of Ancient Greece*. New York: McGraw, 1996.

Denniston, J. D., ed. *Euripides:* Electra. Oxford: Clarendon, 1939. Text in Greek.

Detienne, Marcel. *Dionysos at Large*. Trans. Arthur Goldhammer. Cambridge: Harvard UP, 1989.

———. *Les maîtres de vérité dans la Grèce archaïque*. 2nd ed. Paris: Maspero, 1967.

Detienne, Marcel, and Jean-Pierre Vernant. *Cunning Intelligence in Greek Culture and Society*. 1972. Trans. Janet Lloyd. Atlantic Highlands: Humanities, 1978.

Devereux, George. *The Character of the Euripidean Hippolytos*. Chico: Scholars, 1985.

Diggle, James, ed. *Euripidis fabulae*. 3 vols. Oxford Classical Texts. Oxford: Oxford UP, 1981. Text in Greek.

Dillon, Matthew. "Tragic Laughter." *Classical World* 84 (1991): 345–55.

Dimock, G. E., Jr. "Euripides' *Hippolytus*; or, Virtue Rewarded." *Yale Classical Studies* 25 (1977): 239–58.

Diodorus Siculus. *Bibliotheca Historica. Diodorus of Sicily in Twelve Volumes*. Trans. C. H. Oldfather et al. Cambridge: Harvard UP, 1963–71.

Dodds, E. R., ed. and comm. *Euripides:* Bacchae. 2nd ed. Oxford: Oxford UP, 1960. Text in Greek.

———. *The Greeks and the Irrational*. Berkeley: U of California P, 1951.

Dover, Kenneth J., ed. *Ancient Greek Literature*. 2nd ed. Oxford: Oxford UP, 1997.

———. *Aristophanic Comedy*. Berkeley: U of California P, 1972.

———. *The Greeks and Their Legacy*. Vol. 2 of *Collected Papers*. Oxford: Blackwell, 1988.

Dubois, Page. *Centaurs and Amazons: Women and the Pre-history of the Great Chain of Being*. Ann Arbor: U of Michigan P, 1982.

Duncan, Ronald, trans. *Euripides:* The Trojan Women. Adapt. Jean-Paul Sartre. New York: Vintage, 1967.

Dunn, Francis. *Tragedy's End: Closure and Innovation in Euripidean Drama*. Oxford: Oxford UP, 1996.

Easterling, Patricia E. "Anachronism in Greek Tragedy." *Journal of Hellenic Studies* 105 (1985): 1–10.

———, ed. *The Cambridge Companion to Greek Tragedy*. Cambridge: Cambridge UP, 1997.

———. "Form and Performance." Easterling, *Cambridge Companion* 151–77.

———. "The Infanticide in Euripides' *Medea*." *Yale Classical Studies* 25 (1977): 177–91.

———, ed. Trachiniae: *Sophocles*. Cambridge Greek and Latin Classics. Cambridge: Cambridge UP, 1982.

Easterling, Patricia E., and Bernard Knox, eds. *The Cambridge History of Classical Literature*. Vol. 1: *Greek Drama*. Cambridge: Cambridge UP, 1985.

Ehrenberg, Victor. *The People of Aristophanes: A Sociology of Attic Old Comedy*. Cambridge: Harvard UP, 1951.

Eliot, T. S. "Euripides and Professor Murray." *The Sacred Wood: Essays on Poetry and Criticism*. London: Methuen, 1920. 46–50. Rpt. in *Selected Essays*. By Eliot. Rev. ed. New York: Harcourt, 1950.

England, E. B., ed. *The* Iphigeneia among the Tauri *of Euripides*. London: Macmillan, 1883. Text in Greek.

Erp Taalman Kip, A. Maria van. *Reader and Spectator: Problems in the Interpretation of Greek Tragedy*. Amsterdam: Gieben, 1990.

Errondonea, F. "Deianeira vere DEI-ANEIRA." *Mnemosyne* 55 (1927): 145–64.

Esposito, Stephen, trans. and comm. *Euripides:* The Bacchae. Focus Classical Lib. Newburyport: Focus, 1998.

Euben, J. Peter, ed. *Greek Tragedy and Political Theory*. Berkeley: U of California P, 1986.

Euripides. *The Plays of Euripides*. Trans. Percy Bysshe Shelley (1824), Henry Hart Milman (1865), Robert Potter (1780), and Michael Wodhull (1809). Everyman's Lib. London: Dent, 1906.

Falkner, Thomas M. "The Wrath of Alkmene: Gender, Authority, and Old Age in Euripides' *Children of Heracles*." *Old Age in Greek and Latin Literature*. Ed. Falkner and Judith de Luce. Albany: State U of New York P, 1989. 114–31.

Fantham, Elaine, et al., eds. *Women in the Classical World: Image and Text*. New York: Oxford UP, 1994.

Ferguson, John. *Euripides,* Medea *and* Electra: *A Companion to the Penguin Translation of Philip Vellacott*. Bristol: Bristol Classical, 1987.

Finley, John. *Three Essays on Thucydides*. Cambridge: Harvard UP, 1967.

Fischer-Lichte, Erika. *The Semiotics of Theater*. Trans. Jeremy Gaines and Doris L. Jones. Bloomington: Indiana UP, 1992.

Fitts, Dudley, and Robert Fitzgerald, trans. *The* Alcestis *of Euripides*. New York: Harcourt, 1936.

Foley, Helene. "*Anodos* Drama: Euripides' *Helen* and *Alcestis*." *Innovations of Antiquity*. Ed. Ralph Hexter and Daniel Selden. New York: Routledge, 1992. 133–60. Rpt. in Foley, *Female Acts* 301–32.

———. "The Bacchae." Foley, *Ritual* 205–58.

———. "The Conception of Women in Athenian Drama." Foley, *Reflections* 127–68.

———. *Female Acts in Greek Tragedy*. Princeton: Princeton UP, 2001.

———. "Medea's Divided Self." *Classical Antiquity* 8.1 (1989): 61–85. Rpt. in Foley, *Female Acts* 243–71.

———. "Modern Performance and Adaptation of Greek Tragedy." *Transactions of the American Philological Association* 129 (1999): 1–12. <http://www.apaclassics.org/Publications/PresTalks/FOLEY98.html>.

———. *Reflections of Women in Antiquity*. New York: Gordon, 1981.

———. *Ritual Irony: Poetry and Sacrifice in Euripides*. Ithaca: Cornell UP, 1985.

Friedrich, Rainer. "Drama and Ritual." *Themes in Drama V: Drama and Religion*. Ed. J. Redmond. Cambridge: Cambridge UP, 1983. 159–223.

———. "Everything to Do with Dionysos? Ritualism, the Dionysiac, and the Tragic." Silk 257–83.

Frischer, Bernard. "*Concordia Discors* and Characterization in Euripides' *Hippolytus*." *Greek, Roman and Byzantine Studies* 11 (1970): 85–100.

Frow, John. *Marxism and Literary History*. Cambridge: Harvard UP, 1986.

Frye, Northrop. *The Anatomy of Criticism: Four Essays*. Princeton: Princeton UP, 1957.

Fuqua, Charles. "Heroism, Heracles, and the *Trachiniae*." *Traditio* 36 (1980): 1–81.

Gamel. Mary-Kay. *Alcestis*. Unpublished performance translation, 1988.

——. *Effie and the Barbarians* (version of *Iphigenia among the Taurians*). Unpublished performance translation, 1995.

——. *Electra*. Unpublished performance translation, 1990.

——. *Eye on Apollo* (version of *Ion*). Unpublished performance translation, 1996.

——. *Medea. Types of Drama*. Ed. Sylvan Barnet. New York: Longman, 1998. 99–122.

Gantz, Timothy. *Early Greek Myth: A Guide to Literary and Artistic Sources*. Baltimore: Johns Hopkins UP, 1993.

Gascoigne, George, and Francis Kinwelmersh, trans. *Jocasta*. 1566. Rpt. in *Supposes and Jocasta: Two Plays translated from the Italian [of Lodovico Dolce], the First by Geo. Gascoigne, the Second by Geo. Gascoigne and F. Kinwelmersh*. Ed. John W. Cunliffe. The Belles Lettres Series. Boston: Heath, 1906. Text in English and Italian.

Gibert, John. *Change of Mind in Greek Tragedy*. Hypomnemata 108. Göttingen: Vandenhoeck, 1995.

Goff, Barbara E. *The Noose of Words: Readings of Desire, Violence, and Language in Euripides'* Hippolytos. Cambridge: Cambridge UP, 1990.

Golder, Herbert, and Stephen Scully, eds. *The Chorus in Greek Tragedy and Culture*. Spec. issues of *Arion* 3.1 (1994–95): 1–154, 4.1 (1996): 1–114.

Goldhill, Simon. *Aeschylus: The* Oresteia. Cambridge: Cambridge UP, 1992.

——. "The Audience of Athenian Tragedy." Easterling, *Cambridge Companion* 54–68.

——. "Collectivity and Otherness—The Authority of the Tragic Chorus: Response to Gould." Silk 244–56.

——. "Drama and the City of Athens." Goldhill, *Aeschylus* 1–21.

——. "The Great Dionysia and Civic Ideology." Winkler and Zeitlin 97–129.

——. "Modern Critical Approaches to Greek Tragedy." Easterling, *Cambridge Companion* 324–47.

——. *Reading Greek Tragedy*. Cambridge: Cambridge UP, 1986.

——. "Reading Performance Criticism." McAuslan and Walcot 1–11.

——. "Representing Democracy: Women at the Great Dionysia." *Ritual, Finance, Politics: Festschrift for D. M. Lewis*. Ed. Robin Osborne and Simon Hornblower. Oxford: Oxford UP, 1994. 347–69.

Gould, John. "Hiketeia." *Journal of Hellenic Studies* 93 (1973): 74–103.

——. "Tragedy and the Collective Experience." Silk 217–43.

Graf, Fritz. "Medea, the Enchantress from Afar: Remarks on a Well-Known Myth." Clauss and Johnston 21–43.

Grant, Michael. *Myths of the Greeks and Romans*. New York: Meridian, 1995.

Graves, Robert. *The Greek Myths*. New York: Penguin, 1992.

Green, Richard, and Eric Handley, eds. *Images of the Greek Theatre*. London: British Museum, 1995.

Gregory, Justina. *Euripides and the Instruction of the Athenians*. Ann Arbor: U of Michigan P, 1991.

Grene, David, trans. *Hippolytus*. Grene and Lattimore, *Euripides I*: 157–221.

Grene, David, and Richmond Lattimore, eds. *Euripides I:* Alcestis, The Medea, The Heracleidae, Hippolytus. The Complete Greek Tragedies. Chicago: U of Chicago P, 1955.

———, eds. *Euripides II:* The Cyclops, Heracles, Iphigenia in Tauris, Helen. The Complete Greek Tragedies. Chicago: U of Chicago P, 1956.

———, eds. *Euripides III:* Hecuba, Andromache, The Trojan Women, Ion. The Complete Greek Tragedies. Chicago: U of Chicago P, 1958.

———, eds. *Euripides IV:* Rhesus, The Suppliant Women, Orestes, Iphigenia in Aulis. The Complete Greek Tragedies. Chicago: U of Chicago P, 1958.

———, eds. *Euripides V:* Electra, The Phoenician Women, The Bacchae. The Complete Greek Tragedies. Chicago: U of Chicago P, 1959.

Griffin, Jasper. "Characterization in Euripides: *Hippolytus* and *Iphigenia in Aulis*." *Characterization and Individuality in Greek Literature*. Ed. C. Pelling. Oxford: Oxford UP, 1990. 128–47.

———. "The Social Function of Attic Tragedy." *Classical Quarterly* 48 (1998): 39–61.

Grimal, Pierre. *Penguin Dictionary of Classical Mythology*. Baltimore: Penguin, 1992.

Gruppe, Otto. "Herakles." *Paulys Realencyclopädie der Classischen Alterumswissenschaft*. Ed. August Friedrich von Pauly et al. Stuttgart: Metzler, 1894–1919. Suppl. 3, cols. 910–1121.

Guthrie, W. K. C. *The Sophists*. New York: Cambridge UP, 1991.

Hall, Edith. *Inventing the Barbarian*. Oxford: Oxford UP, 1989.

Hall, Edith, Fiona Macintosh, and Oliver Taplin, eds. Medea *in Performance, 1500–2000*. Oxford: Legenda, 2000.

Halleran, Michael, trans. and comm. *Euripides:* Heracles. Focus Classical Lib. Newburyport: Focus, 1988.

———, trans. and comm. *Euripides'* Hippolytus. Focus Classical Lib. Newburyport: Focus, 2001.

———, trans. and comm. *Euripides:* Hippolytus. Warminster: Aris, 1995. Dual lang. ed.

———. *The Stagecraft in Euripides*. London: Croom Helm, 1985.

Hamilton, Edith, trans. *Three Greek Plays:* Prometheus Bound, Agamemnon, The Trojan Women. 1937. New York: Norton, 1965.

Harriott, Rosemary. "Aristophanes' Audience and the Plays of Euripides." *Bulletin of the Institute of Classical Studies* 9 (1962): 1–8.

Harris, Stephen, and Gloria Platzner. *Classical Mythology: Images and Insights*. 2nd ed. Mountain View: Mayfield, 1998.

Harrison, Tony. *Medea: A Sex-War Opera, in Dramatic Verse 1973–1985.* Newcastle upon Tyne: Bloodaxe, 1985.

Hartigan, Karelisa V. *Ambiguity and Self-Deception: The Apollo and Artemis Plays of Euripides.* Frankfurt: Lang, 1991.

———. *Greek Tragedy on the American Stage.* Westport: Greenwood, 1995.

Havelock, Eric A. *Preface to Plato.* Cambridge: Harvard UP, 1963.

HD [Hilda Doolittle]. Ion: *A Play after Euripides.* Rev. ed. Redding Ridge: Black Swan, 1986.

Heath, Malcolm. *The Poetics of Greek Tragedy.* Stanford: Stanford UP, 1987.

———. *Political Comedy in Aristophanes.* Hypomnemata Suppl. Göttingen: Vanden-hoeck, 1987.

Henderson, Jeffrey. "Women and the Athenian Dramatic Festivals." *Transactions of the American Philological Association* 121 (1991): 133–47.

Henrichs, Albert. "Human Sacrifice in Greek Religion: Three Case Studies." *Le sacrifice dans l'antiquité.* Ed. J. Rudhardt and O. Reverdin. Geneva: Entretiens Hardt 27, 1981. 195–235.

———. "'Why Should I Dance?' Choral Self-Referentiality in Greek Tragedy." *Arion* 3 (1995): 56–111.

Herington, C. J. *Poetry into Drama: Early Tragedy and the Greek Poetic Tradition.* Berkeley: U of California P, 1985.

Herodotus. *The Histories.* Trans. Aubrey de Sélincourt. Rev. and introd. John Marincola. London: Penguin, 1996.

Hesiod. *Hesiod, the Homeric Hymns, and Homerica.* Trans. Hugh G. Evelyn-White. Loeb Classical Lib. London: Heinemann; Cambridge: Harvard UP, 1914. Dual lang. ed.

Hester, D. A. "Deianiera's 'Deception Speech.'" *Antichthon* 14 (1980): 1–8.

Hoey, T. F. "Ambiguity in the Exodus of Sophocles' *Trachiniae.*" *Arethusa* 10 (1977): 269–94.

———. "The Date of the *Trachiniae.*" *Phoenix* 33 (1979): 210–32.

Holst-Warhaft, Gail. *Dangerous Voices: Women's Laments and Greek Literature.* London: Routledge, 1992.

Holt, Philip. "The End of the Trachinae and the Fate of Herakles." *Journal of Hellenic Studies* 109 (1989): 69–90.

Homer. *Homer: The Odyssey.* 1919. Trans. A. T. Murray. Rev. George E. Dimock. 2nd ed. 2 vols. Loeb Classical Lib. Cambridge: Harvard UP, 1995. Dual lang. ed.

Hornblower, Simon, and Anthony Spawforth, eds. *The Oxford Classical Dictionary.* 3rd ed. Oxford: Oxford UP, 1996.

Howatson, M. C., ed. *The Oxford Companion to Classical Literature.* 2nd ed. Oxford: Oxford UP, 1989.

Jacoby, Felix, ed. and comm. *Die Fragmenta der Griechischen Historiker.* 1923. Leiden: Brill, 1958. Text in Greek.

Jebb, Richard C. *Sophocles: The Plays and Fragments.* Part 5: *The Trachiniae.* 1892. Cambridge: Cambridge UP, 1908; Amsterdam: Hakkert, 1962. Dual lang. ed.

Jeffers, Robinson. Medea: *Freely Adapted from the* Medea *of Euripides.* New York: Random, 1946.

Johnston, Sarah Iles. "Corinthian Medea and the Cult of Hera Akraia." Claus and John-
    ston 44–70.

Joint Association of Classical Teachers. *The World of Athens: An Introduction to Clas-
    sical Athenian Culture*. Cambridge: Cambridge UP, 1984.

Jones, D. M. *"Euripides' Alcestis."* Wilson, *Twentieth Century Interpretations* 57–64.

Jones, John. *On Aristotle and Greek Tragedy*. Oxford: Oxford UP, 1962.

Just, Roger. *Women in Athenian Law and Life*. London: Routledge, 1989.

Kalke, Christine. "The Making of a Thyrsus: The Transformation of Pentheus in Euripi-
    des' *Bacchae*." *American Journal of Philology* 106 (1985): 409–26.

Kamerbeek, J. C. *The Plays of Sophocles*. Part 2: *The Trachiniae*. Leiden: Brill, 1970.
    Text in Greek.

Kassel, R., and C. Austin, eds. *Poetae Comici Graeci*. Berlin: de Gruyter, 1983.

Kearns, Emily. *The Heroes of Attica*. Bulletin Suppl. 57. London: U of London, Insti-
    tute of Classical Studies, 1989.

Kennelly, Brendan, trans. *Medea*. Newcastle upon Tyne: Bloodaxe, 1991.

——, trans. *The Trojan Women*. Newcastle upon Tyne: Bloodaxe, 1993.

Kerrigan, John. "Medea Studies: Euripides to Pasolini." *Revenge Tragedy: Aeschylus to
    Armageddon*. Oxford: Oxford UP, 1996. 88–110.

Kirk, Geoffrey S., trans. The Bacchae *of Euripides*. Englewood Cliffs: Prentice, 1970.

——. "Homer." Easterling and Knox 1–50.

Kirk, John W., and Ralph A. Bellas. *The Art of Directing*. Belmont: Wadsworth,
    1985.

Kitto, H. D. F. *Form and Meaning in Drama: A Study of Six Greek Plays and of* Ham-
    let. London: Methuen, 1956.

——. *Greek Tragedy: A Literary Study*. 1939. 3rd ed. London: Methuen, 1961.

Knox, Bernard M. W. "Divine Intervention in Euripidean Thought." *Studi di Filologica
    Classica in Onore di Giusto Monaco*. Vol. 1. Palermo: Università di Palermo,
    1991. 223–30.

——. "Euripides: The Poet as Prophet." Burian, *Directions* 1–12.

——. "The *Hippolytus* of Euripides." *Yale Classical Studies* 13 (1952): 1–31. Rpt. in
    Knox, *Word* 205–30.

——. "The *Medea* of Euripides." *Yale Classical Studies* 25 (1977): 193–225. Rpt. in
    Knox, *Word* 295–322.

——. "Myth and Attic Tragedy." Knox, *Word* 3–24.

——. Rev. of *Aeschylus:* Suppliants, trans. Janet Lembke; *Aeschylus:* Seven against
    Thebes, trans. Anthony Hecht and Helen Bacon; and *Aeschylus:* Prometheus
    Bound, trans. James Scully and C. John Herington. *New York Review of Books*
    Nov. 1975: 27–30. Rpt. in Knox, *Word* 56–63.

——. *Word and Action: Essays on the Ancient Theater*. Baltimore: Johns Hopkins UP,
    1979.

Kovacs, David, trans. *Euripides*. Vol. 1: Cyclops, Alcestis, Medea. Vol. 2: Children of
    Heracles, Hippolytus, Andromache, Hecuba. Vol. 3: Suppliant Women, Electra,

Heracles. Vol. 4: Trojan Women, Iphigenia among the Taurians, Ion. Loeb Classical Lib. Cambridge: Harvard UP, 1994–2000. Dual lang. ed.

——. The Heroic Muse: Studies in the Hippolytus and Hecuba of Euripides. Baltimore: Johns Hopkins UP, 1987.

——. "Shame, Pleasure, and Honor in Phaedra's Great Speech (Euripides' Hippolytus 375–87)." American Journal of Philology 101 (1980): 287–303.

Kraus, Kristina S. "Logos Men est Arcaios: Stories and Story-Telling in Sophocles' Trachiniae." Transactions of the American Philological Association 121 (1991): 75–98.

Lan, David, trans. Euripides: Ion. London: Methuen, 1994.

Lattimore, Richmond, trans. Alcestis. Grene and Lattimore, Euripides I: 1–53.

——, trans. Four Comedies by Aristophanes. Ann Arbor: U of Michigan P, 1969.

——, trans. The Trojan Women. Grene and Lattimore, Euripides III: 121–82.

Lesky, Albin. Alkestis, der Mythus und das Drama. Sitzungsbericht der Akademie der Wissenschaften zu Wien. Phil.-Hist. Klasse 203.2 (1925): 1–86.

——. Greek Tragedy. Trans. H. A. Frankfort. New York: Barnes, 1965.

——. A History of Greek Literature. Trans. James Willis and Cornelis de Heer. New York: Crowell, 1966.

——. "What Is Tragedy?" Lesky, Greek Tragedy 1–26.

Lexicon Iconographicum Mythologiae Classicae. Zurich: Artemis, 1981– .

Ley, Graham. A Short Introduction to the Ancient Greek Theater. Chicago: U of Chicago P, 1991.

Linforth, Ivan M. "The Pyre on Mount Oeta in Sophocles' Trachiniae." University of California Publications in Classical Philology 14 (1951): 255–67.

Lloyd, G. E. R. Magic, Reason, and Experience. Cambridge: Cambridge UP, 1979.

Lloyd, Michael. The Agon in Euripides. Oxford: Clarendon, 1992.

Loraux, Nicole. The Children of Athena: Athenian Ideas about Citizenship and the Division between the Sexes. Trans. Carole Levine. Princeton: Princeton UP, 1993.

——. "Herakles: The Super-Male and the Feminine." Before Sexuality: The Construction of Erotic Experience in the Ancient Greek World. Ed. David M. Halperin et al. Princeton: Princeton UP, 1990. 21–52.

——. "Kreousa the Autochthon: A Study of Euripides' Ion." Winkler and Zeitlin 168–206.

——. Tragic Ways of Killing a Woman. Trans. Anthony Forster. Cambridge: Harvard UP, 1987.

Lord, Louis. "Literary Criticism of Euripides in the Earlier Scholia." Diss. Yale U, 1908.

Luce, T. James, ed. Ancient Writers: Greece and Rome. New York: Scribner's, 1982.

Lumley, Lady Jane, trans. Iphigenia at Aulis. Ed. Harold H. Child. Malone Soc. Reprints. London: Chiswick, 1909.

Luschnig, Celia A. E. The Gorgon's Severed Head: Studies of Alcestis, Electra, and Phoenissae. Leiden: Brill, 1995.

——. Time Holds the Mirror: A Study of Knowledge in Euripides' Hippolytus. Mnemosyne Suppl., vol. 102. Leiden: Brill, l988.

——. Tragic Aporia: A Study of Euripides' Iphigenia at Aulis. Ramus Monographs 3. Berwick: Aureal, 1988.

MacDowell, Douglas M. *The Law in Classical Athens*. Aspects of Greek and Roman Life. Ithaca: Cornell UP, 1978.

Macintosh, Fiona. "Tragedy in Performance: Nineteenth and Twentieth Century Productions." Easterling, *Cambridge Companion* 284–323.

MacKinnon, Kenneth. *Greek Tragedy into Film*. London: Croom Helm, 1986.

Mahon, Derek, trans. The Bacchae: *After Euripides*. Oldcastle: Gallery, 1991.

March, Jennifer R. *The Creative Poet: Studies on the Treatment of Myths in Greek Poetry*. Bulletin Suppl. 49. London: U of London, Inst. of Classical Studies, 1987.

Martin, Thomas. *Overview of Archaic and Classical Greek History*. New Haven: Yale UP, 1996.

Mastronarde, Donald. "Actors on High: The Skene Roof, the Crane, and the Gods in Attic Drama." *Classical Antiquity* 9 (1990): 247–94.

McAuslan, Ian, and Peter Walcot, eds. *Greek Tragedy*. Oxford: Oxford UP, 1993.

McCall, Marsh. "The *Trachiniae*: Structure, Focus, and Heracles." *American Journal of Philology* 93 (1972): 142–63.

McClure, Laura. *Spoken like a Woman: Speech and Gender in Athenian Drama*. Princeton: Princeton UP, 1999.

McDermott, Emily. *Euripides' Medea: The Incarnation of Disorder*. University Park: Pennsylvania State UP, 1989.

McDonald, Marianne. *Ancient Sun, Modern Light: Greek Drama on the Modern Stage*. New York: Columbia UP, 1992.

———. *Euripides in Cinema: The Heart Made Visible*. Philadelphia: Centrum, 1983.

McDonald, Marianne, and Kenneth MacKinnon. "Cacoyannis vs. Euripides: From Tragedy to Melodrama." *Drama: Beiträge zum antiken Drama und seiner Rezeption*. Stuttgart: M and P, 1993. 222–34.

McLeish, Kenneth, trans. *After the Trojan War: Women of Troy, Hecuba, Helen. Three Plays by Euripides*. Bath: Absolute, 1995.

Meagher, Robert Emmet, trans. *Euripides: Hekabe*. Wauconda: Bolchazy-Carducci, 1995.

Mee, Charles L. *History Plays*. Baltimore: Johns Hopkins UP, 1998.

———. Orestes. Mee, *Plays* 87–158.

———. *Trojan Women: A Love Story*. Mee, *Plays* 159–250.

Meltzer, Gary S. "The 'Just Voice' as Paradigmatic Metaphor in Euripides' *Hippolytus*." *Helios* 23.2 (1996): 173–90.

Merkelbach, Reinhold, and M. L. West, eds. *Fragmenta Hesiodea*. London: Oxford UP, 1967. Text in Greek.

Michelini, Ann N. *Euripides and the Tragic Tradition*. Madison: U of Wisconsin P, 1987.

———. "Euripides: Conformist, Deviant, Neo-conservative?" *Arion* 5.1 (1997): 208–22.

———. "The Expansion of Myth in Late Euripides: *Iphigeneia at Aulis*." Cropp, Lee, and Sansone 41–57.

———. "Political Themes in Euripides' *Suppliants*." *American Journal of Philology* 115.2 (1994): 219–52.

————. "Replaying the Other." Rev. of *Playing the Other*, by Froma I. Zeitlin. *Arion* 7.2 (1999): 154–73.

Miller, Jonathan. *Subsequent Performances*. New York: Viking, 1986.

Mills, Sophie. *Theseus, Tragedy, and the Athenian Empire*. Oxford: Oxford UP, 1995.

Mitchell, Robin N. "Miasma, Mimesis, and Scapegoating in Euripides' *Hippolytus*." *Classical Antiquity* 10.1 (1991): 97–122.

Morford, Mark, and Robert Lenardon. *Classical Mythology*. 6th ed. New York: Oxford UP, 1999.

Morwood, James, trans. and ed. Bacchae *and Other Plays*. Introd. Edith Hall. Oxford World Classics. Oxford: Oxford UP, 2000.

————, trans. and ed. Medea *and Other Plays*. Introd. Edith Hall. Oxford World Classics. Oxford: Oxford UP, 1998.

Mossman, Judith. *Wild Justice: A Study of Euripides'* Hecuba. Oxford: Clarendon, 1995.

Mueller, Martin. *Children of Oedipus and Other Essays on the Imitation of Greek Tragedy*. Toronto: U of Toronto P, 1980.

Murray, Gilbert, trans. *The* Alcestis *of Euripides*. London: Allen, 1915.

————. *Euripides and His Age*. 1913. 2nd ed. Oxford: Oxford UP, 1946.

————, trans. *The* Medea *of Euripides*. London: Allen, 1907.

Nagy, Gregory. *Comparative Studies in Greek and Indic Meter*. Cambridge: Harvard UP, 1974.

————, trans. "The Homeric Hymn to Demeter." <http://www.stoa.org/diotima/anthology/demeter.shtml>.

————. *Pindar's Homer: The Lyric Possession of the Epic Past*. Baltimore: Johns Hopkins UP, 1990.

Nauck, Augustus, ed. *Tragicorum Graecorum Fragmenta*. Suppl. Bruno Snell. 2nd ed. Hildesheim: Georg Olms, 1964. Text in Greek.

Nelson, Marilyn, trans. *Hecuba*. Slavitt and Bovie, *Euripides 1*: 71–146.

Nietzsche, Friedrich. *Beyond Good and Evil*. Trans. Walter Kaufmann. New York: Vintage, 1966.

————. The Birth of Tragedy *and* The Case of Wagner. Trans. W. Kaufmann. New York: Vintage, 1966.

————. *Daybreak. Thoughts on the Prejudices of Morality*. Trans. R. J. Hollingdale. Cambridge: Cambridge UP, 1982.

Nussbaum, Martha C. *The Fragility of Goodness: Luck and Ethics in Greek Tragedy and Philosophy*. Cambridge: Cambridge UP, 1986.

————. Introduction. C. K. Williams vii–xliv.

Otto, Walter Friedrich. *Dionysus, Myth and Cult*. Trans. and introd. Robert B. Palmer. Bloomington: Indiana UP, 1965.

Ovid. *The Metamorphoses*. Trans. Rolfe Humphries. Bloomington: Indiana UP, 1955.

Owen, A. S., ed. *Euripides'* Ion. Oxford: Clarendon, 1939. Text in Greek.

Padilla, Mark W. "Gifts of Humiliation: *Charis* and Tragic Experience in the *Alcestis*." *American Journal of Philology* 121 (2000): 179–211.

———. "The Gorgonic Archer: Danger of Sight in Euripides' *Heracles.*" *Classical World* 86 (1992): 1–12.

———. "Herakles and Animals in Athenian Comedy and Satyr Drama." Bonnet, Jurdain-Annequin, and Pirenne-Delforge 217–30.

———. "Heroic Paternity in Euripides' *Heracles.*" *Arethusa* 27 (1994): 279–302.

———. *The Myths of Herakles in Ancient Greece: Survey and Profile.* Lanham: UP of America, 1998.

Parca, Maryline. "Of Nature and Eros: Deianeira in Sophocles' *Trachiniae.*" *Illinois Classical Studies* 17 (1992): 175–92.

Parker, Robert. *Athenian Religion: A History.* Oxford: Oxford UP, 1996.

Parry, Adam. *Logos and Ergon in Thucydides.* New York: Arno, 1981.

Parry, Milman. *The Making of Homeric Verse: The Collected Poems of Milman Parry.* Ed. Adam Parry. Oxford: Oxford UP, 1971.

Pasolini, Paolo Pier, dir. *Medea.* Janus Film, 1970.

Pelling, Christopher, ed. *Greek Tragedy and the Historian.* Oxford: Clarendon, 1997.

Philips, F. Carter. "Heracles." *Classical World* 71 (1978): 431–40.

Pickard-Cambridge, Arthur. *The Dramatic Festivals of Athens.* 2nd ed. Rev. John Gould and David Lewis. Oxford: Oxford UP, 1988.

Pindar. *The Odes of Pindar.* Trans. John Sandys. 2nd ed. Rev. London: Heinemann; New York: Putnam, 1919. Dual lang. ed.

Plato. *The Collected Dialogues of Plato, Including the Letters.* Ed. Edith Hamilton and Huntington Cairns. Bollingen ser. 71. Princeton: Princeton UP, 1961.

———. *Plato Symposium.* Ed. Kenneth Dover. Cambridge: Cambridge UP, 1980. Text in Greek.

Plato. *Republic.* Trans. Robin Waterfield. Oxford: Oxford UP, 1993.

Platter, Charles. "Heracles, Deianeira, and Nessus: Reverse Chronology and Human Knowledge in Bacchylides 16." *American Journal of Philology* 115 (1994): 337–49.

Plutarch. *Plutarchi Moralia.* Ed. F. H. Sandback. Vol. 7. Leipzig: Teubner, 1967.

Podlecki, Anthony J. "Could Women Attend the Theater in Ancient Athens?" *Ancient World* 21 (1990): 27–43

———, trans. and comm. *Euripides: Medea.* Focus Classical Lib. Newburyport: Focus, 1991.

———. *The Political Background of Aeschylean Tragedy.* Ann Arbor: U of Michigan P, 1966.

Pomeroy, Sarah, et al., eds. *Ancient Greece: A Political, Social, and Cultural History.* New York: Oxford UP, 1999.

Poole, Adrian. *Tragedy: Shakespeare and the Greek Example.* Oxford: Blackwell, 1987.

Pope, Alexander, trans. The Iliad *of Homer.* 1715. Ed. Steven Shankman. London: Penguin, 1996.

Porter, John R. *Studies in Euripides' Orestes.* Leiden: Brill, 1994.

Powell, Anton, ed. *Euripides, Women, and Sexuality.* London: Routledge, 1990.

Powell, Barry. *Classical Myth.* 2nd ed. Upper Saddle River: Prentice, 1998.

Pozzi, Dora C. "Hero and Antagonist in the Last Scene of Euripides' *Heraclidae*." *Helios* 20 (1993): 29–41.

Price, Theodora Hadzisteliou. *Kourotrophos: Cults and Representations of Greek Nursing Deities*. Studies of the Dutch Archaeological and Historical Society 8. Leiden: Brill, 1978.

Pucci, Pietro. *The Violence of Pity in Euripides'* Medea. Ithaca: Cornell UP, 1993.

Rabinowitz, Nancy Sorkin, ed. and trans. *Alcestis*. Blondell, Gamel, Rabinowitz, and Zweig 91–145.

———. *Anxiety Veiled: Euripides and the Traffic in Women*. Ithaca: Cornell UP, 1993.

———. "How Is It Played? The Male Actor of Greek Tragedy: Evidence of Misogyny or Gender-Bending?" *Didaskalia Supplement* 1 (1995) <http://didaskalia.berkeley.edu/supplements/supp1/Rabinowitz.html>.

———. "Tragedy and the Politics of Containment." *Pornography and Representation in Greece and Rome*. Ed. Amy Richlin. Oxford: Oxford UP, 1992. 36–53.

Reckford, Kenneth. "Concepts of Demoralization in the *Hecuba*." Burian, *Directions* 112–28.

Rehm, Rush. *Greek Tragic Theatre*. New York: Routledge, 1992.

———. *Marriage to Death*. Princeton: Princeton UP, 1994.

———. "Performing the Chorus: Choral Action, Interaction, and Absence in Euripides." *Arion* 4.1 (1996): 45–60.

Reid, Jane Davidson, with Chris Rohmann, eds. *Oxford Guide to Classical Mythology in the Arts, 1300–1990s*. 2 vols. Oxford: Oxford UP, 1993.

Rhodes, P. J. *The Athenian Boule*. Oxford: Clarendon, 1972.

Riffaterre, Michael. "Transposing Presuppositions on the Semiotics of Literary Translation." *Texte: Revue de Critique et de Théorie Littéraire* 4 (1985): 99–110. Rpt. in *Theories of Translation: An Anthology of Essays from Dryden to Derrida*. Ed. Rainer Schulte and John Biguenet. Chicago: U of Chicago P, 1992. 204–17.

Roach, Joseph R. *The Player's Passion: Studies in the Science of Acting*. Ann Arbor: U of Michigan P, 1993.

Robinson, John Mansley. *An Introduction to Early Greek Philosophy: The Chief Fragments and Ancient Testimony, with Connecting Commentary*. Boston: Houghton, 1968.

Roche, Paul, trans. *Euripides: Ten Plays*. New York: Signet, 1998.

Roisman Hanna. *Nothing Is as It Seems: The Tragedy of the Implicit in Euripides'* Hippolytus. Lanham: Rowman, 1999.

Romilly, Jacqueline de. *La modernité d'Euripide*. Paris: PUF, 1986.

———. *A Short History of Greek Literature*. Trans. Lillian Doherty. Chicago: U of Chicago P, 1985.

Rorty, Amélie Oksenberg, ed. *Essays on Aristotle's Poetics*. Princeton: Princeton UP, 1992.

Rose, Peter W. *Sons of the Gods, Children of Earth: Ideology and Literary Form in Ancient Greece*. Ithaca: Cornell UP, 1992.

Rubin, Gayle. "The Traffic in Women: Notes on the 'Political Economy' of Sex." *Towards an Anthropology of Women*. Ed. Rayne R. Reiter. New York: Monthly Review, 1975.

Rudkin, David, trans. *Euripides:* Hippolytus. London: Heinemann, 1980.

Saïd, Suzanne. "Bibliographie tragique, 1900–1988: Quelques orientations." *Métis* 3.1–2 (1988): 410–512.

Sale, William. *Existentialism and Euripides: Sickness, Tragedy and Divinity in the Medea,* Hippolytus *and the* Bacchae. Berwick, Victoria, Austral.: Aureal, 1977.

Schefold, Karl. *Myth and Legend in Early Greek Art.* New York: Abrams, 1966.

Schleiermacher, Friedrich. "Methoden des Übersetzens." *Friedrich Schleiermacher's sämmtliche Werke, Dritte Abtheilung: Zur Philosophie.* Vol. 2. Berlin: Reimer, 1938. Rpt. as "From 'On the Different Methods of Translating.'" Trans. Waltraud Bartscht. *Theories of Translation: An Anthology of Essays from Dryden to Derrida.* Ed. Rainer Schulte and John Biguenet. Chicago: U of Chicago P, 1992. 36–54.

Scully, Stephen. "Orchestra and Stage in Euripides' *Suppliant Women*." *Arion* 4.1 (1996): 61–84.

Seaford, Richard. "Dionysiac Drama and the Dionysiac Mysteries." *Classical Quarterly* 31 (1981): 252–71.

——, trans. and comm. *Euripides:* Bacchae. Warminster: Aris, 1996. Dual lang. ed.

——. *Reciprocity and Ritual: Homer and Tragedy in the Developing City-State.* Oxford: Oxford UP, 1994.

——. "The Social Function of Attic Tragedy: A Response to Jasper Griffin." *Classical Quarterly* 50 (2000): 30–44.

——. "The Structural Problem of Marriage in Euripides." A. Powell 151–76.

——. "The Tragic Wedding." *Journal of Hellenic Studies* 107 (1987): 106–30.

Segal, Charles. "The *Bacchae* as Metatragedy." Burian, *Directions* 156–74.

——. "Chorus and Community in Euripides' *Bacchae*." *Poet, Public, and Performance in Ancient Greece.* Ed. Lowell Edmunds and Robert Wallace. Baltimore: Johns Hopkins UP, 1997. 65–86.

——. "Classics, Ecumenicism, and Greek Tragedy." *Transactions of the American Philological Society* 125 (1995): 1–26.

——. *Dionysiac Poetics and Euripides'* Bacchae. 2nd ed. Princeton: Princeton UP, 1997.

——. *Euripides and the Poetics of Sorrow: Art, Gender, and Commemoration in* Alcestis, Hippolytus, *and* Hecuba. Durham: Duke UP, 1993.

——. *Interpreting Greek Tragedy: Myth, Poetry, Text.* Ithaca: Cornell UP, 1986.

——. "The Menace of Dionysus: Sex Roles and Reversals in Euripides' *Bacchae*." *Women in the Ancient World: The Arethusa Papers.* Ed. J. Peradotto and J. Sullivan. Albany: State U of New York P, 1984. 195–212.

——. "Metatragedy: Art, Illusion, Imitation." C. Segal, *Dionysiac Poetics* 215–71.

——. "Pentheus and Hippolytus on the Couch and on the Grid: Psychoanalytic and Structuralist Renderings of Greek Tragedy." *Classical World* 72 (1978): 129–48. Rpt. in C. Segal, *Interpreting* 268–93.

——. "Shame and Purity in Euripides' *Hippolytus*." *Hermes* 98 (1970): 278–99.

——. "Sophocles' *Trachiniae*: Myth, Poetry, and Heroic Values." *Yale Classical Studies* 25 (1977): 99–158.

——. *Tragedy and Civilization: An Interpretation of Sophocles.* Martin Classical Lectures 26. Cambridge: Harvard UP, 1981.

———. "The Tragedy of the *Hippolytus*: The Waters of Ocean and the Untouched Meadow." *Harvard Studies in Classical Philology* 70 (1965): 117–69.

———. "The Two Worlds of Euripides' Helen." C. Segal, *Interpreting* 222–67.

Segal, Erich, ed. *Euripides: A Collection of Critical Essays*. Englewood Cliffs: Prentice, 1968.

———, ed. *Oxford Readings in Greek Tragedy*. Oxford: Oxford UP, 1983.

Sfyroeras, Pavlos. "The Ironies of Salvation: The Aigeus Scene in Euripides' *Medea*." *Classical Journal* 90 (1995): 125–42.

Shapiro, H. A. "*Hêrôs Theos*: The Death and Apotheosis of Herakles." *Classical World* 77 (1983): 7–18.

———. *Myth into Art: Poet and Painter in Classical Greece*. New York: Routledge, 1994.

Silk, M. S., ed. *Tragedy and the Tragic: Greek Theatre and Beyond*. Oxford: Oxford UP, 1996.

Simon, Bennett. *Mind and Madness in Ancient Greece: The Classical Roots of Modern Psychiatry*. Ithaca: Cornell UP, 1978.

Simon, Erika. *The Ancient Greek Theatre*. London: Routledge, 1988.

Singer, June. *Androgyny: Towards a New Theory of Sexuality*. London: Routledge, 1977.

Slavitt, David R., and Palmer Bovie, eds. *Euripides 1:* Medea, Hecuba, Andromache, The Bacchae. Penn Greek Drama Series. Philadelphia: U of Pennsylvania P, 1997.

———, eds. *Euripides 2:* Hippolytus, Suppliant Women, Helen, Electra, Cyclops. Penn Greek Drama Series. Philadelphia: U of Pennsylvania P, 1997.

———, eds. *Euripides 3:* Alcestis, Daughters of Troy, The Phoenician Women, Iphigenia at Aulis, Rhesus. Penn Greek Drama Series. Philadelphia: U of Pennsylvania P, 1998.

———, eds. *Euripides 4:* Children of Heracles, The Madness of Heracles, Iphigenia in Tauris, Orestes. Penn Greek Drama Series. Philadelphia: U of Pennsylvania P, 1999.

Smith, Susan Harris. *Masks in Modern Drama*. Berkeley: U of California P, 1984.

Snell, Bruno. *Scenes from Greek Drama*. Sather Classical Lectures. Berkeley: U of California P, 1964.

Solmsen, Friedrich. *Intellectual Experiments of the Greek Enlightenment*. Princeton: Princeton UP, 1975.

Sommerstein, Alan. "Notes on Euripides' *Hippolytus*." *Bulletin of the Institute of Classical Studies* 37 (1990): 23–41.

Sophocles. *The Three Theban Plays*. Trans. Robert Fagles. Introd. and comm. Bernard Knox. New York: Penguin, 1984.

Sourvinou-Inwood, Christiane. "Medea at a Shifting Distance: Images and Euripidean Tragedy." Clauss and Johnston 253–96.

Soyinka, Wole. The Bacchae *of Euripides: A Communion Rite*. New York: Norton, 1973.

Spolin, Viola. *Theater Games for Rehearsal*. Evanston: Northwestern UP, 1985.

Stanford, W. B. *Greek Tragedy and the Emotions: An Introductory Study*. London: Routledge, 1983.

Stanislavski, Konstantin. *An Actor Prepares*. Trans. Elizabeth Reynolds Hapgood. New York: Theatre Arts, 1936.

———. *Creating a Role*. Trans. Elizabeth Reynolds Hapgood. New York: Theatre Arts, 1961.

Steadman, Peter, dir. *Medea*. New York Greek Drama Company, FCA, 1986.

Stinton, T. C. W. "The Apotheosis of Heracles from the Pyre." *Papers Given at a Colloquium on Greek Drama in Honour of R. P. Winnington-Ingram*. Suppl. 15. Ed. Lyn Rodley. London: Soc. for the Promotion of Hellenic Studies, 1987. 1–16.

———. "The Scope and Limits of Allusion in Greek Tragedy." Cropp et al. 67–102.

Storey, Ian C. "Tragedy in the Pit: Euripides' *Medea*." 1996 <http://didaskalia.berkeley .edu/issues/vol3no1/storey.html>.

Strauss, Barry S. *Fathers and Sons in Athens: Ideology and Society in the Era of the Peloponnesian War*. Princeton: Princeton UP, 1993.

Taplin, Oliver. "Comedy and the Tragic." Silk, *Tragedy and the Tragic* 188–202.

———. *Comic Angels*. Oxford: Oxford UP, 1993.

———. *Greek Tragedy in Action*. Berkeley: U of California P, 1978.

———. *The Stagecraft of Aeschylus: The Dramatic Use of Exits and Entrances in Greek Tragedy*. Oxford: Oxford UP, 1977.

———. "Tragedy and Trugedy." *Classical Quarterly* 33 (1983): 331–33.

Taylor, Don. *Directing Plays*. London: Routledge, 1996.

———. *Euripides: The War Plays*. London: Methuen, 1990.

Thalmann, W. G. *Conventions of Form and Thought in Early Greek Epic Poetry*. Baltimore: Johns Hopkins UP, 1984.

Thomas, Rosalind. *Literacy and Orality in Ancient Greece*. Cambridge: Cambridge UP, 1992.

Thompson, Stith. *Motif-Index of Folk Literature*. 2nd ed. 5 vols. Bloomington: Indiana UP, 1955–58.

Thucydides. The History of the Peloponnesian War: *The Unabridged Crawley Translation*. Trans. Richard Crawley. New York: Modern Lib., 1951.

Trendall, A. D., and T. B. L. Webster. *Illustrations of Greek Drama*. London: Phaidon, 1971.

Vellacott, Philip, trans. The Bacchae *and Other Plays*. Baltimore: Penguin, 1954.

———. *Ironic Drama: A Study of Euripides' Method and Meaning*. Cambridge: Cambridge UP, 1975.

———, trans. Medea *and Other Plays*. Baltimore: Penguin, 1963.

———, trans. Orestes *and Other Plays*. Baltimore: Penguin, 1972.

———, trans. *Three Plays*. Baltimore: Penguin, 1953.

Venuti, Lawrence. *The Translator's Invisibility: A History of Translation*. London: Routledge, 1995.

Verbanck-Piérard, Annie. "Le double culte d'Héraklès: Légende ou réalité." *Entre hommes et dieux: Le convive, le héros, le prophète*. Ed. Annie-France Laurens. Centre de Recherches d'Histoire Ancienne 86. Lire des polythéismes 2. Annales Littéraires de l'Université de Besançon 391. Paris: Belles Lettres, 1989. 43–64.

Vermeule, Emily Townsend, trans. *Electra*. Grene and Lattimore, *Euripides V*: 1–66.

Vernant, Jean-Pierre. *Myth and Society in Ancient Greece*. Trans. Janet Lloyd. Atlantic Highlands: Humanities, 1980.

——. *Myth and Thought among the Greeks*. London: Routledge, 1983.

——. *The Origins of Greek Thought*. Ithaca: Cornell UP, 1982.

Vernant, Jean-Pierre, and Pierre Vidal-Naquet. *Tragedy and Myth in Ancient Greece*. 1971. Trans. Janet Lloyd. Atlantic Highlands: Humanities, 1981.

Verrall, A. W. *Essays on Four Plays of Euripides:* Andromache, Helen, Heracles, Orestes. Cambridge: Cambridge UP, 1905.

——. *Euripides the Rationalist: A Study in the History of Art and Religion*. Cambridge: Cambridge UP, 1895.

Vickers, Brian. *Towards Greek Tragedy: Drama, Myth, Society*. London: Longman, 1973.

Visser, Margaret. "Medea: Daughter, Sister, Wife and Mother." Cropp et al. 149–66.

Vollkommer, Rainer. *Herakles in the Art of Classical Greece*. Oxford: Oxford U Committee for Archaeology, 1988.

Walcot, Peter. *Greek Drama in Its Theatrical and Social Context*. Cardiff: U of Wales P, 1976.

Walker, Charles R., trans. *Iphigenia in Aulis*. Grene and Lattimore, *Euripides IV*: 209–307.

Walker, Henry J. *Theseus and Athens*. Oxford: Oxford UP, 1995.

Walsh, George. *The Varieties of Enchantment: Early Greek Views of the Nature and Function of Poetry*. Chapel Hill: U of North Carolina P, 1984.

Walton, J. Michael. *The Greek Sense of Theatre: Tragedy Reviewed*. 2nd ed. Amsterdam: Harwood, 1996.

——. *Greek Theatre Practice*. Westport: Greenwood, 1980.

——. *Living Theatre: A Handbook of Classical Performance and Modern Production*. New York: Greenwood, 1987.

Warner, Rex, trans. *The Medea*. Grene and Lattimore, *Euripides I*: 55–108.

——, trans. *Three Great Plays of Euripides*. New York: Meridian, 1958.

Way, Arthur S., trans. *Euripides*. 4 vols. Loeb Classical Lib. London: Heinemann; New York: Putnam, 1912–25. Dual lang. ed.

Webster, T. B. L. *Greek Theatre Production*. 2nd ed. London: Methuen, 1970.

——. *The Tragedies of Euripides*. London: Methuen, 1967.

Weir, Peter, dir. *Picnic at Hanging Rock*. Videocassette. Home Vision Cinema, 1975.

West, M. L., ed. *Iambi et Elegi Graeci, Ante Alexandrum Cantati*. 1971. 2nd ed. Vol. 1. Oxford: Clarendon, 1989. Text in Greek.

Whitman, Cedric H. *Euripides and the Full Circle of Myth*. Cambridge: Harvard UP, 1974.

——. *Sophocles: A Study of Heroic Humanism*. Cambridge: Harvard UP, 1951.

Wilamowitz-Möllendorff, Ulrich von. *Euripides:* Herakles. 1893. 3 vols. Darmstadt: Wissenschaftliche Buchgesellschaft, 1981–85. Text in Greek.

Wiles, David. *Greek Theatre Performance: An Introduction*. Cambridge: Cambridge UP, 2000.

———. *The Masks of Menander*. Cambridge: Cambridge UP, 1991.

———. *Tragedy in Athens: Performance Space and Theatrical Meaning*. Cambridge: Cambridge UP, 1997.

Wilkins, John. "The State and the Individual: Euripides' Plays of Voluntary Self-Sacrifice." A. Powell 177–94.

———. "The Young of Athens: Religion and Society in the *Herakleidae* of Euripides." *Classical Quarterly* 40 (1990): 329–39.

Williams, Bernard. *Shame and Necessity*. Berkeley: U of California P, 1993.

Williams, C. K., trans. The Bacchae *of Euripides: A New Version*. Introd. Martha Nussbaum. New York: Farrar, 1990.

Williams, C. K., and G. W. Dickerson, trans. *Sophocles:* Women of Trachis. New York: Oxford UP, 1978.

Williams, Dyfri. "Herakles, Peisistratos and the Alcmeonids." *Image et céramique grecque. Actes du Colloque de Rouen, 25–26 Nov. 1982*. Ed. F. Lissarrague and F. Thelamon. Rouen: Publications de l'Université de Rouen 96, 1983. 131–40.

Wilner, Eleanor, trans., with Inés Azar. *Medea*. Slavitt and Bowie, *Euripides 1*: 1–70.

Wilson, John R., ed. *Twentieth Century Interpretations of Euripides'* Alcestis: *A Collection of Critical Essays*. Englewood Cliffs: Prentice, 1968.

Winkler, John. "The Ephebe's Song: *Tragoidia* and *Polis*." Winkler and Zeitlin 20–62.

Winkler, John, and Froma Zeitlin, eds. *Nothing to Do with Dionysos? Athenian Drama in Its Social Context*. Princeton: Princeton UP, 1990.

Winnington-Ingram, R. P. "Euripides: *Poietes Sophos*." *Arethusa* 2 (1969): 127–42.

———. *Euripides and Dionysus: An Interpretation of* The Bacchae. Cambridge: Cambridge UP, 1948.

———. "*Hippolytus*: A Study in Causation." *Euripide*. Fondation Hardt pour l' Étude de l'Antiquité Classique, Entretiens tome 6. Geneva: Vandoeuvres, 1960. 169–97.

Wolff, Christian. "Euripides." Luce 233–66.

Woodford, Susan. "Cults of Heracles in Attica." *Studies Presented to G. M. A. Hanfmann*. Ed. D. Mitten. Harvard University Monographs in Art and Archaeology. Mayence: Fogg Art Museum, 1971. 211–25.

Woodruff, Paul, trans. and comm. *Euripides:* The Bacchae. Indianapolis: Hackett, 1998.

Wyckoff, Elizabeth, trans. *Antigone. Sophocles II*. Ed. David Grene and Richmond Lattimore. The Complete Greek Tragedies. Chicago: U of Chicago P, 1942. 157–204.

———, trans. *The Phoenician Women*. Grene and Lattimore, *Euripides V*: 67–140.

Wyke, Maria. "Classics and Contempt: Redeeming Cinema for the Classical Tradition." *Arion* 3rd ser. 6.1 (1998): 124–36.

Yunis, Harvey. *A New Creed: Fundamental Religious Beliefs in the Athenian Polis and Euripidean Drama*. Hypomnemata 91. Göttingen: Vandenhoeck, 1988.

Zeitlin, Froma I. "The Closet of Masks: Role-Playing and Myth-Making in the *Orestes* of Euripides." *Ramus* 9.1 (1980): 51–77.

———. "Mysteries of Identity and Designs of the Self in Euripides' *Ion*." Zeitlin, *Playing* 285–338.

———. *Playing the Other: Gender and Society in Classical Greek Literature*. Chicago: U of Chicago P, 1996.

———. "Playing the Other: Theater, Theatricality, and the Feminine in Greek Drama." Winkler and Zeitlin 63–96. Rpt. in Zeitlin, *Playing* 441–74.

———. "The Power of Aphrodite: Eros and the Boundaries of the Self in the *Hippolytus*." Burian, *Directions* 52–111. Rpt. in Zeitlin, *Playing* 219–84.

———. "Thebes: Theater of Self and Society in Athenian Drama." Winkler and Zeitlin 130–67.

———. "Travesties of Gender and Genre in Aristophanes' *Thesmophoriazusae*." Foley, 169–217. Rpt. in Zeitlin, *Playing* 375–416.

INDEX

Modern Language Association of America

Approaches to Teaching World Literature

Joseph Gibaldi, series editor

Achebe's Things Fall Apart. Ed. Bernth Lindfors. 1991.

Arthurian Tradition. Ed. Maureen Fries and Jeanie Watson. 1992.

Atwood's The Handmaid's Tale *and Other Works*. Ed. Sharon R. Wilson, Thomas B. Friedman, and Shannon Hengen. 1996.

Austen's Pride and Prejudice. Ed. Marcia McClintock Folsom. 1993.

Balzac's Old Goriot. Ed. Michal Peled Ginsburg. 2000.

Baudelaire's Flowers of Evil. Ed. Laurence M. Porter. 2000.

Beckett's Waiting for Godot. Ed. June Schlueter and Enoch Brater. 1991.

Beowulf. Ed. Jess B. Bessinger, Jr., and Robert F. Yeager. 1984.

Blake's Songs of Innocence and of Experience. Ed. Robert F. Gleckner and Mark L. Greenberg. 1989.

Boccaccio's Decameron. Ed. James H. McGregor. 2000.

British Women Poets of the Romantic Period. Ed. Stephen C. Behrendt and Harriet Kramer Linkin. 1997.

Brontë's Jane Eyre. Ed. Diane Long Hoeveler and Beth Lau. 1993.

Byron's Poetry. Ed. Frederick W. Shilstone. 1991.

Camus's The Plague. Ed. Steven G. Kellman. 1985.

Cather's My Ántonia. Ed. Susan J. Rosowski. 1989.

Cervantes' Don Quixote. Ed. Richard Bjornson. 1984.

Chaucer's Canterbury Tales. Ed. Joseph Gibaldi. 1980.

Chopin's The Awakening. Ed. Bernard Koloski. 1988.

Coleridge's Poetry and Prose. Ed. Richard E. Matlak. 1991.

Dante's Divine Comedy. Ed. Carole Slade. 1982.

Dickens' David Copperfield. Ed. Richard J. Dunn. 1984.

Dickinson's Poetry. Ed. Robin Riley Fast and Christine Mack Gordon. 1989.

Narrative of the Life of Frederick Douglass. Ed. James C. Hall. 1999.

Eliot's Middlemarch. Ed. Kathleen Blake. 1990.

Eliot's Poetry and Plays. Ed. Jewel Spears Brooker. 1988.

Shorter Elizabethan Poetry. Ed. Patrick Cheney and Anne Lake Prescott. 2000.

Ellison's Invisible Man. Ed. Susan Resneck Parr and Pancho Savery. 1989.

Dramas of Euripides. Ed. Robin Mitchell-Boyask. 2002.

Faulkner's The Sound and the Fury. Ed. Stephen Hahn and Arthur F. Kinney. 1996.

Flaubert's Madame Bovary. Ed. Laurence M. Porter and Eugene F. Gray. 1995.

García Márquez's One Hundred Years of Solitude. Ed. María Elena de Valdés and Mario J. Valdés. 1990.

Goethe's Faust. Ed. Douglas J. McMillan. 1987.

Hebrew Bible as Literature in Translation. Ed. Barry N. Olshen and Yael S. Feldman. 1989.

Homer's Iliad *and* Odyssey. Ed. Kostas Myrsiades. 1987.

Ibsen's A Doll House. Ed. Yvonne Shafer. 1985.

Works of Samuel Johnson. Ed. David R. Anderson and Gwin J. Kolb. 1993.

Joyce's Ulysses. Ed. Kathleen McCormick and Erwin R. Steinberg. 1993.

Kafka's Short Fiction. Ed. Richard T. Gray. 1995.

Keats's Poetry. Ed. Walter H. Evert and Jack W. Rhodes. 1991.

Kingston's The Woman Warrior. Ed. Shirley Geok-lin Lim. 1991.

Lafayette's The Princess of Clèves. Ed. Faith E. Beasley and Katharine Ann
     Jensen. 1998.

Works of D. H. Lawrence. Ed. M. Elizabeth Sargent and Garry Watson. 2001.

Lessing's The Golden Notebook. Ed. Carey Kaplan and Ellen Cronan Rose. 1989.

Mann's Death in Venice *and Other Short Fiction*. Ed. Jeffrey B. Berlin. 1992.

Medieval English Drama. Ed. Richard K. Emmerson. 1990.

Melville's Moby-Dick. Ed. Martin Bickman. 1985.

Metaphysical Poets. Ed. Sidney Gottlieb. 1990.

Miller's Death of a Salesman. Ed. Matthew C. Roudané. 1995.

Milton's Paradise Lost. Ed. Galbraith M. Crump. 1986.

Molière's Tartuffe *and Other Plays*. Ed. James F. Gaines and
     Michael S. Koppisch. 1995.

Momaday's The Way to Rainy Mountain. Ed. Kenneth M. Roemer. 1988.

Montaigne's Essays. Ed. Patrick Henry. 1994.

Novels of Toni Morrison. Ed. Nellie Y. McKay and Kathryn Earle. 1997.

Murasaki Shikibu's The Tale of Genji. Ed. Edward Kamens. 1993.

Pope's Poetry. Ed. Wallace Jackson and R. Paul Yoder. 1993.

Shakespeare's Hamlet. Ed. Bernice W. Kliman. 2001.

Shakespeare's King Lear. Ed. Robert H. Ray. 1986.

Shakespeare's Romeo and Juliet. Ed. Maurice Hunt. 2000.

Shakespeare's The Tempest *and Other Late Romances*. Ed. Maurice Hunt. 1992.

Shelley's Frankenstein. Ed. Stephen C. Behrendt. 1990.

Shelley's Poetry. Ed. Spencer Hall. 1990.

Sir Gawain and the Green Knight. Ed. Miriam Youngerman Miller and
     Jane Chance. 1986.

Spenser's Faerie Queene. Ed. David Lee Miller and Alexander Dunlop. 1994.

Stendhal's The Red and the Black. Ed. Dean de la Motte and Stirling Haig. 1999.

Sterne's Tristram Shandy. Ed. Melvyn New. 1989.

Stowe's Uncle Tom's Cabin. Ed. Elizabeth Ammons and Susan Belasco. 2000.

Swift's Gulliver's Travels. Ed. Edward J. Rielly. 1988.

Thoreau's Walden *and Other Works*. Ed. Richard J. Schneider. 1996.

Voltaire's Candide. Ed. Renée Waldinger. 1987.

Whitman's Leaves of Grass. Ed. Donald D. Kummings. 1990.

Woolf's To the Lighthouse. Ed. Beth Rigel Daugherty and Mary Beth Pringle. 2001.

Wordsworth's Poetry. Ed. Spencer Hall, with Jonathan Ramsey. 1986.

Wright's Native Son. Ed. James A. Miller. 1997.